OpenLayers 2.10

Beginner's Guide

Create, optimize, and deploy stunning cross-browser web maps with the OpenLayers JavaScript web-mapping library

Erik Hazzard

BIRMINGHAM - MUMBAI

OpenLayers 2.10
Beginner's Guide

First published: March 2011

Production Reference: 1110311

Published by Packt Publishing Ltd.
32 Lincoln Road
Olton
Birmingham, B27 6PA, UK.

ISBN 978-1-849514-12-5

www.packtpub.com

Cover Image by Jose Argudo (josemanises@gmail.com)

Credits

Author
Erik Hazzard

Reviewers
Xurxo Méndez Pérez
Alan Palazzolo
Ian Turton
Couzic Mikael

Acquisition Editor
Usha Iyer

Development Editor
Maitreya Bhakal

Technical Editors
Pallavi Kachare

Indexers
Hemangini Bari
Rekha Nair

Editorial Team Leader
Aanchal Kumar

Project Team Leader
Priya Mukherji

Project Coordinator
Jovita Pinto

Proofreader
Steve Maguire

Graphics
Nilesh Mohite

Production Coordinator
Adline Swetha Jesuthas

Cover Work
Adline Swetha Jesuthas

About the Author

Erik Hazzard is a web developer—designer, Open Source advocate, and VI user. He loves to learn, teach, and occasionally blogs on his website at `http://vasir.net/`. As a professional web developer of five years, Erik specializes in Python and JavaScript, using open source software whenever possible. When he's not developing web applications, he's often developing or designing video games.

He works at FREAC (Florida Resources and Environmental Analysis Center), a great place with great people that does all kinds of GIS and web development work.

I'd like to thank the developers of OpenLayers, who continually do a fantastic job of developing the best web-mapping framework. I'd like to also thank my friends and mentors Ian Johnson and David Arthur for giving me the confidence and support I needed to get into web development. I'd like to thank Georgianna Strode and Stephen Hodge for their guidance, advice, and providing me with the opportunity to become a better web developer. I could not have written this book without the help of the great team at Packt; I hope every author can be as lucky as me to have such an excellent group of people to work with. I'd like to thank my parents for their never ending support. Lastly, I'd like to thank my love, Alisen, for her understanding and taking the time to help me make sure that the book is as easy to read as possible.

About the Reviewers

Xurxo Méndez Pérez was born in 1983 in Ourense, a little town in the south of Galicia, Spain. He lived there until he started the study for a degree in IT in the University of A Coruña, which finalized in 2008.

For the last two years he has been working, at the Computer Architecture Group of the University of A Coruña developing GIS applications (making intensive use of many OGC standards) like Sitegal and SIUXFor (web GIS based applications to manage land properties and promote their good uses in the Galician region), MeteoSIX (a GIS system that provides access to geolocated observed and forecasted meteorological data in Galicia) and others.

He also has large experience (3+ years) as a developer of mobile applications, having played first with JavaME, but nowadays he specializes in Google Android, with more than a dozen developed applications, some of them combining concepts like GIS and geolocation, real time responsiveness, and multiuser needs.

Alan Palazzolo has been building web applications big and small for over five years, most of which have been with the open source, content management system Drupal, and along the way has picked up some experience in data visualization and mapping. He is a strong believer and advocate for the open source methodology in software and in life. He was involved in starting a Free Geek chapter in the Twin Cities, and constantly tries to use technology, and specifically the Internet, to enhance the lives of those that are less fortunate than most.

Ian Turton is a geography researcher at the Pennsylvania State University. He became a geographer by accident nearly 20 years ago and hasn't managed to escape yet. During that period he was a co-founder of the GeoTools open source Java toolkit that is now used as the basis of many geographic open source projects. He continues to serve on the Project Steering Committee for the project as well as committing new code and patches. He has also taught the very popular course "Open Web Mapping" using open standards and open source programs at the Pennsylvania State University and the University of Leeds.

www.PacktPub.com

Support files, eBooks, discount offers, and more

You might want to visit www.PacktPub.com for support files and downloads related to your book.

Did you know that Packt offers eBook versions of every book published, with PDF and ePub files available? You can upgrade to the eBook version at www.PacktPub.com and as a print book customer, you are entitled to a discount on the eBook copy. Get in touch with us at service@packtpub.com for more details.

At www.PacktPub.com, you can also read a collection of free technical articles, sign up for a range of free newsletters and receive exclusive discounts and offers on Packt books and eBooks.

http://PacktLib.PacktPub.com

Do you need instant solutions to your IT questions? PacktLib is Packt's online digital book library. Here, you can access, read and search across Packt's entire library of books.

Why Subscribe?

- Fully searchable across every book published by Packt
- Copy and paste, print and bookmark content
- On demand and accessible via web browser

Free Access for Packt account holders

If you have an account with Packt at www.PacktPub.com, you can use this to access PacktLib today and view nine entirely free books. Simply use your login credentials for immediate access.

Table of Contents

Preface

Web mapping is the process of designing, implementing, generating, and delivering maps on the World Wide Web and its products. OpenLayers is a powerful, community driven, open source, pure JavaScript web-mapping library. With it, you can easily create your own web map mashup using WMS, Google Maps, and a myriad of other map backends. Interested in knowing more about OpenLayers? This book is going to help you learn OpenLayers from scratch.

OpenLayers 2.10 Beginner's Guide will walk you through the OpenLayers library in the easiest and most efficient way possible. The core components of OpenLayers are covered in detail, with examples, structured so that you can easily refer back to them later.

The book starts off by introducing you to the OpenLayers library and ends with developing and deploying a full-fledged web map application, guiding you through every step of the way.

Throughout the book, you'll learn about each component of the OpenLayers library. You'll work with backend services like WMS, third-party APIs like Google Maps, and even create maps from static images. You'll load data from KML and GeoJSON files, create interactive vector layers, and customize the behavior and appearance of your maps.

There is a growing trend in mixing location data with web applications. *OpenLayers 2.10 Beginner's Guide* will show you how to create powerful web maps using the best web mapping library around.

This book will guide you to develop powerful web maps with ease using the open source JavaScript library OpenLayers.

What you need for this book

The only thing you'll need for this book is a computer and text editor. Your operating system will come with a text editor, and any will do, but if you are using Windows I recommend using Notepad++ (`http://notepad-plus-plus.org/`), VI if you are using Linux, and Textmate if on OSX. An Internet connection will be required to view the maps, and you'll also need a modern web browser such as Firefox, Google Chrome, Safari, or Opera. While a modern browser is required to get the most of the library, OpenLayers even provides support for non standards based browsers such as Internet Explorer (even IE6, to some extent).

No knowledge of **Geographic Information Systems** (**GIS**) is required, nor is extensive JavaScript experience. A basic understanding of JavaScript syntax and HTML / CSS will greatly aid in understanding the material, but is not required.

What this book covers

Chapter 1: *Getting Started with OpenLayers*. This chapter will introduce OpenLayers and some programming concepts behind it. It covers how to create a map, walking through how to set up the code and configure various settings.

Chapter 2: *Squashing Bugs with Firebug*. This chapter will cover setting up the Firebug plugin, which we'll use throughout the book, so that we can do simple debugging and better understand how OpenLayers works behind the scenes.

Chapter 3: *The 'Layers' in OpenLayers*. Here, we'll cover one of the core classes of OpenLayers—the Layer class. We'll discuss what a 'Layer' is, how to work with layers and the different layer classes.

Chapter 4: *Wrapping our Heads Around Projections*. This chapter will cover a few basic geography concepts and why understanding them will help us use OpenLayers. We'll also cover projections, why they are used, and how to use them.

Chapter 5: *Interacting With Third Party APIs*. This chapter will focus on creating an OpenLayers map using different third party APIs, such as Google Maps and OpenStreetMaps.

Chapter 6: Taking Control of Controls. We'll cover another core class of OpenLayers, the Control class. We'll cover what controls are and discuss the various types of controls, along with how to work with the events.

Chapter 7: *Giving Controls Some Style*. This chapter will walk through how OpenLayers uses CSS to style controls.

Chapter 8: *Charting the Map Class*. This chapter will discuss another core component of OpenLayers—the Map class. We'll learn about how to map functions and their properties, along with how to set up multiple maps on the same page.

Chapter 9: *Using Vector Layers*. Here, we'll learn what a Vector layer is and how it works. We'll also cover how to work with the data, such as KML files.

Chapter 10: *Vector Layer Style Guide*. In this chapter we'll cover how to style the vector layer and how to use the Rule and Filter classes.

Chapter 11: *Creating Web Map Applications*. This final chapter will go over how to build a web-mapping application from scratch, and how to use the OpenLayers build file.

Who this book is for

This book is for anyone who has any interest in using maps on their website, from hobbyists to professional web developers. OpenLayers provides a powerful, but easy-to-use, pure JavaScript and HTML (no third-party plug-ins involved) toolkit to quickly make cross-browser web maps. A basic understanding of JavaScript will be helpful, but there is no prior knowledge required to use this book. If you've never worked with maps before, this book will introduce you to some common mapping topics and gently guide you through the OpenLayers library. If you're an experienced application developer, this book will also serve as a reference to the core components of OpenLayers.

How to read this book

This book is primarily designed to be read from start to finish, with chapters building on each other and increasing in complexity. At the same time, however, the chapters are modular so that each can also serve as reference once you've learned the material. This book should preferably be read straight through first, of course, and then serve as a reference later.

Conventions

In this book, you will find several headings appearing frequently.

To give clear instructions of how to complete a procedure or task, we use:

Time for action – heading

1. Action 1
2. Action 2
3. Action 3

Instructions often need some extra explanation so that they make sense, so they are followed with:

What just happened?

This heading explains the working of tasks or instructions that you have just completed.

You will also find some other learning aids in the book, including:

Pop quiz – heading

These are short questions intended to help you test your own understanding.

Have a go hero – heading

These set practical challenges and give you ideas for experimenting with what you have learned.

You will also find a number of styles of text that distinguish between different kinds of information. Here are some examples of these styles, and an explanation of their meaning.

Code words in text are shown as follows: "You can download it as either a `tar.gz` or `.zip`."

A block of code is set as follows:

```
Lines [21] to [23]
  if(!map.getCenter()){
    map.zoomToMaxExtent();
  }
```

When we wish to draw your attention to a particular part of a code block, the relevant lines or items are set in bold:

```
var wms_layer = new OpenLayers.Layer.WMS(
  'WMS Layer Title',
  'http://vmap0.tiles.osgeo.org/wms/vmap0',
```

```
    {layers: 'basic'},
    {}
);
```

New terms and **important words** are shown in bold. Words that you see on the screen, in menus or dialog boxes for example, appear in the text like this: "By default, your map adds an **argParser** control which will try to pull information from a permalink.".

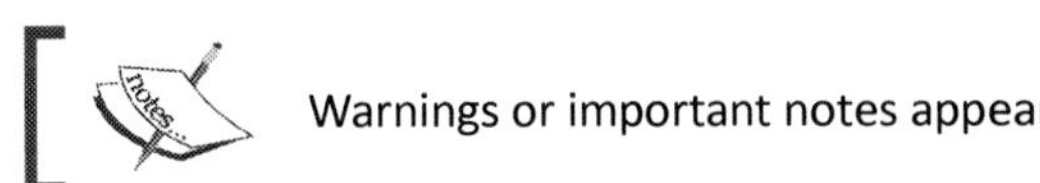

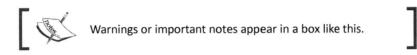

Warnings or important notes appear in a box like this.

Reader feedback

Feedback from our readers is always welcome. Let us know what you think about this book—what you liked or may have disliked. Reader feedback is important for us to develop titles that you really get the most out of.

To send us general feedback, simply send an e-mail to `feedback@packtpub.com`, and mention the book title via the subject of your message.

If there is a book that you need and would like to see us publish, please send us a note in the **SUGGEST A TITLE** form on `www.packtpub.com` or e-mail `suggest@packtpub.com`.

If there is a topic that you have expertise in and you are interested in either writing or contributing to a book, see our author guide on `www.packtpub.com/authors`.

Customer support

Now that you are the proud owner of a Packt book, we have a number of things to help you to get the most from your purchase.

Downloading the example code for this book

You can download the example code files for all Packt books you have purchased from your account at `http://www.PacktPub.com`. If you purchased this book elsewhere, you can visit `http://www.PacktPub.com/support` and register to have the files e-mailed directly to you.

Errata

Although we have taken every care to ensure the accuracy of our content, mistakes do happen. If you find a mistake in one of our books—maybe a mistake in the text or the code—we would be grateful if you would report this to us. By doing so, you can save other readers from frustration and help us improve subsequent versions of this book. If you find any errata, please report them by visiting `http://www.packtpub.com/support`, selecting your book, clicking on the **errata submission form** link, and entering the details of your errata. Once your errata are verified, your submission will be accepted and the errata will be uploaded on our website, or added to any list of existing errata, under the Errata section of that title. Any existing errata can be viewed by selecting your title from `http://www.packtpub.com/support`.

Piracy

Piracy of copyright material on the Internet is an ongoing problem across all media. At Packt, we take the protection of our copyright and licenses very seriously. If you come across any illegal copies of our works, in any form, on the Internet, please provide us with the location address or website name immediately so that we can pursue a remedy.

Please contact us at `copyright@packtpub.com` with a link to the suspected pirated material.

We appreciate your help in protecting our authors, and our ability to bring you valuable content.

Questions

You can contact us at `questions@packtpub.com` if you are having a problem with any aspect of the book, and we will do our best to address it.

1
Getting Started with OpenLayers

Within the past few years, the popularity of interactive web maps has exploded. In the past, creating interactive maps was reserved for large companies or experts with lots of money. But now, with the advent of free services like Google and Yahoo! Maps, online mapping is easily accessible to everyone. Today, with the right tools, anyone can easily create a web map with little or even no knowledge of geography, cartography, or programming.

Web maps are expected to be fast, accurate, and easy to use. Since they are online, they are expected to be accessible from anywhere on nearly any platform. There are only a few tools that fulfill all these expectations.

OpenLayers is one such tool. It's free, open source, and very powerful. Providing both novice developers and seasoned GIS professionals with a robust library, OpenLayers makes it easy to create modern, fast, and interactive web-mapping applications.

In this chapter we will

- Learn what OpenLayers is
- Discuss some web mapping application concepts
- Make our First Map
- Cover concepts behind OpenLayers, such as Object Oriented Programming
- Provide information on resources outside of this book

What is OpenLayers?

OpenLayers is an open source, **client side** JavaScript **library** for making interactive web maps, viewable in nearly any web browser. Since it is a client side library, it requires no special server side software or settings—you can use it without even downloading anything! Originally developed by Metacarta, as a response, in part, to Google Maps, it has grown into a mature, popular framework with many passionate developers and a very helpful community.

Why use OpenLayers?

OpenLayers makes creating powerful web-mapping applications easy and fun. It is very powerful but also easy to use—you don't even need to be a programmer to make a great map with it. It's open source, free, and has a strong community behind it. So if you want to dig into the internal code, or even improve it, you're encouraged to do so. Cross browser compatibility is handled for you—it even works in IE6.

OpenLayers is not tied to any proprietary technology or company, so you don't have to worry so much about your application breaking (unless you break it). At the time of writing, support for modern mobile and touch devices is in the works (with many proof of concept examples), and should be in the official library in the near future—if they aren't by the time you're reading this.

OpenLayers allows you to build entire mapping applications from the ground up, with the ability to customize every aspect of your map—layers, controls, events, etc. You can use a multitude of different map server backends together, including a powerful vector layer. It makes creating map 'mashups' extremely easy.

What, technically, is OpenLayers?

We said OpenLayers is a **client side** JavaScript **library**, but what does this mean?

Client side

When we say client side we are referring to the user's computer, specifically their web browser. The only thing you need to have to make OpenLayers work is the OpenLayers code itself and a web browser. You can either download it and use it on your computer locally, or download nothing and simply link to the JavaScript file served on the site that hosts the OpenLayers project (`http://openlayers.org`). OpenLayers works on nearly all browsers and can be served by any web server or your own computer. Using a modern, standard-based browser such as Firefox, Google Chrome, Safari, or Opera is recommended.

Library

When we say **library** we mean that OpenLayers is an **API** (**Application Programmer Interface**) that provides you with tools to develop your own web maps. Instead of building a mapping application from scratch, you can use OpenLayers for the mapping part, which is maintained and developed by a bunch of brilliant people.

For example, if you wanted to write a blog you could either write your own blog engine, or use an existing one such as WordPress or Blogger and build on top of it. Similarly, if you wanted to create a web map, you could write your own from scratch, or use software that has been developed and tested by a group of developers with a strong community behind it.

By choosing to use OpenLayers, you do have to learn how to use the library (or else you wouldn't be reading this book), but the benefits greatly outweigh the costs. You get to use a rich, highly tested and maintained code base, and all you have to do is learn how to use it. Hopefully, this book will help you with that.

OpenLayers is written in **JavaScript**, but don't fret if you don't know it very well. All you really need is some knowledge of the basic syntax, and we'll try to keep things as clear as possible in the code examples.

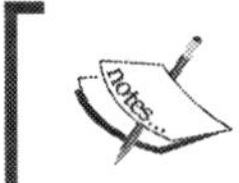

If you are unfamiliar with JavaScript, Mozilla provides phenomenal JavaScript documentation at `https://developer.mozilla.org/en/javascript`.

Anatomy of a web-mapping application

First off—what is a 'web-mapping application'? To put it bluntly, it's some type of Internet application that makes use of a map. This could be a site that displays the latest geo-tagged images from Flickr (we'll do this in Chapter 11), a map that shows markers of locations you've traveled to, or an application that tracks invasive plant species and displays them. If it contains a map and it does something, you could argue that it is a web map application. The term can be used in a pretty broad sense.

So where exactly does OpenLayers fit in? We know OpenLayers is a client side mapping library, but what does that mean? Let's take a look at the following screenshot:

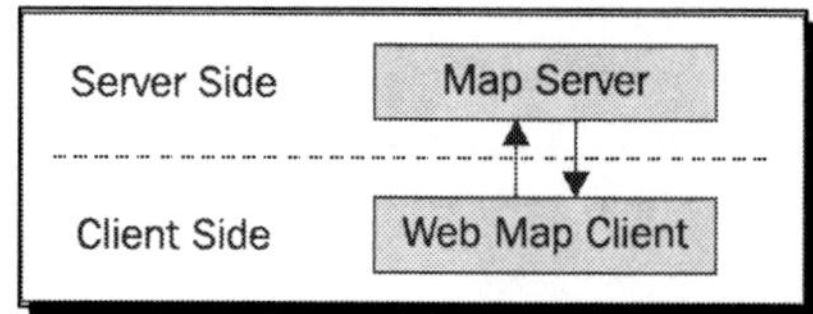

This is called the **Client / Server Model** and it is, essentially, the core of how all web applications operate. In the case of a web map application, some sort of map client (e.g., OpenLayers) communicates with some sort of web map server (e.g., a WMS server or the Google Maps backend).

Web map client

OpenLayers lives on the client side. One of the primary tasks the client performs is to get map images from a map server. Essentially, the client has to ask a map server for what you want to look at. Every time you navigate or zoom around on the map, the client has to make new requests to the server—because you're asking to look at something different.

OpenLayers handles this all for you, and it is happening via asynchronous JavaScript (**AJAX**) calls to a map server. To reiterate—the basic concept is that OpenLayers sends requests to a map server for map images every time you interact with the map, then OpenLayers pieces together all the returned map images so it looks like one big, seamless map. In Chapter 2, we'll cover this concept in more depth.

Web map server

A map server (or map service) provides the map itself. There are a myriad of different map server backends. A small sample includes WMS, Google Maps, Yahoo! Maps, ESRI ArcGIS, WFS, and OpenStreet Maps. If you are unfamiliar with those terms, don't sweat it. The basic principle behind all those services is that they allow you to specify the area of the map you want to look at (by sending a request), and then the map servers send back a response containing the map image. With OpenLayers, you can choose to use as many different backends in any sort of combination as you'd like.

OpenLayers is not a web map server; it only consumes data from them. So, you will need to be able to access some type of web map service. Don't worry though. Fortunately, there are a myriad of free and/or open source web map servers available that are remotely hosted or easy to set up yourself, such as MapServer.

[ Throughout this book, we'll often use a freely available web mapping service from OSGeo, so don't worry about having to provide your own.]

With many web map servers you do not have to do anything to use them—just supplying a URL to them in OpenLayers is enough. OSGeo, OpenStreet Maps, Google, Yahoo!, and Bing Maps, for instance, provide access to their map servers (although, some commercial restrictions may apply with various services in some situations).

Relation to Google / Yahoo! / and other mapping APIs

The Google, Yahoo!, Bing, and ESRI Mappings API allow you to connect with their map server backend. Their APIs also usually provide a client side interface (at least in the case of Google Maps).

The Google Maps API, for instance, is fairly powerful. You have the ability to add markers, plot routes, and use KML data (things you can also do in OpenLayers)—but the main drawback is that your mapping application relies totally on Google. The map client and map server are provided by a third party. This is not inherently a bad thing, and for many projects, Google Maps and the like are a good fit.

However, there are quite a few drawbacks.

- You're not in control of the backend
- You can't really customize the map server backend, and it can change at any time
- There may be some commercial restrictions, or some costs involved
- These other APIs also cannot provide you with anything near the amount of flexibility and customization that an open source mapping application framework (i.e., OpenLayers) offers

Layers in OpenLayers

So, what's with the **Layer** in OpenLayers? Well, OpenLayers allows you to have multiple different 'backend' servers that your map can use. To access a web map server, you create a **layer** object and add it to your map with OpenLayers.

For instance, if you wanted to have a Google Maps and a WMS service displayed on your map, you would use OpenLayers to create a GoogleMaps **layer** object and a WMS **layer** object, and then add them to your OpenLayers map. We'll soon see an example with a WMS layer, so don't worry if you're a little confused.

What is a Layer?

Like layers of an onion, each layer is above and will cover up the previous one; the order that you add in the layers is important. With OpenLayers, you can arbitrarily set the overall transparency of any layer, so you are easily able to control how much layers cover each other up, and dynamically change the layer order at any time.

For instance, you could have a Google map as your base layer, a layer with satellite imagery that is semi-transparent, and a vector layer all active on your map at once. A vector layer is a powerful layer that lets us add markers and various geometric objects to our maps—we'll cover it in Chapter 9. Thus, in this example, your map would have three separate layers. We'll go into much more depth about layers and how to use and combine them in Chapter 3.

The OpenLayers website

The website for OpenLayers is located at `http://openlayers.org/`. To begin, we need to download a copy of OpenLayers (or, we can directly link to the library—but we'll download a local copy). You can download the compressed library as either a `.tar.gz` or `.zip`, but both contain the same files.

OpenLayers: Free Maps for the Web

Get OpenLayers Now!!
Latest code:

- Link to the hosted version
- 2.10 (Stable): .tar.gz | .zip
- 2.10 Release Notes
- Class Documentation, More documentation
- See examples of OpenLayers Usage: Release Examples (2.10), Development Examples (trunk)

About...
OpenLayers makes it easy to put a dynamic map in any web page. It can display map tiles and markers loaded from any source. OpenLayers has been developed to further the use of geographic information of all kinds. OpenLayers is completely free, Open Source JavaScript, released under a BSD-style License (also known as the Clear BSD).

Let's go over the links:

- **Link to the hosted version**: If you do not want to actually download OpenLayers, you can instead link to the OpenLayers library by adding this script URL to your site in a <script> tag.
- **2.10 (Stable)** `.tar.gz` **or** `.zip`: This should show the latest stable release (2.10 at the time of writing). You can download it as either a `tar.gz` or `.zip`; if you are unsure of which to get, you should download the `.zip` version.
- **2.10 Release Notes**: This highlights things that have changed, bugs that have been fixed, etc.
- **Class documentation, more documentation**: These are links to the API documentation, which we will make heavy use of throughout the book. I recommend opening it up and keeping it up while working through the examples.
- **See examples...**: OpenLayers provides a rich array of examples demonstrating features of the library; if you're ever stuck or looking for a good example—go here.

Time for action – downloading OpenLayers

Let's download the OpenLayers library. After you're done, you should have the OpenLayers library files set up on your computer.

1. Go to the OpenLayers website (`http://openlayers.org`) and download the `.zip` version (or if you prefer the `.tar.gz` version).
2. Extract the file you just downloaded. When you extract it, you'll end up with a folder called OpenLayers-2.10 (or whatever your version is).

3. Open up the OpenLayers folder. Once inside, you'll see a lot of folders and files, but the ones we are concerned with right now is a file called `OpenLayers.js` and two folders, `/img` and `/theme`. We'll be copying these to a new folder.

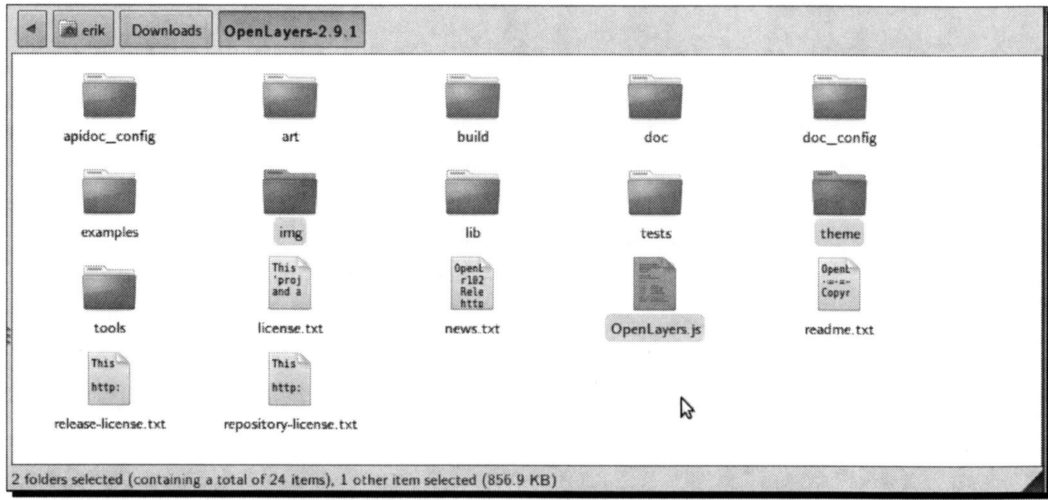

4. Create a new folder outside the OpenLayers directory; we'll use `~/code/` (if you are on Windows, then `c:/code`). You can name the folder whatever you like, but we'll refer to it as the `code` folder. Inside the code folder, copy over the `OpenLayers.js` and two folders (`/img` and `/theme`) from the previous step. Your new folder structure should look similar to this:

What just happened?

We just 'installed' OpenLayers by copying over a pre-built, compressed JavaScript file containing the entire OpenLayers library code and two directories containing assets (images and stylesheets). To use OpenLayers, you'll need at a minimum the `OpenLayers.js` file and the `img` and `theme` folders.

If you open the `OpenLayers.js` file, you'll notice it is nearly unreadable. This is because this is a **minified** version, which basically means extra white space and unnecessary characters have been stripped out to cut down on the file size. While it is no longer readable, it is a bit smaller and thus requires less time to download. If you want to look at the uncompressed source code, you can view it by looking in the OpenLayers source code folder you extracted.

You can, as we'll see in the last chapter of this book, build your own custom configurations of the library, including only the things you need. But for now, we'll just use the entire library. Now that we have our OpenLayers library files ready to use, let's make use of them!

Making our first map

The process for creating a map with OpenLayers requires, at a minimum, the following things:

- Including the OpenLayers library files
- Creating an HTML element that the map will appear in
- Creating a map object from the Map class
- Creating a layer object from a Layer class
- Adding the layer to the map
- Defining the map's extent (setting the area the map will initially be displaying)

Now we're finally ready to create our first map!

Time for action – creating your first map

Let's dive into OpenLayers and make a map! After you finish this section, you should have a working map, which uses a publicly available WMS server backend from OSGeo.

1. Navigate to the `code` directory that contains the `OpenLayers.js` file, `/img` and `/theme` directories. Create a file here called `index.html`. This directory (`/code`) will be referred to as our root directory, because it is the base (root) folder where all our files reside.

2. Add in the following code to `index.html` and save the file as an `.html` file—if you are using Windows, I suggest using Notepad++. Do not try to edit the file in a program like Microsoft Word, as it will not save properly. The following code will also be used as the base template code for many future examples in this book, so we'll be coming back to it a lot.

The lines numbers in the code are for demonstration purposes; do not type them in when you are writing your code.

```
<!DOCTYPE html>
<html lang='en'>
<head>
    <meta charset='utf-8' />
    <title>My OpenLayers Map</title>
    <script type='text/javascript' src='OpenLayers.js'></script>
    <script type='text/javascript'>

        var map;

        function init() {
            map = new OpenLayers.Map('map_element', {});
            var wms = new OpenLayers.Layer.WMS(
                'OpenLayers WMS',
                'http://vmap0.tiles.osgeo.org/wms/vmap0',
                {layers: 'basic'},
                {}
            );

            map.addLayer(wms);
            if(!map.getCenter()){
                map.zoomToMaxExtent();
            }
        }

    </script>
</head>

<body onload='init();'>
    <div id='map_element' style='width: 500px; height: 500px;'>
    </div>
</body>
</html>
```

3. Open up `index.html` in your web browser. You should see something similar to:

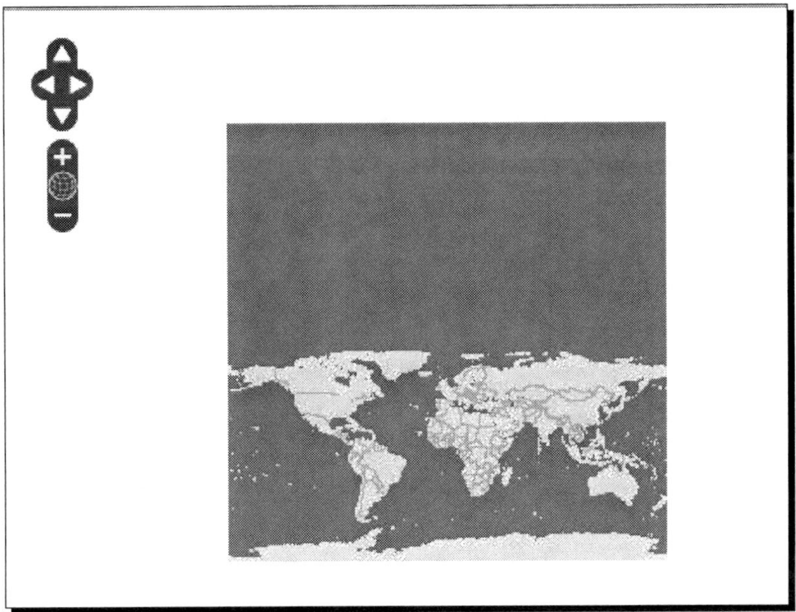

What just happened?

We just created our first map using OpenLayers! If it did not work for you for some reason, try double checking the code and making sure all the commas and parentheses are in place. You can also refer to the *Preface* where a link to code samples used in the book is given. By default, we're given a few controls if we don't specify any. We will use the file we created as a template for many examples throughout the book, so save a copy of it so you can easily reference it later.

The control on the left side (the navigation buttons) is called the **PanZoom** control. You can click the buttons to navigate around the map, drag the map with your mouse/use the scroll wheel to zoom in, or use your keyboard's arrow keys. We'll cover controls in far greater detail in Chapter 6.

How the code works

Now, let's take a look at the code—line by line. Before we do that, let's include a quick reference to the line numbers at which the requirements from the previous section occur at. These are the core things that you need to do to have a functioning map.

We'll denote line numbers with brackets—[x], where x is the line number.

1. **Including the OpenLayers library files:**

   ```
   Line [6]
     <script type='text/javascript' src='OpenLayers.js'></script>
   ```

2. **Creating an HTML element for our map:**

   ```
   Lines [30] and [31]
     <div id='map_element' style='width: 500px; height: 500px'>
   </div>
   ```

3. **Creating a map object from the Map class:**

   ```
   Line [12]
     map = new OpenLayers.Map('map_element', { });
   ```

4. **Creating a layer object from a Layer class:**

   ```
   Lines [13] to [18]
     var wms_layer = new OpenLayers.Layer.WMS(
       'WMS Layer Title',
       'http://vmap0.tiles.osgeo.org/wms/vmap0',
       {layers: 'basic'},
       {}
     );
   ```

5. **Adding the layer to the map:**

   ```
   Line [20]
     map.addLayer(wms_layer);
   ```

6. **Defining the map's extent:**

   ```
   Lines [21] to [23]
     if(!map.getCenter()){
       map.zoomToMaxExtent();
     }
   ```

Understanding the code—Line by line

Lines [1] to [5]: Sets up the HTML page. Every HTML page needs an `<html>` and `<head>` tag, and the extraneous code you see specifies various settings that inform your browser that this is an HTML5 compliant page. For example, we include the `DOCTYPE` declaration in line [1] to specify that the page conforms to standards set by the WC3. We also specify a `<title>` tag, which contains the title that will be displayed on the page.

> This is the structure that all our code examples will follow, so this basic code template will be implicitly assumed in all examples that follow throughout the book.

Line [6]: `<script type='text/javascript' src='OpenLayers.js'></script>`

This includes the OpenLayers library. The location of the file is specified by the `src='OpenLayers.js'` attribute. Here, we're using a **relative path**. As the `index.html` page is in the same folder as the `OpenLayers.js` file, we don't have to worry about specifying the path to it. The file could be either on your computer or another computer—it doesn't matter much, as long as the browser can load it.

We can also use an **absolute path**, which means we pass in a URL that the script is located at. `OpenLayers.org` hosts the script file as well; we could use the following line of code to link to the library file directly:

```
<script type='text/javascirpt' src='http://openlayers.org/api/
OpenLayers.js'></script>
```

Notice how the src specifies an actual URL—this is how we use **absolute paths**. Either way works, however, throughout the book we'll assume that you are using a relative path and have the OpenLayers library on your own computer/server. If you use the hosted OpenLayers library, you cannot be sure that it will always be available, and it may change overnight (and changes when the library is updated)—so using a local copy is recommended.

Line [7]: Starts a `<script>` block. We'll set up all our code inside it to create our map. Since the OpenLayers library has been included in line [5], we are able to use all the classes and functions the library contains.

Line [8]: `var map;`

Here we create a global variable called `map`. In JavaScript, anytime we **create** a variable we need to place `var` in front of it to ensure that we don't run into **scope** issues (what functions can access which variables). When **accessing** a variable, you do not need to put `var` in front of it.

Since we are defining map as a variable at the global level (outside of any functions), we can access it anywhere in our code. Soon we will make this map variable our map object, but right now it is just an empty global variable.

Line [11]: Creates a function called `init`. When the page loads (via `body onload='init();'` on line [29]), this function will get called. This function contains all of our code to set up our OpenLayers map. If you are familiar with JavaScript, you do not have to put all the code in a function call—you could, for instance, just put the code at the bottom of the page and avoid a function call all together. Creating a function that gets called when the page loads is a common practice and so we will be doing it throughout the book.

Line [12]: `map = new OpenLayers.Map('map_element', { });`

Remember that global map variable? Well, now we're making it a map object, created from the `OpenLayers.Map` class. It is also referred to as an instance of the Map class. We'll talk about what this means later in this chapter in the *Object Oriented Programming* section. The map object is the crux of our OpenLayers application— we call its functions to tell the map to zoom to areas, fire off events, keep track of layers, etc.

Now, let's look at the right hand side of the equal sign (`=`): `new` means that we are creating a new object from the class that follows it. `OpenLayers.Map` is the class name which we are creating an object from. Notice that something is inside the parenthesis: `('map_element', {})`. This means we are passing two things into the class (called arguments, and you pass them in separated by a comma). Every class in OpenLayers expects different arguments to be passed into it, and some classes don't expect anything.

The **Map** class expects two parameters. The first argument, `map_element`, is the ID of the HTML element that the map will appear in. The second argument, `{ }`, are the map **options**, consisting of `key:value` pairs (e.g., `{key:value}`). This is also called **JavaScript Object Notation**, a way to create objects on the fly. We'll cover this in more depth very shortly in the next section. Also, you are not required to include this argument if it is empty (even though we just did it), but we are just doing it here for consistency.

Because we passed in `map_element` as the first parameter, we will have an HTML element (almost always a <div>) with the ID of `map_element`. The HTML element ID can be anything, but for the sake of clarity and to avoid confusion, we call it `map_element`.

Line [13]: `var wms = new OpenLayers.Layer.WMS(`

Here, we create a layer object for the map to use from the WMS subclass of the Layer class. In OpenLayers, every map needs to have at least one layer. The layer points to the 'back end', or the server side map server, as we discussed earlier. The layer can be any of a multitude of different services, but we are using WMS here. WMS, which stands for **Web Map Service**, is an international standard defined by the **Open Geospatial Consortium** (**OGC**).

The arguments we can pass in for layers are dependent on the layer class—we cover layers in detail in Chapter 3. If you don't want to wait, you can also check out the documentation at `http://dev.openlayers.org/docs/files/OpenLayers/Layer-js.html` to see what arguments different layers of classes expect.

Notice we don't include everything on one line when creating our layer object—this improves readability, making it easier to see what we pass in. The only difference is that we are also adding a new line after the commas which separate arguments, which doesn't affect the code (but does make it easier to read).

Line [14]: `'WMS Layer Title',`

This is the first parameter passed in; the layer's title. Most layer classes expect the first parameter passed in to be the title of the layer. This title can be anything you would like, the main purpose of it is for human readability—it is displayed in controls such as the layer list.

Line [15]: `'http://vmap0.tiles.osgeo.org/wms/vmap0',`

The URL is the second parameter that the WMS layer class expects to receive. For now, we're using a publicly available WMS service from OSGeo. We will cover in depth the WMS in Chapter 3. For now, all you need to know is that this is the base URL, which the layer will be using.

Line [16]: `{layers: 'basic'},`

The third parameter is an anonymous object containing the layer **properties** (similar in format to the previous **options** object on line [12]), and is specific to the WMS layer class. These are the things that are actually added (more or less) straight into the GET call to the map server backend when OpenLayers makes requests for the map images.

JavaScript object notation

In OpenLayers, we pass in **anonymous objects** to classes a lot. In JavaScript, **anonymous objects** are comma separated `key:value` pairs, and are set up in the format of `{key1:value1, key2:value2}`. They are, basically, objects that are created without deriving from a class. This format is also referred to as **JavaScript Object Notation.**

When we say `key1:value1`, it's similar to saying `"key1 = value1"`, but we use a colon instead of an equals sign. We can also create an anonymous object and pass it in instead of creating it on the line, for example:

```
var layer_parameters = {layers: 'basic'};
var wms = new OpenLayers.Layer.WMS('layer_title', 'url',
layer_parameters, …);
```

With a WMS layer, we need to pass in, at a minimum, a `layers` key. In this case it has the value of `'basic'`. This `layer` parameter specifies layers that exist on the map server. So, when you ask the WMS server from a map image with the layer `'basic'`, it sends you back an image that is composed of that layer. You can also ask for multiple layers from the map server. In this case, we only want the WMS service to give us back an image that contains a layer called `'basic'`.

Let's get back to the code.

Line [17]: `{ }`

The fourth parameter is an optional **options** object, an anonymous object in the format we just discussed. These properties are generally shared by every OpenLayers Layer class. For instance, regardless of the Layer type (e.g., WMS or Google Layer), you can pass in an opacity setting (e.g., `{opacity: .8}` for 80 percent opacity). So, regardless of whether you are working with a WMS or a Vector layer, this opacity property can apply to either layer.

> Since this is the last thing passed into the Layer object creation call, make sure there is not a leading trailing comma. Trailing commas are a common error and are often tedious to debug.

This **options** object is optional, but we will often use it, so it's a good habit to keep our code consistent and provide an empty object (by `{}`), even if we aren't passing anything into it yet.

Line [18]: `);`

This simply finalizes the object creation call.

Line [20]: `map.addLayer(wms);`

Now that we have a `wms_layer` object created, we need to add it to the map object. Notice we are calling a function of the map object. There are actually a few ways to go about adding a layer to a map object. We can use the above code (by calling `map.addLayer`), where we pass in an individual layer, or we could use `map.addLayers`:

```
map.addLayers( [layer1, layer2, ...] );
```

Here, we pass an array of layers. Both methods are equally valid, but it may be easier to pass in an array when you have multiple layers.

You can also create the layer objects before you create the map object and pass the layer objects into the map when you create it, for instance:

```
map = new OpenLayers.Map('map_element', {layers: [layer1, layer2,
...]});
```

All ways are valid, but we will usually use `addLayer` or `addLayers` throughout the book.

Line [21] - [23]:

```
if(!map.getCenter()){
  map.zoomToMaxExtent();
}
```

Finally, we must specify the map's viewable area. Here, the actual code that moves the map is `map.zoomToMaxExtent()`, which zooms the map to the map's maximum extent. It is inside an `if` statement. This `if` statement checks to see whether the map already has a center point.

The reason why we add in this check is because, by default, your map can accept a specially formatted URL that can contain an extent and layers to turn on/off. This is, in more common terms, referred to as a `permalink`. If we did not check to see if a center has already been set, permalinks would not work.

By default, your map adds an **argParser** control which will try to pull information from a permalink. We cover this in Chapter 6, but to see it in action now you can simply add the following to your URL, which will zoom the map to the same coordinate and zoom level: `?zoom=4&lat=56&lon=-116`

So, your URL might look like `c:/code/index.html?zoom=4&lat=56&lon=-116`

There are a few ways to set the map's extent. If you know you want to show everything, the `map.zoomToMaxExtent()` function is a quick and good way to do it. There are other ways as well, such as

```
map.zoomToExtent(new OpenLayers.Bounds([minx,miny,maxx,maxy]);
```

There are even more ways though. If you know a specific location you want the map to start at, this is another way to do it:

```
map.setCenter(new OpenLayers.LonLat(x,y));
map.zoomTo(5);
```

Where `x,y` are the Lon/Lat values, and `5` is the zoom level you wish to zoom to. By default, your map will have 16 zoom levels, which can be configured by setting the `numZoomLevels` property when creating your map object.

More ways exist, but these are the most common strategies. The basic idea is that you need to specify a center location and zoom level—setting the extent accomplishes this, as does explicitly setting the center and zoom level.

Line [24]: }

This simply finishes the `init()` function.

Lines [26], [27]:

These lines close the script tag and head tag.

Line [29]: `<body onload='init();'>`

This starts the body tag. When the page is finished loading, via the `onload='init();'` attribute in the `body` tag, it will call the JavaScript `init()` function. We have to wait until the page loads to do this because we cannot use the map div (or any HTML element) until the page has been loaded. Another way to do this would be to put the `init()` call in a JavaScript tag at the bottom of the page (which would not be called until the page loads), but both methods accomplish the same thing.

When browsers load a page, they load it from top to bottom. To use any **DOM** (**Document Object Model**) elements (any HTML element on your page) in JavaScript, they first have to be loaded by the browser. So, you cannot reference HTML with JavaScript before the browser sees the element. It'd be similar to trying to access a variable that hasn't yet been created. Even though we have JavaScript code that references the `map_element` div at the top of the page, it is not actually executed until the page is loaded (hence the need for the `onload` and `init()` function call).

Line [30] and [31]: `<div id='map_element' style='width: 500px; height: 500px'></div>`

To make an OpenLayers map, we need an HTML element where the map will be displayed in. Almost always this element will be a `div`. You can give it whatever ID you would like, and the ID of this HTML element is passed into the call to create the map object. You can style the div however you would like—setting the width and height to be 100 percent, for instance, if you wanted a full page map. It would be best to style the elements using CSS, but styling the div in line like this works as well.

Lines [32] and [33]: These lines finalize the page by closing the remaining tags.

Behind the scenes—Object Oriented Programming (OOP)

Now, let's talk about how this stuff works from a more theoretical and technical level. OpenLayers employs **Object Oriented Programming** (**OOP**) techniques, meaning that to use with the library, we create **objects** from built in **classes** that OpenLayers provides.

What does this mean? You already are familiar with what classes and objects are, but you just may not know it. Think of the concepts of a **class** and **object** in terms of the parts of speech. For example, think of what the abstract idea of a noun means—a person, place, thing, or idea. Noun itself (the abstract idea) is a **class**. But the actual, concrete words that qualify as a noun are **objects**.

Interaction happens with objects

Ironman and **Batman** are two separate words (or, in terms of OOP, two **objects**), but they belong to the same noun **class**. A class is primarily used to generate objects; we interact with objects. Consider these two sentences:

"Noun was in a fight with noun."

"Ironman was in a fight with Batman."

Now, the second sentence is more of an actual sentence. We use the words **Ironman** and **Batman** in the sentence (which are objects; they are instances of the noun class). We don't use noun (a class) in the sentence, because interacting with a class like this doesn't make much sense. This is one of the important concepts of OOP—we interact with objects, and we generate objects through classes.

MadLibs

Madlibs, for those unfamiliar with it, is a game where you are given text with some missing words. The point is to come up with words to fill in the blanks, but each blank can only contain a certain type of word (noun, adjective, verb, and so on). The type of word is a **class** and the actual word you insert is an **object**.

Time for Action – play MadLibs

Finish this sentence, by replacing verb and noun with verb and noun 'objects':

I verb up to the noun. It's about 7 or 8 o'clock. I looked at my noun. I was there, to verb on my throne as prince of noun(place).

What Just Happened?

You just did a Madlibs, demonstrating some of the concepts of OOP. As you can see, it doesn't make much sense to read the sentence as "I verb up to the noun". Since verb and noun are classes, we don't use the actual term verb or noun in the sentence.

So, the idea would be to generate separate objects, one of the class noun and one of the class verb. For example, the previous sentence could be completed like: "I pulled up to the house". Pulled and house are objects that are instances of the verb and noun classes, respectively.

We use words that belong to those classes, which are **objects**. Another term used when referring to objects is **instance**, which is used to designate the class the object is derived from, for example, **Frodo** (a person / hobbit) is an instance of a noun.

Programming with OOP

The same concept applies to programming. The only thing we can really do with a class is to create an object from it. Objects are derived from classes—you can interact and do things with objects, but not with classes. So, in OpenLayers, we need to create objects from the built in classes to be able to really do anything. The main thing we need are map and layers objects. If we want to create an OpenLayers map, we need a map object, and we create it in the following manner:

```
var map = new OpenLayers.Map( … );
```

The `new` declaration means that we want to create a new object from the `OpenLayers.Map` class. The ellipsis (`...`) in the parenthesis presents things we pass into the class to create our object, called **arguments**. Each class expects different arguments to be passed into it. It is similar to the Madlibs example—the noun class accepts only certain words. If we were to create a word object in JavaScript, the code may look something like this:

```
var my_word_object = new Noun('Ironman');
```

Here, we pass in `'Ironman'` to the noun class, and now we have our word object. Because the Noun class only accepts nouns, this would work fine. If we try to pass in a verb, for instance, it would not work because the noun class cannot accept things that are verbs. Similarly, the **Map** class expects different arguments to be passed into it than the **Layer** class does.

Subclasses

There are also subclasses, which are classes derived from another class and inherit all the attributes from the 'base' class it inherits from. Subclasses can also override properties and methods that they inherit.

For instance, let's say we have a Dog class that is a subclass of the Animal class. The Dog class would inherit all the attributes of the base Animal class—such as, perhaps, a speak method. Now, the Dog class would override the speak method and it would bark (or 'yap' annoyingly) when called. The Dog class might also provide additional methods that weren't in the base Animal class, such as, perhaps, a wag_tail method.

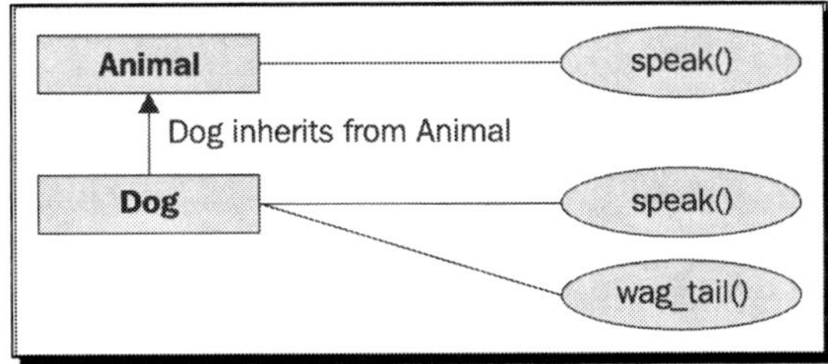

'Base' class and 'Subclasses' are both classes; the terminology just helps to clear up what class inherits from what other class.

There are many subclasses in OpenLayers, for example, the GoogleMap Layer class is a subclass of the base **Layer** class, and the **Navigation** control class is a subclass of the base **Control** class. Subclasses are still classes, and the exact same concept applies; we still need to generate objects from the class to use it.

The previous section was just an introduction to OOP. While you don't necessarily need to know a whole lot more about OOP concepts to use this book, a great resource to learn more about the concepts can be found at `http://en.wikipedia.org/wiki/Object-oriented_programming`.

Classes are easy to spot in OpenLayers code. By convention, in OpenLayers (and many other places) class names are `CamelCased`, which means the first letter of each word is capitalized, while objects are not. For example, `MyClass` would be an example of a class name, while `my_object` would be an example of an object.

Now what?

Our coverage of the sample code was not meant to be extremely thorough; just enough to give you an idea how it works. We'll be covering OOP concepts in more detail throughout the chapters, so if anything is bit unclear, don't worry too much.

As OpenLayers is a library and provides functions for you, it is important to know what those functions are and what they do. There are many places to do this, but the best source is the API docs.

API docs

The API documentation is always up to date and contains an exhaustive description of all the classes in OpenLayers. It is usually the best first place to go when you have a question. You can access the documentation at `http://dev.openlayers.org/docs/files/OpenLayers-js.html`. It is continually updated and contains a wealth of information. We will constantly refer to it throughout the book, so keep the link handy! Sometimes, however, the API docs may not seem clear enough, but there are plenty of other resources out there to help you.

Where to go for help

Books are great, but they're basically just a one way form of communication. If you have any questions that the book does not answer, Google is the best first place to go. Mailing lists and IRC are other great resources. Sometimes it's hard to formulate the right question, but there is help!

This book's website

The extension website for this book can be found at `http://vasir.net/openlayers_book`. Current, up to date corrections and code fixes, along with more advanced tutorials and explanations, can be found there—and also on my blog at `http://vasir.net/blog`. You can also grab the code and more information about this book at Packt Publishing's website for the book, located at `https://www.packtpub.com/openlayers-2-1-javascript-web-mapping-library-beginners-guide/book`.

Mailing lists

The OpenLayers mailing list is an invaluable resource that lets you not only post questions, but also browse questions others have asked (and answered). There are two main OpenLayers news groups—Users and Dev. The **Users** list is where the majority of questions are asked. **Dev** is reserved for development of the OpenLayers library itself. If you have questions about how to use OpenLayers, they belong in the Users list, not the Dev list. You can subscribe to the mailing list at `http://lists.osgeo.org/mailman/listinfo/openlayers-users`.

There are various ways to browse the content, and I prefer to use Nabble. You can view the lists at `http://osgeo-org.1803224.n2.nabble.com/OpenLayers-f1822462.html`.

Please do a thorough search before posting questions, as it is likely that a question similar to yours has already been asked and solved. If you have a question about using OpenLayers, please use the User list. Please do not post questions to the Dev list, unless it has to do strictly with development of the OpenLayers library itself.

When posting a question, please be as thorough as possible, stating your problem, what you have done, and the relevant source code (e.g. "I have a problem with using a WMS layer. I have tried this and that, and here is what my source code looks like..."). A good guideline for asking questions in a way that will best elicit a response can be found at `http://www.catb.org/~esr/faqs/smart-questions.html`.

IRC

Internet Relay Chat (IRC) is another great place to go if you have questions about OpenLayers. IRC is used for group communication; a big chat room, essentially. If you have exhausted Google and the mailing list, IRC provides you with real time with other people interested in OpenLayers.

Generally, the people who hang out in the OpenLayers chat room are very friendly, but please try to find an answer before asking in IRC. The server is `irc.freenode.net` and the chat room is `#openlayers`. You can download an IRC client online; a good Windows one is mIRC (`http://mirc.com`). More information about how to use IRC can be found at `http://www.mirc.com/install.html`.

OpenLayers source code repository

Traditionally, OpenLayers has used SVN as its revision management system. At the time of writing, however, the source code repository location is hosted at GitHub. You can access the entire code repository at `http://github.com/openlayers/openlayers`.

Feel free to download a copy and play around with it yourself. There is a process to actually get your code permanently added to the official source code base, but it cannot hurt to download a copy of the code base and look around it yourself to figure out how it's really working!

Summary

In this chapter we were introduced to OpenLayers and learned a bit about it.

We saw what Web Map Applications are and how they work. After that, we created our first map with OpenLayers, then analyzed how the code works. Then we covered a fundamental concept, Object Oriented Programming, which we'll need to know about while really working with OpenLayers. Lastly, resources for help and information outside this book were provided.

Now that we have a basic handle on OpenLayers, we'll jump straight into debugging OpenLayers. By doing so, we'll cover more thoroughly many of the concepts that we've discussed, such as how OpenLayers requests and receives map images, and how it puts them together.

2

Squashing Bugs With Firebug

OpenLayers is, at a fundamental level, not doing anything that is conceptually too hard to grasp. It gets map images from a server, and puts them together. From a technical level, however, there is a lot of work going on, and it might seem magical how it all works together so well.

Fortunately, there are many tools to dispel any potential magical thinking we might have and show us how OpenLayers is working behind the scenes. Firebug, a free and open source plugin for Firefox, is one such great tool. Speeding up development time, viewing network communication, and squashing bugs are just a few things that Firebug, and other web development tools, do that make them hard to live without.

To really use OpenLayers effectively and to its full potential, we need to understand how it works. In this chapter, we'll try our best to do just that, by using web development tools to examine OpenLayers' inner workings. By doing so, we'll accomplish two things. First, we'll become familiar with these tools which will significantly help us when developing our maps. Secondly, and more importantly for now, we'll gain a better understanding of how OpenLayers works.

Throughout this chapter we'll cover:

- What Firebug and other development tools are
- Setting up Firebug
- Each of the Firebug Panels
- Using the JavaScript Command Line Console panel

What is Firebug?

Firebug is a free, open source addon for Firefox. If you do not have Firefox, I recommend downloading it (it is also free and open source). However, other modern and standards based browsers, such as Google's Chrome, Apple's Safari, and Opera, also work well and have great built in developer tools.

Firebug, and other web development tools, makes the web development process much easier and quicker. What do I mean by this? With these tools, we can change anything on our site, on the fly, without editing or saving any files. We can type in JavaScript code with a command line interface and execute it immediately. We can view all the requests that our web page sends to servers, along with the server's reply. For example, if our map isn't able to get back map images from the server, we could examine the requests our page is making and find out if we have any typos or haven't set up our map layer properly.

Using these tools makes it a lot easier to develop not only an OpenLayers mapping application, but any web application, and makes it easier to fix any bugs we encounter in the process. We'll focus on Firebug in this chapter and refer back to it throughout the book, but other tools such as Google's Chrome and Apple's Safari's built in developer tools work just as well (although some functionality may vary).

Setting up Firebug

Since Firebug is an extension of Firefox, you'll need to first install Firefox. You can download it for free at `http://getfirefox.com`. After that, Firebug can be freely downloaded at `http://getfirebug.com`. When you click on the link to download Firebug, Firefox will prompt you with a message asking if you wish to install the plugin. After installing, all you have to do is restart Firefox and you'll be good to go.

Time for Action – downloading Firebug

If you do not already have an up to date version of Firefox installed, please do so now. After you have installed Firefox, set up Firebug by following these steps:

1. Go to `http://getfirebug.com`.
2. Click on the **Install Firebug for Firefox** button. Once you click this, you should see a message similar to this:

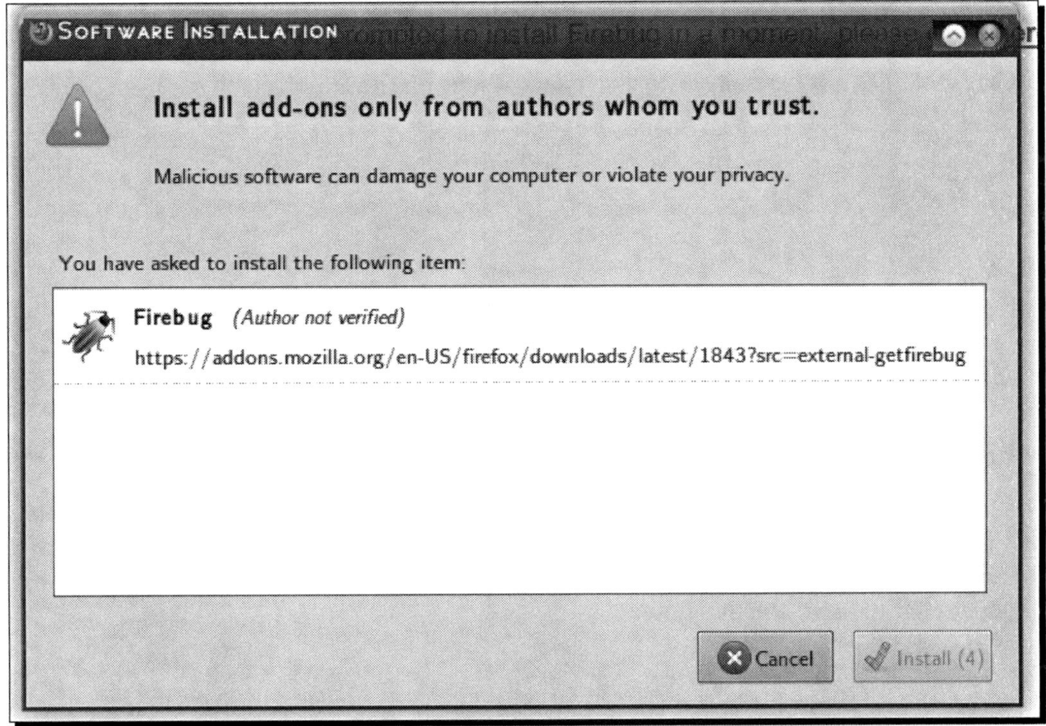
Software Installation
Install add-ons only from authors whom you trust.
Malicious software can damage your computer or violate your privacy.
You have asked to install the following item:
Firebug (Author not verified)
https://addons.mozilla.org/en-US/firefox/downloads/latest/1843?src=external-getfirebug
Cancel
Install (4)

3. Click **Install**, wait for it to finish installing, and then restart Firefox.

4. Now that Firebug is installed, you should see a Firebug icon on the bottom right side of your screen.

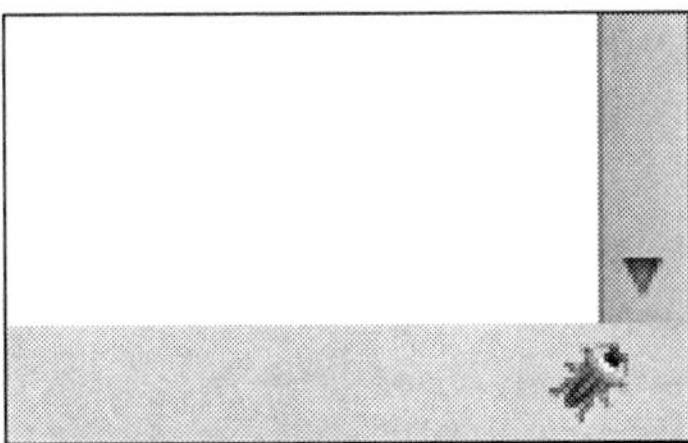

What Just Happened?

When Firebug is not enabled, the **Firebug Icon** is gray. When it is in enabled, it has an orange color—this is just a quick way for you to tell if Firebug is enabled or not for the current page you're on.

When you click on the Firebug icon (near the bottom right of your browser's window), Firebug will open and you can start using it. But before we start, let's take a look at what Firebug looks like after initially installing it and clicking on the Firebug icon:

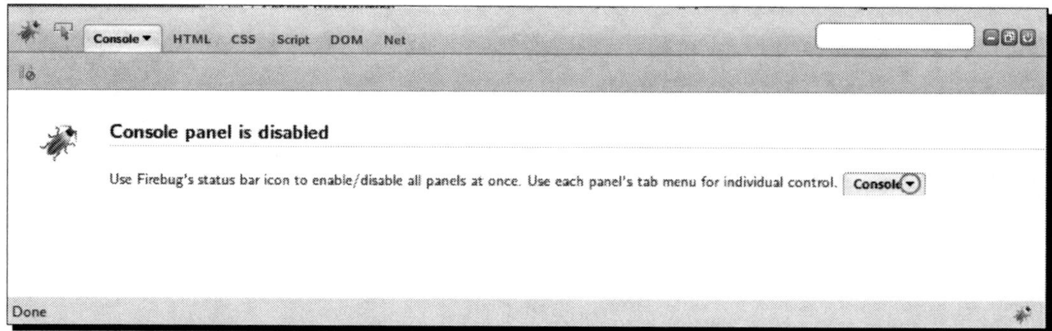

The top row contains two icons (a **Firebug icon** and a **Page Inspector** icon), multiple **panels** that provide specific functionality (they look and act similar to tabs, but the technical term is "panels"), a search box, and finally minimize, maximize, and close the buttons. Let's go over the items, left to right, one at a time.

The position of the icons may change over time as Firebug is updated; but the general functionality should remain (more or less) the same.

Firebug controls

Firebug icon: The Firebug icon on the top left contains various commands and options related to Firebug when you click on it.

Page Inspector icon: This icon, a cursor inside a rectangle, is the **HTML Inspector**. When you click on it, your mouse cursor will identify HTML elements on the web page. So, when you mouse over anything on a website, the element will be outlined in blue and the **HTML** panel will open up and show you the element your mouse is over.

Panels

The next set of controls is called **panels**; each panel provides a different type of function. The panels act like tabs (the two terms can be used interchangeably), but Firebug refers to them as 'panels' in the documentation. Let's go over each panel, since they are, essentially, what makes up Firebug.

Console panel

Firebug's **Console panel** is where we'll spend most of our time. It acts as a powerful JavaScript command line, or interpreter, which means we can type in JavaScript code and execute it right away—no need to save or edit any files.

One thing that makes this so useful is that we can interact directly with the **DOM** (**Document Object Model**—any HTML element on the webpage), including any existing JavaScript code the page contains. So, this means we're able to interact with our OpenLayers map on the fly, issuing command and testing code to instantly see what works and what doesn't. As you can imagine, this saves a ton of time!

By default, the Console panel is disabled. To enable it, click on the arrow near the **Console** text and select **Enabled**.

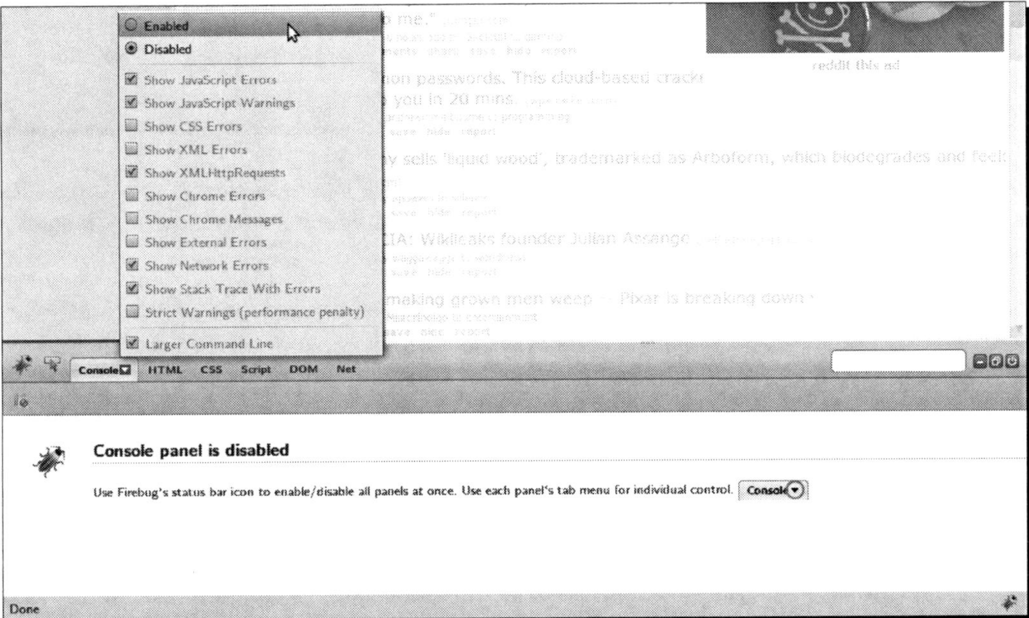

HTML panel

The HTML panel provides not just a display of the HTML source code, but also the ability to quickly edit any HTML element and its associated style. You can add and remove HTML elements, edit HTML attributes, and change nearly anything about the page without having to save any files. It's great for development.

How it works

Firebug automatically builds a tree structure from your HTML code, allowing you to expand and hide each HTML tag. It is important to note that the code you see in the HTML panel is generated HTML code—the code in the panel may not be exactly the same as the page's source code.

HTML panel contents

Here is what the HTML tab looks like when Firebug is opened while viewing a webpage:

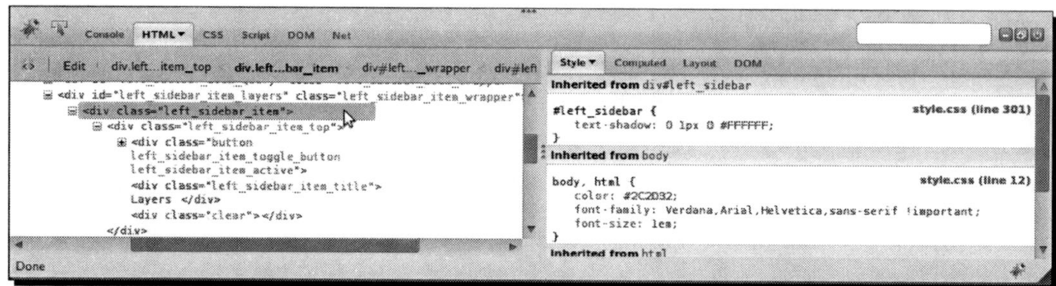

On the left side, Firebug shows us the HTML of the page. We can right click on any tag and do various things—such as copying the HTML to the clipboard, deleting the element, changing the tag attributes, and more.

On the right side, we see the associated style information for the element we have selected. Here, we can modify or add properties and they will instantly appear on the page. In this example we selected a `div` element with a class of `'left_sidebar_item'`. Looking at the CSS on the right side, there is no definition for the `'left_sidebar_item'` class (if there was, we would see something called `.left_sidebar_item`, with a period in front of it to indicate that it is indeed a class). We do, however, see a definition for `#left_sidebar`, which is a parent div of the currently selected div.

> If you are unfamiliar with HTML or CSS, the w3schools site is a great resource. For more information on HTML, visit `http://www.w3schools.com/html/default.asp` and for CSS visit `http://www.w3schools.com/css/default.asp`.

What does this mean? Well, Firebug lists all inherited style information, and parent element styles propagate down to all their child elements (each child has all its parent's styles, unless the child overrides a style, which doesn't happen in this example). That's why we also see the `body, html` definition, and every div will display that, since every div sits inside the `<html>` and `<body>` tags of the web page.

By double clicking on pretty much anything in the HTML or CSS list you can quickly change values and names. Any change you make will immediately show up on the page, which makes it very easy to change style in real time and see how the page is affected without having to edit and save any files. Play around with it a bit—if you mess anything up, you can just reload the page.

When editing pages with Firebug, any changes you make will disappear when you refresh the page. You are not editing the actual web server's files with Firebug—instead, you are editing a copy that is on your computer that only you can see when you make changes to it. So, if you make any changes and want them to be saved, you'll have to edit your actual source code.

CSS panel

This panel provides similar functionality as the CSS sidebar in the **HTML panel** we just talked about. It also provides the option to edit any CSS document associated with the page, not just the style of a selected element. We need not talk much about this panel, and for the purposes of this book we won't spend much time here. But if you are a web designer, this is another powerful panel that can greatly speed up your development time.

Script panel

The Script panel is very powerful. Not only does it allow you to view all the JavaScript code associated with the page, it is a great real-time code debugger. You can set watch expressions, view the stack, set breakpoints, etc. If those terms are foreign, don't worry, we won't be spending much time with this panel.

However, before we move on to the next panel I want to quickly talk about enabling **breaking on errors**. With this option enabled, Firebug will stop the web page whenever a JavaScript error is encountered. This makes it very easy to quickly pinpoint where your page is blowing up at. To enable it, simply click on the pause-button icon.

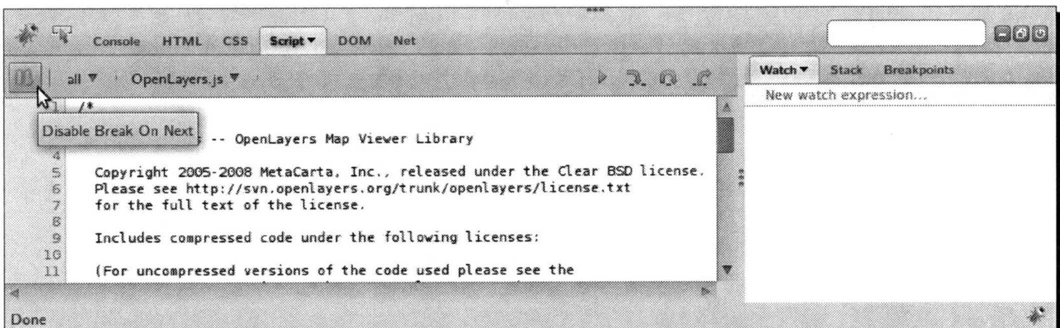

Keep note of when you enable it—I've been frustrated more than once when developing because I forgot that it had been enabled. When it is enabled, the `Script` text will glow yellow, as demonstrated in the above screenshot. You can also enable/disable it through the Console panel.

Unfortunately (depending on your viewpoint), we can't go much more in depth with these tools, as it is outside the scope of this book. But please feel free to play around with them, as Firebug's powerful debugger is a great resource. More information on it can be found at `http://getfirebug.com/errors`.

DOM panel

The next panel is the Document Object Model panel, or **DOM** panel. The DOM is, basically, a representation of HTML elements as objects. The DOM panel automatically sets up a tree structure to represent our HTML page, allowing us to view everything our HTML page contains. We can also see JavaScript variables and their values, as well as functions, objects, and more. When using the DOM panel, attributes and properties are colored black, and functions and methods are colored green.

We won't go much more in depth here, but the DOM panel is a very valuable tool, especially when you want to take a peek at JavaScript components. By using the DOM panel (and assuming we are looking at a page that includes OpenLayers), we can quickly see all of OpenLayer's classes, functions, etc. It is not a replacement for the API docs, but serves as a good, quick way to view such information.

Net panel

Firebug's **Net** panel is a tool we will often use throughout this book. Basically, it provides a way for us to monitor network activity by viewing all the requests and responses the web page is making. We can see any Asynchronous JavaScript (**AJAX**) request the page makes. Without AJAX, we would have to refresh our entire page anytime we wanted to do anything with our OpenLayers map. So, for example, every time you zoom in, OpenLayers makes a series of **requests** to the map server to get new map images, and the map server's **response** is a new map image that OpenLayers then displays. This request/response method is handled via AJAX—without it, we would have to refresh the entire page after every request.

AJAX is a method by which, through JavaScript, you can send a request to a server and receive a response without actually refreshing the page. Traditionally, if you want your web page to get an update from the server, you would need to have the page itself send a request.

The Net panel allows us to see the URL that is being requested, the GET or POST parameters, the server's response, the size of the response in KB, and the time it took to complete the request. You may also have to enable the Net panel—it can be enabled in a similar way we enabled the Console panel, by clicking on the arrow next to the **Net** text on the top tab. Let's take a look at what the Net panel looks like for the example from Chapter 1:

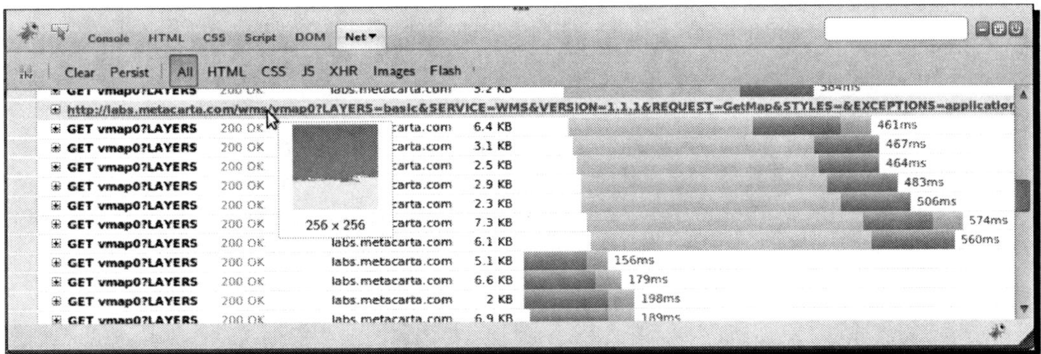

Before we talk about the requests being made, take a look at the toolbar above the lists of requests—the one that contains the links **Clear**, **Persist**, **All**, **HTML**, etc. Clicking on **Clear** will do what its name implies—clears out the list of requests. Clicking on **Persist** will cause the list of requests to persist, or not get deleted, on page reloads.

The next grouping of links allows us to filter the requests by type. Because we are getting back only images from the map server in this case, all the requests you see would belong to the **Images** option. If the **CSS** option was clicked, we would not see those requests, as they are not CSS files.

Now, let's break down the actual **request list**.

Request list

The request list shows us all the requests the page makes. Each URL in the previous screenshot is a URL that OpenLayers is making a request to. By clicking on the **+** (plus) sign next to each request, we can get more information about the request, including the full request URL and the response. When we click on the plus sign, we get a box with **Params**, **Headers**, **Response**, and **Cache** tabs. The **Params** tab lists all the parameters, or key/value pairs the URL contains. The **Response** tab provides us with the server's response to our request. For the purpose of this book, we do not need to worry about the other two tabs.

Parameters

Take a look again at the list—before we mouse over the text in the screenshot, the titles contain **GET vmap0?LAYERS**. The **GET** specifies that the request type is GET, which basically means we are embedding variables inside the URL itself with `key=value` pairs, separated by a `&` sign.

When we mouse over a URL, we can see more of it—as in the previous screenshot, we see a bunch of variables in the format `key=value&key=value& . . .`. These values correspond to the values listed in the **Params** tab when you expand the URL.

If you take a look at the link we have our mouse over, you'll notice that the URL is the same as the URL from the example in Chapter 1, `http://labs.metacarta.com/wms/vmap0`. However, there is an additional text after `vmap0`; a question mark followed by `key=value` pairs. The question mark signifies the start of the `key=value` pairs in a GET request.

Let's take a look at some of the variables the URL contains.

```
?LAYERS=basic&SERVICE=wms . . .
```

The `LAYERS` key should look familiar, as we specified in Chapter 1. In that example, we used the code:

```
{layers: 'basic'},
```

When we defined the `key:value` pair, we were essentially telling OpenLayers what to pass into the actual URL it generates. From the generated URL, we can see that it did indeed pass over the right layer name. Now, as we discussed earlier, this layer name, `basic`, is the layer we want from the WMS service. The layer name we pass in here affects what image the WMS server responds with. In this case, we'll get back an image with the layer named `basic`.

Notice that there are many more parameters (separated by `&` signs) than what we passed in. OpenLayers automatically adds these parameters for you, so we get back the right image of a map without us having to manually build each URL.

To see the entire `key:value` pairs, or parameters, expand the URL and look at the **Params** tab.

Note that these GET variables, such as LAYERS and SERVICE are specific to WMS. Other layer types will use different values.

BBOX parameter

One of the important variables to take a look at in the URL is the **BBOX**, or **Bounding Box**, parameter. Expand one of the URLs by clicking on the plus sign next to it and take a look in the **Params** tab. This BBOX number is the extent of that individual map image piece. You'll see a number in the following format:

```
minx, miny, maxx, maxy
```

These four numbers form a rectangle that contains the extent of the map image. A number example might be something like `-73.5, 39.3, -67.5, 45`. These numbers will depend on the projection your map is in—but don't worry too much about that for now.

If you look at the BBOX parameter of other URLs, you'll notice that part (or all) of the BBOX values change for each request. URLs that are grouped together in the request list share some values for their BBOX parameter. It is analogous to a grid; each request returns an individual cell of the grid. (This functionality is not the same for all Layer types in OpenLayers, but this basic concept holds for the majority of Layer types, including the WMS layer in this example.)

Pop Quiz– panel

1. What panel would you use if you wanted to execute JavaScript code?
   a. The Net panel
   b. The Console panel
   c. The DOM panel
   d. The HTML panel

Panel conclusion

Each panel serves a certain purpose and all of Firebug's panels are extremely useful, but throughout the book we will be mainly focusing on the following panels:

- Console panel (Command Line JavaScript)
- HTML panel
- Net panel

These three panels will be used the most throughout the book. We'll occasionally come back to the other panels, but we won't spend a whole lot of time with them. However, before we conclude this chapter, let's get a bit more familiar with the **Console panel**, since we'll be making heavy use of it in the coming chapters.

Using the Console panel

We talked a bit about what the console panel is—essentially, a JavaScript command line. We can execute any JavaScript code we want, and interact with any page element. There are two primary components to the Console panel—the **console log area** and the **input area.**

The **console log area** will display information about any errors, along with displaying any code that is entered. The **input area** allows us to either enter a single line of code or, by clicking on the red arrow on the right side of the input box, multiple lines of code.

Before we start using the console with our maps, let's get familiar with the console by executing some JavaScript code.

Time for Action – executing code in the Console

We're going to do some basic JavaScript coding via the Firebug console; specifically, just calling a built in `alert()` function to display an alert.

1. Open up Firefox. It doesn't matter at this point what website (if any) that you go to, since we will be writing a stand alone code.

2. Open up Firebug by clicking on the Firebug icon. Go to the **Console** panel. If it is not enabled, enable it.

3. Now, at the bottom of your screen you'll see an area where you can enter code, designated by **>>>**. Clicking anywhere after that will allow you to enter the code.

4. Type in the following code, and then hit *Enter*.

   ```
   alert('Narwhals like bacon');
   ```

5. You should see an alert box pop up with the text `Narhwals like bacon` (or whatever string you passed into the `alert` function). After the code is executed, it will appear in the log above the input line.

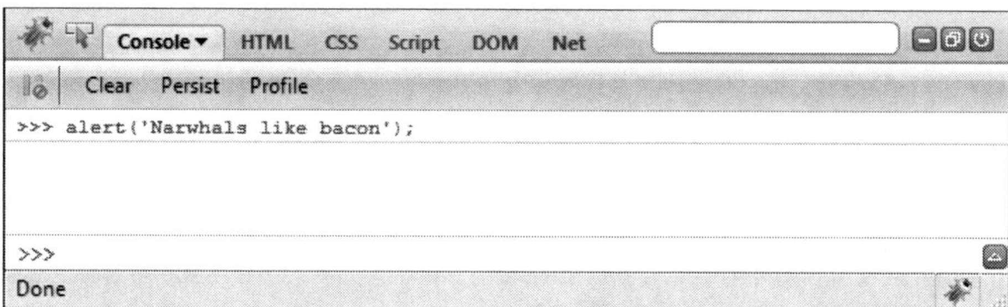

What Just Happened?

We just executed some JavaScript code without having to edit and save any files. Although we did a simple alert, we are really not limited by what we can do. Anything that we could save in a JavaScript file, we could enter in the Console.

You'll also notice that the same code that we typed in appeared in the log area. We'll also get an error message if any errors occur with the code—go ahead and try it! Instead of typing `alert('My alert');` type something like `fakealert('Boom');`. This will give you a reference error, since nowhere is the function `fakealert()` defined—`alert()`, on the other hand, is a built in function, so we can call it from any page.

That's pretty much to it! The rest just builds on those principles. Let's go ahead and do just one more thing, something only slightly more involved, before jumping into manipulating an OpenLayers page.

Time for Action – creating object literals

We're going to introduce object literals and get acclimated with how to manipulate them now, so we can better work with OpenLayers code.

1. Open up Firefox and Firebug's Console panel (enabling it if it disabled)—again, it doesn't matter right now what page you're on.

2. Click on the red arrow on the bottom right, above the Firebug icon. This will open up a side panel where we can type in multiple lines of code. The code will not be executed when we press *Enter*, like in single line mode. Instead, we can execute the code by either pressing *Ctrl + Enter* or clicking **Run**.

3. Type in the following code, and then execute it by pressing *Ctrl+Enter* or clicking **Run**.

   ```
   var my_parameters = {'answer': 42, 'question': null};
   console.log(my_parameters);
   ```

4. The above code should display, in the console log area, something similar to **Object { answer=42 }**. Click on it, and the DOM panel will open, showing you all the information about the object you just created.

5. Click on the Console panel to get back to it. In the input box, add the following code to the existing code and execute it:

   ```
   console.log(my_parameters.answer);
   ```

6. You should see a line of output in the console area containing the number **42**.

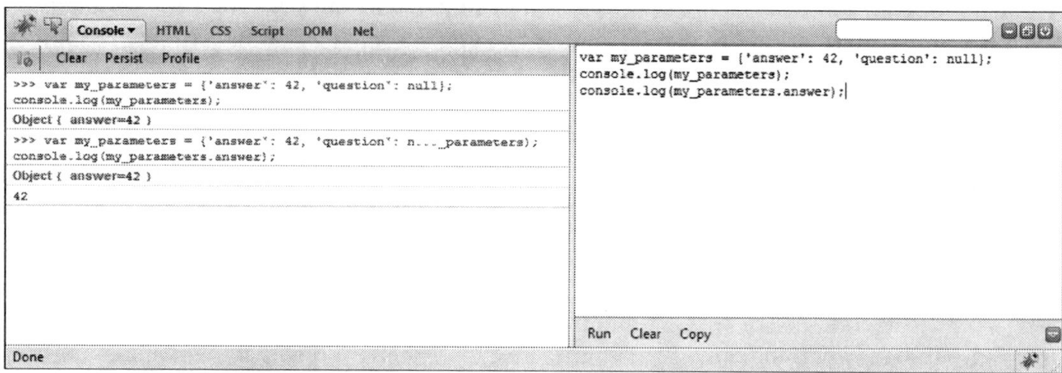

What Just Happened?

We just created what is called in JavaScript an anonymous object, or **object literal**. Now, we have discussed how objects are created from classes, and in JavaScript we need to use the `new` keyword to instantiate an object from a class. But there is no `new` keyword here!

Object literals

The key concept here is that we are just creating a single object that does not derive from a class. Since object literals (anonymous objects) do not derive from a class, it is, essentially, an empty object. It contains *only* what we explicitly define. The value associated with a key can be almost anything—a string, integer, function, array, or even another object literal.

We encountered object literals in Chapter 1 when we discussed **JavaScript Object Notation**—they were the `{key:value}` pairs used to define the parameters and options of our layer and objects. The only difference is that we did not assign a variable to them; we simply passed them in when we created our layer object.

Object literals are extremely useful for a variety of tasks, and it is a great way to package information in an easy to use form. They are in the form of `{key:value, key2:value2}`. We can access any property of an object literal by using **dot notation**, in the form of `my_object_literal.key`. The key, like before, is the `key` part of the `key:value` pair. In the above code, we call `console.log(my_parameters.answer);` and the value of the key `answer` is displayed in the console's log area.

console.log(): The Firebug function `console.log()` is a function that will, essentially, display what you pass into it in the console log. You can pass in variables, strings, objects; anything, and it will display in the log. It comes in handy often, so getting familiar with it is a good idea.

We will use object literals frequently when making our maps—so if they don't make much sense yet, don't worry. The basic idea to grasp, and the primary way we will use them, is that they are essentially `key:value` pairs. Before we end this chapter, let's do one quicker example where we interact with an OpenLayers map using the Console panel.

Time for Action – interacting with a map

We'll use the map we created in Chapter 1 to do this example, interacting with our OpenLayers map by calling various functions of the map.

1. Open up the map from Chapter 1 in Firefox. Enable Firebug and the Console panel. If you would like, you can take a look at the Net panel and view the network activity to see the requests your page is making.

2. Go to the Console panel, input and then execute the following code:

   ```
   console.log(map);
   ```

3. You should see the map object information come up in the console log. Click on it, and take a moment to look over the various attributes it has. Near the bottom, you can see a list of all the functions that belong to it (which are also referred to as methods).

   Take note of the function names, as we'll be using them.

4. Go back to the Console panel, type in and execute the following code:

   ```
   map.zoomIn();
   map.getExtent();
   ```

5. Take note of the extent. Clear out the code you typed in, then type in the following and execute it:

   ```
   map.zoomToMaxExtent();
   map.getExtent();
   ```

6. Now, let's take a look at some properties of the map object. We can access the map properties using the `dot notation`, which we discussed previously. Clear any code you've typed so far, input and execute the following code:

```
console.log(map.id);
console.log(map.numZoomLevels);
```

7. Refer back to the functions of the map object (by running `console.log(map);` then clicking on the output in the log area). Try playing around with different functions and attributes the map object has. To access the functions, you just need to type in `map.function();`.

   You can also access the properties of the map by typing `map.key`, where `key` would be something like `id` (so the full code would be `map.id`). The attributes are black in the DOM panel, and the functions are colored green.

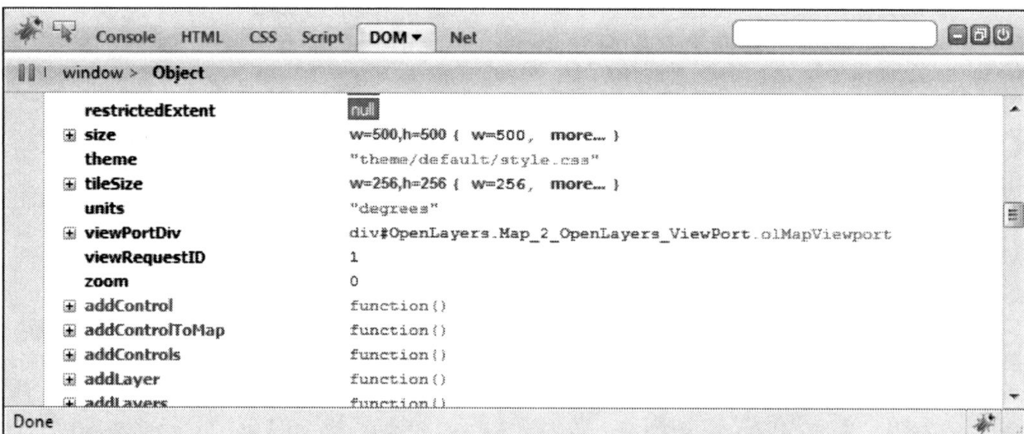

What Just Happened?

We just executed some functions of our map and accessed some properties of it. All we have to do is call our object, `map`, followed by a period, then a function or property it owns. Using this dot notation (e.g., `map.zoomIn();`), we can access any property or function of the map object.

We also saw how the DOM panel comes in handy, and took a look at functions that we can call, which the map object owns. Any function listed there can be called via `map.functionname();`, but some functions require parameters to be passed in or they will not work. But where can we go to figure out more information about the functions and what they require?

Have a Go Hero – experiment with functions

Try to call different functions that you see listed in the **DOM** tab. Many functions will not work unless you pass certain arguments into them, but don't be afraid of errors! Poke around the various functions and properties and try to interact with them using the **Console** tab like in the example above.

API documentation

The API documentation for the Map class, which our map object derives from (and thus, inherits all the functions and properties of the class) provides more detailed explanations of the properties, functions, and what we can do with them. They can be found at `http://dev.openlayers.org/apidocs`. Even though Firebug is a great resource to quickly interact with code and learn from it, the API docs present an extra level of information that Firebug cannot necessarily provide.

Summary

In this chapter, we learned more about how OpenLayers works. We learned how to set up and use Firebug and other Web Development tools.

We then took a look at the panels that Firebug provides and what they are used for. Finally, we spent time with the Console panel—something you'll be making extensive use of throughout this book (and when you're developing your own web maps).

This chapter aimed to provide some foundational knowledge of web development tools for getting into both OpenLayers and general web development. Web development tools, like Firebug, are one of the biggest assets in our toolkit. They speed up development time, help us identify bugs, interact with our code better, and much more.

Firebug and such tools can also degrade performance if you are just browsing the web, so it is probably best to leave them disabled unless you're using them.

For the code exercises in the following chapters, it will be very beneficial if you use Firebug to first test the code, to see what it's doing. That way, you immediately know, so to say, where each piece of the puzzle fits in; you know what each line of code actually does, and how it affects the entire project.

In the next chapter, we'll really dive into OpenLayers, covering perhaps the most fundamental topic in OpenLayers: the Layer class.

3
The 'Layers' in OpenLayers

Maps can contain an overwhelming amount of information, but some maps don't show enough. Figuring out just what information to display on a map is certainly an art form, and creating printed maps with just the right balance of information is quite difficult.

Fortunately, creating maps for the web is slightly easier in this respect, because we can let the user determine what information they want to see. Imagine two people looking at a city map—one person just cares about the bus routes, while the other wants to only know about bicycle routes. Instead of creating two maps, we could create a single map with two different layers, one for each route. Then the user can decide if they want to see the bus routes, bicycle routes, both, or none at all.

OpenLayers provides us with a variety of layer types to choose from and use. We can do all sorts of things—such as changing layer opacity, turning the layers on or off, changing the layer order, and much more.

In this chapter we'll go over what Layers are—both in the abstract and concrete sense (via OpenLayer's **Layer** class). By the end, you will possess enough expertise to use different types of Layers on your map and interact with them. In this chapter, we will:

- Learn what layers are
- Show the difference between base layers and overlay layers
- Talk about the WMS layer class
- Learn about the layer class properties
- Cover other types of layers
- Discuss layer class functions

What's a layer?

A **layer** is basically a way to show multiple levels of information independent of each other. Layers are not just a mapping or cartography concept; graphic designers and digital artists make heavy use of layers.

Imagine a printed-out map of a city. Let's say you also have two sheets of transparent paper. One sheet has blue lines that indicate bus routes, and the other sheet contains green lines that indicate bicycle routes. Now, if you placed the transparent sheet of paper with bicycle routes on top of the map, you would see a map of the city with the bicycle routes outlined.

Putting on or taking off these transparent pieces of paper would be equivalent to turning a layer on or off. The order you place the sheets on top of each other also affects what the map will look like—if two lines intersect, you would either see the green line on top or the blue line on top. That's the basic concept of a layer.

Layers in OpenLayers

OpenLayers is a JavaScript framework, and as discussed earlier is built using **Object Oriented Programming**. When we want to actually create a layer, we create (or instantiate) an object from an OpenLayers **Layer** class.

OpenLayers has many different Layer classes, each allowing you to connect to a different type of map server 'back end.' For example, if you wanted to connect to a WMS map server, you would use the `Layer.WMS` class, and if you wanted to use Google Maps you'd use the `Layer.Google` class. Each layer object is independent of other layer objects, so doing things to one layer won't necessarily affect the other.

How many layers can I have?

The safest maximum amount of layers you can have on a map at one time depends largely on the user's machine (i.e., their processing power and memory). Too many layers can also overwhelm users; many popular web maps (e.g., Google and Yahoo!) contain just a few layers. If you need to use tons of layers (say, more than fifty), it might be a better idea to create/destroy them as necessary, as having too many layers may slow down your map on some machines.

Whatever the purpose of your web map application is, you will need at least one layer to have a usable map. An OpenLayers map without any layers would be sort of like an atlas without any maps. You need at least one layer—at least one **Base layer**. All other layers that 'sit above' the base layer are called **Overlay layers**. These are the two 'types' of layers in OpenLayers.

Base layer

A base layer is at the very bottom of the layer list, and all other layers are on top of it. This would be our printed out map from the earlier example. The order of the other layers can change, but the base layer is always below the overlay layers. By default, the first layer that you add to your map acts as the base layer. You can, however, change the property of any layer on your map to act as the base layer (by setting the `isBaseLayer` property to `True`).

You may also have *multiple* base layers. However, only *one* base layer can be active at a time. When one base layer is turned on, all the other base layers are turned off. Overlay layers (non base layers), however, do not behave this way—turning on or off overlay layers will not affect other overlay layers. Base layers are similar to radio buttons—only one can be active at a time. Overlay layers are similar to check boxes—you can have as many on or off as you'd like.

> At the time of writing, there was a discussion to remove the 'base layer' terminology and replace it with 'mutually exclusive layers.' If this is the case when you are reading this, the ideas and concepts work the same as the base layer/overlay concept.

Overlay layers

Any layer that is not a base layer is called an overlay layer. Like we talked about, the order that you add layers to your map is important. Every time you add a layer to the map, it is placed above the previous one.

> Throughout the rest of this book, we'll be using the map we created in Chapter 1's example as a sort of template. The only thing that will change is that you will not be using the lines of code that create the WMS layer and add it to the map. You will need to delete those lines of code yourself, or refer to the template from the book's website at `http://vasir.net/openlayers_book/`.

Time for Action – creating a map with multiple layers

Let's create a map with two WMS layers. One layer will act as our base layer, and the other will be an overlay layer containing labels for country, state, and city names.

1. Create a copy of the file you made for the last example of Chapter 1 and remove the existing WMS layer code (or, use the template from `http://vasir.net/openlayers_book/`). You can name it whatever you'd like, but we'll refer to it as `chapter3_ex1_wms_layers.html`. Make sure it is in the same directory as your `OpenLayers.js` file.

1. First we're going to remove everything that was in the `init()` function. Your function should now look like this:

```
function init() {
}
```

2. Next, inside the `init()` function, we're going to setup our map object like before:

```
map = new OpenLayers.Map('map_element', {});
```

3. Now we're going to create our first layer. We'll use a WMS layer and ask the WMS server for the layer `'basic'` (a layer on the WMS service). We'll also explicitly set it to be a base layer.

```
var wms_layer_map = new OpenLayers.Layer.WMS(
  'Base layer',
  'http://vmap0.tiles.osgeo.org/wms/vmap0',
  {layers: 'basic'},
  {isBaseLayer: true}
);
```

4. Let's create a second layer object now. It will also be a WMS layer. This time, we're going to ask for a few different layers from the WMS service—a bunch of labels. We're also going to set the `transparent` property to `true`, so the map images which the server sends back will be transparent. We'll also set the opacity to be 50 percent (by setting the `opacity` to `.5`). This layer will be an **overlay** layer.

```
var wms_layer_labels = new OpenLayers.Layer.WMS(
  'Location Labels',
  'http://vmap0.tiles.osgeo.org/wms/vmap0',
  {layers: 'clabel,ctylabel,statelabel',
  transparent: true},
  {opacity: .5}
);
```

5. Time to add the layers to the map. We'll use the `addLayers` function and pass in an array of layer objects.

```
map.addLayers([wms_layer_map, wms_layer_labels]);
```

6. Now, let's add a **Layer Switcher** control that will show us the layers on the map.

```
map.addControl(new OpenLayers.Control.LayerSwitcher({}));
```

7. Finally, we need to set the map center information. This last step needs to be repeated for all further examples throughout the book—you need to be sure to include it even if it isn't explicitly asked for. All our maps will need to have their extent set somehow, and this is one standard way to do so (refer to Chapter 1 for more explanation).

```
if(!map.getCenter()){
  map.zoomToMaxExtent();
}
```

8. Save the file, and then open it up in your web browser (preferably Firefox, since we'll be using Firebug). Because we're just working with HTML and JavaScript, you don't need to place this on a server or anything. You can simply open the file with your web browser directly from the folder. You should see something like this:

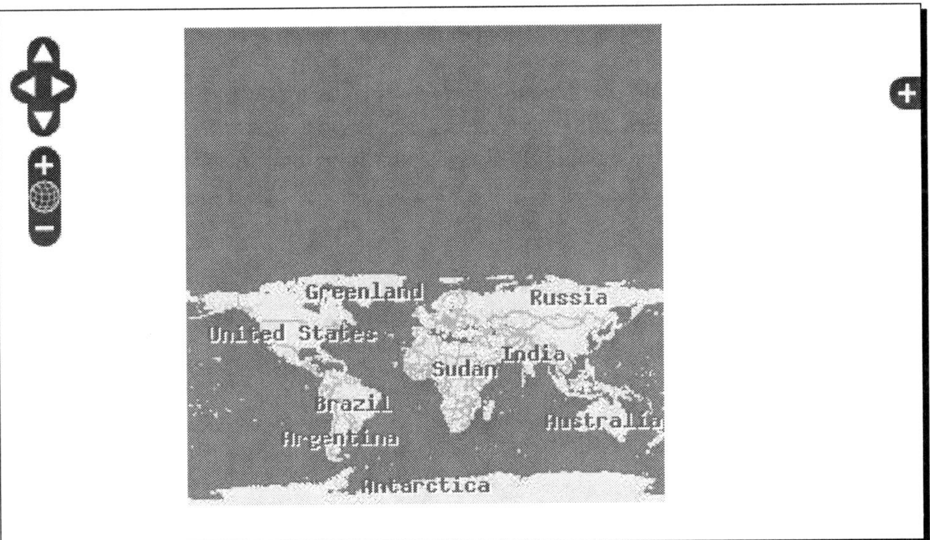

What Just Happened?

We just created a map with two WMS layers and a **Layer Switcher Control** that allows us to turn on and off layers. **Controls** are what OpenLayers provides that allows us to actually interact with the map and layers. To use controls, we create objects from different Control classes. By default, all maps get a Navigation control object which allows us to pan and zoom the map. In Chapter 6, we'll cover controls in depth.

In the previous example, our layer objects were called wms_base_layer and wms_overlay_layer. Throughout this book, this will be the format I will use to name objects—all lowercase with underscores (_), no spaces. You can, of course, use whichever convention you like, as long as your naming scheme is consistent.

Creating layer objects

The process to work with layers consists of two steps:

1. Create the layer object.
2. Add the layer object to the map. You can use either map.addLayer(layer) to add an individual layer, or map.addLayers([layer1, layer2, ...]) to add an array of layers, like in the previous example.

These two steps can actually be combined into one step (by instantiating the layer object when calling the addLayer function—this works, but I don't recommend it as it makes it a little harder to work with the layer object). By now, we have a bit of experience instantiating objects from the WMS Layer class. Let's take a look at the code that creates our wms_base layer object.

```
var wms_layer_map = new OpenLayers.Layer.WMS(
  'Base layer',
  'http://vmap0.tiles.osgeo.org/wms/vmap0',
  {layers: 'basic'},
  {isBaseLayer: true}
);
```

Each item inside the parentheses, after OpenLayers.Layer.WMS(, are called **arguments** which we pass in while creating the object. But how did I know what arguments to pass in?

We didn't write the class, so we don't know what it expects to take in. So, as with nearly any third party library, we have to refer to the documentation to see what arguments the class expects. OpenLayers has great documentation, and we'll be using it throughout the book.

Since we're using a WMS Layer, let's take a look at the documentation for the WMS class at http://dev.openlayers.org/docs/files/OpenLayers/Layer/WMS-js.html.

Layer.WMS class

There's a lot of information in the API docs, but let's look specifically at the section titled **Constructor**. This will tell us how to create a WMS layer object. The process varies for different types of layer but let's focus on the WMS class for now. Take a look at the **Parameters** sub section—this specifies what arguments this specific class expects to take in:

Parameters	Description
name	{String} A name for the layer.
url	{String} Base url for the WMS (e.g. `http://vmap0.tiles.osgeo.org/wms/vmap0`).
params	{Object} An object with key/value pairs representing the GetMap query string parameters and parameter values.
options	{Object} Hashtable of extra options to tag onto the layer.

The parameters tell us about the order of arguments to pass in, and what each argument means. The word in between the curly brackets ({ }) refers to the data type of parameter. So, `{string}` means the parameter should be a string.

Let's take a look at the `wms_base_layer` layer instantiation code and see how we use the four parameters.

WMS layer parameters:

The four WMS layer parameters are as follows:

Name

The first parameter is the layer's **name** and it should be a string. We pass in `'Base Layer'`. Notice how we enclose `Base Layer` in quotes—this is how we signify that it is a string. The title can be anything that you like—if you have a layer switcher control, the title will show up in it. Keep in mind that there is a comma after the closing quote, which means that we're done with this first argument and are ready to proceed to the next one.

This **name** parameter is present in nearly all Layer classes.

URL

The **URL** is the second parameter, and it should also be a string. It specifies the URL of the web map server. We pass in `'http://vmap0.tiles.osgeo.org/wms/vmap0'`. This URL parameter is present in most Layer classes.

Params

Params is the third parameter, and it is an anonymous objector consisting of key:value pairs. This parameter specifies *server side* settings that affect the map image, which the WMS server returns. The key:value pairs you pass in here will be appended (more or less) to the URL that OpenLayers generates when it makes requests to the map server.

For example, in the previous example when creating the `wms_layer_labels` we passed in `{layers: 'clabel,ctylabel,statelabel'}`. In this case, we are asking the WMS server to give us back a map image with the *server side* layers called '`clabel,ctylabel,statelabel`' turned on. We specify multiple *server side* layers—it doesn't matter what or how many server side layers we request though, because the WMS Layer object on the *client side* is still considered by OpenLayers to be a single layer object. This **params** parameter is present in most Layer classes.

Possible params keys and values

The possible keys and values for this **params** object depend on the map server you are working with. Unfortunately, covering them all for all layer types is outside the scope of this book. We'll only be using a few WMS parameters throughout this book—`layers` (to specify what layers the WMS service should give us), `transparent` (to ask for transparent images, for things such as label layers), and `srs` (to specify the projection).

For now, at least, our main concerns are just figuring out what layer names are on the WMS server. To figure this out, you can issue a `GETCAPABILITIES` request in the URL (`SERVICE=WMS` must also be specified). For instance, to get the possible layers from the WMS service we've been using so far go to the following URL:

```
http://vmap0.tiles.osgeo.org/wms/vmap0?SERVICE=WMS&REQUEST=GETCAPABIL
ITIES
```

If you are interested in more information about WMS, the specifications can be found at `http://www.opengeospatial.org/standards/wms`.

Options

Options is the last parameter and is an anonymous object that specifies the layer object's settings. You are *not* required to pass in this parameter.

The **options** object contains properties for the client side OpenLayers Layer object. These are the settings for the layer object itself, so all Layer classes have this parameter. To define various properties of the OpenLayers Layer object, we use this `options` argument. Properties include settings such as `isBaseLayer`, `opacity`, and `visibility`. Since the layer properties are client side settings, the WMS server (or whichever map server the layer uses) doesn't know about them.

The possible values are, basically, anything that you find in the API documentation for either the base **Layer** class (at `http://dev.openlayers.org/docs/files/OpenLayers/Layer-js.html`), or the specific subclass you're working with, e.g., the **WMS Layer Class**, at `http://dev.openlayers.org/docs/files/OpenLayers/Layer/WMS-js.html`.

> You can use this **options** parameter to initialize any of the layer parameters described in the API—the best way to get more familiar with it is to just play around with the different properties listed in the docs. The Layer class docs can be found at `http://dev.openlayers.org/docs/files/OpenLayers/Layer-js.html`.

Parameters versus arguments

These two terms are often confused and used interchangeably (but usually, that's ok). **Parameters** are what the items are called during the class or function definition, but when we call the function, the actual values of the parameters are referred to as **arguments**. For example, this is how we create a function in JavaScript:

```
function add_numbers(a, b){
  return a + b;
}
```

This is referred to as the `add_numbers` function definition. Here `a` and `b` are referred to as **parameters**. Now, take a look at how we call it:

```
var the_sum = add_numbers(13, 37);
```

Here, `13` and `37` are referred to as the **arguments**. In the `add_numbers` function, `13` acts as `a` and `37` acts as `b`.

Both terms are technically talking about the same thing. **Parameter** is the term to use when talking about function definitions, and **argument** is the term to use when talking about function calls. The distinction is sort of like that of a meteoroid (when it's in space), a meteor (when it's in the atmosphere), and a meteorite (when it hits the ground)—these three terms refer to the same object.

Now, let's take a look at some of the different arguments we can pass in when creating our layer objects.

Time for Action – configuring the options parameter

The **options** parameter is something that is present in all Layer classes, so let's get a bit more familiar with it. I suggest opening up the Layer documentation and following along, and even trying to add in the options yourself from the possible list of layer properties (at `http://dev.openlayers.org/docs/files/OpenLayers/Layer-js.html`).

1. Use the template (or code from Chapter 1 with the WMS layer code removed). We'll be adding some WMS layers, and we'll refer to this file as `chapter_3_ex2_options_config.html`.

2. First we'll add in a layer that contains the `'basic'` layer from the WMS server, like in the previous example.

```
// Setup our two layer objects
var wms_layer_map = new OpenLayers.Layer.WMS(
  'Base layer',
  'http://vmap0.tiles.osgeo.org/wms/vmap0',
  {layers: 'basic'},
  {isBaseLayer: true}
);
```

3. Next we'll create another layer object. We'll create a layer using labels, like in the previous example. This time though, let's set the layer's options to include `visibility: false`. This will cause the layer to be hidden by default. The layer definition should now look like:

```
var wms_layer_labels = new OpenLayers.Layer.WMS(
  'Location Labels',
  'http://vmap0.tiles.osgeo.org/wms/vmap0',
  {layers: 'clabel,ctylabel,statelabel',
  transparent: true},
  {visibility: false, opacity:0.5}
);
```

4. Time to create another layer. We'll set the layer **params** to ask the WMS service for the `stateboundary` layer. Then, we'll specify the **options** so that it won't display in the layer switcher control (via `displayInLayerSwitcher: false`) and set a minimum scale at which it will be visible (via `minScale`). That means this layer will only show up once we've reached a certain scale. Add the following to your `init()` function.

```
var wms_state_lines = new OpenLayers.Layer.WMS(
  'State Line Layer',
  'http://labs.metacarta.com/wms/vmap0',
  {layers: 'stateboundary',
```

```
    transparent: true},
    {displayInLayerSwitcher: false,
    minScale: 13841995.078125}
);
```

5. Now let's add a layer that will show a different layer from the WMS service and we'll set the layer object's opacity to `.8` (or 80 percent):

```
var wms_water_depth = new OpenLayers.Layer.WMS(
  'Water Depth',
  'http://labs.metacarta.com/wms/vmap0',
  {layers: 'depthcontour',
  transparent: true},
  {opacity:0.8}
);
```

6. Finally, we'll create a layer object that shows some road layers from the WMS service and has an **options** object containing the `transitionEffect: resize` property. This causes the layer to have a 'resize' animation when zooming in or out.

```
var wms_roads = new OpenLayers.Layer.WMS(
  'Roads',
  'http://labs.metacarta.com/wms/vmap0',
  {layers: 'priroad,secroad,rail',
  transparent: true},
  {transistionEffect:'resize'}
);
```

7. Now we just add the layers to the map (replace the previous `addLayers` function call with this one):

```
map.addLayers([
   wms_layer_map,
   wms_layer_labels,
   wms_state_lines,
   wms_water_depth,
   wms_roads]);
```

8. Save the file and then open it in your web browser.

9. Zoom in a few times around the Gulf of Mexico. You'll start to notice black contour lines in the ocean when you zoom in, and you should see a resize effect from the base ground layer. Depending on where you zoom, you should see something like this:

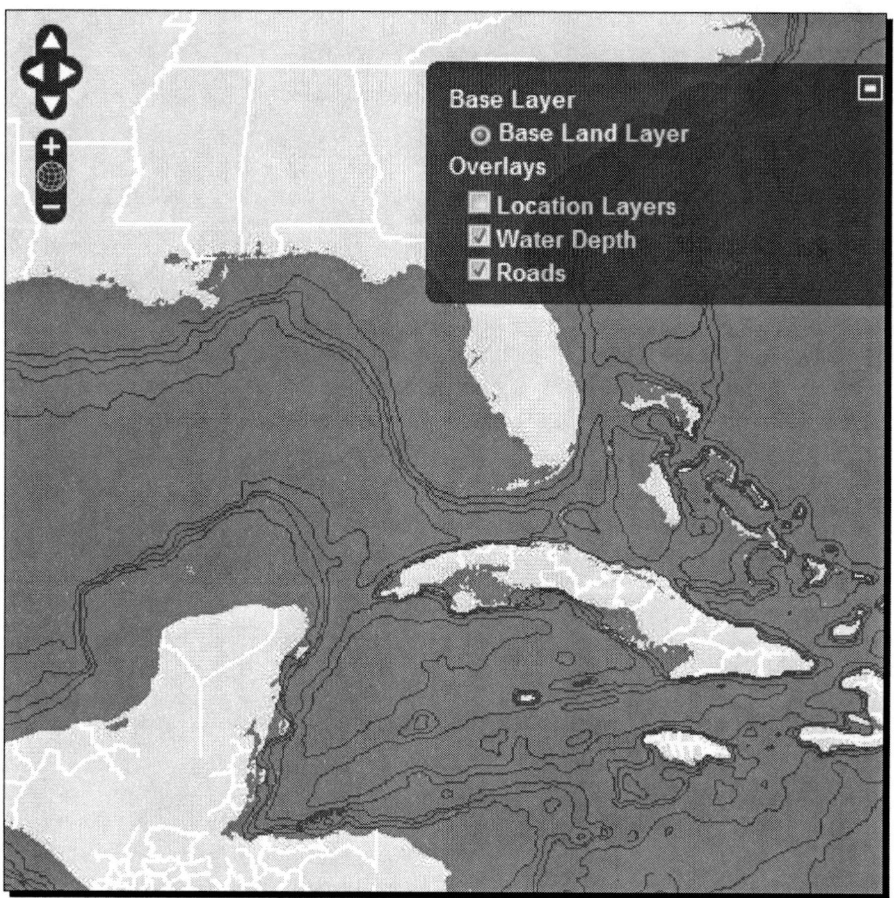

What Just Happened?

We just created another map with a few more layers and demonstrated some more layer options. The map looks slightly different than the first example's map because we are using different WMS server side layers (which are configured in each layer's **params** argument).

For now, let's focus on the fourth argument passed in—the **options** argument. This argument is used in all Layer classes, so when we move on to other types of Layers you'll be able to use all the same properties we're talking about. The **options** argument controls the layer's object's properties.

Configuring layer options

Let's take a look at a couple of the layer's `options` argument we passed in during the previous example.

> Pay close attention to the commas. Both arguments and key:value pairs are separated by a comma, but make sure you do not have a comma after the last pair. Trailing commas will usually break your map and are usually a pain to debug—so if your map isn't working and you don't see any helpful error messages in Firebug, check for trailing commas. A great site to help with your code is `http://jslint.com`.

wms_state_lines layer options

This layer's **options** are:

```
{ displayInLayerSwitcher: false, minScale: 13841995.078125}
```

The first property, `displayInLayerSwitcher`, can be either `true` or `false`, and determines if the layer will appear in the layer switcher control (if there is a layer switcher control). In our example, we do have a layer switcher control and you'll notice that we don't see it in the list of layers. The layer is still there, and we can programmatically turn it on or off through the `setVisibility()` function, e.g. `wms_state_lines.setVisibility(false);`. In fact, when you turn on or off a layer through the layer switcher control, this `setVisibility` function is what is being called. This property is useful when you want to include layers in your map that you don't want to let the user control.

The second property is `minScale: 13841995.078125`. The value for this property is float, a number that can contain a decimal point. This `minScale` property determines the minimum scale the map must be at before the layer is displayed, which basically means how far we must be zoomed in before the layer will be turned on. There is also a `maxScale` property which determines how far we can zoom in before the layer is turned off. The term for this behavior is referred to as **scale dependency**.

Scale dependency

Scale dependency can be controlled either from the client or server side (or both). You'll notice that the `wms_water_depth` layer (with black contour lines in the water to specify depth) does not turn on until we start to zoom in. We haven't set the `minScale` property for the `wms_water_depth` layer, so why don't we see it at all zoom levels? The reason is WMS server has its own scale dependencies on the server side, so even if we wanted to see this layer when the map is zoomed out we can't because the server does not allow it.

When we set the `minScale` or `maxScale` properties on a layer, we are specifying client side scale dependency—so even if the server allows it, we're telling OpenLayers not to show it. To determine the current scale of the map, you can call the `map.getScale();` function which will show you the current scale value.

wms_layer_labels layer options

This layer's **options** property consists of:

```
{visibility: false,  opacity:0.5}
```

The visibility property

We've already covered the first property, so let's talk about the `visibility` property. Its value can be either `true` (by default) or `false`. This visibility property controls if a layer is visible or not. Setting it to `false` will make it hidden, but the user can turn it on by enabling it in the layer switcher control. The `map.getVisibility();` and `map.setVisibility({{Boolean}});` functions refer to this property. `{{Boolean}}` means we can pass in a Boolean, in other words, we can pass in either `true` or `false`.

The opacity property

The next property is `opacity`. It accepts a float with values between 0 and 1. A value of 0 means the layer will be completely transparent, and a value of 1 means the layer will be completely opaque. We set it to `0.5` here, so it will be 50 percent opaque. If you turn on the layer in the map (you can click on the layer in the layer switcher to enable it), you'll notice the labels are sort of see-through. This opacity setting helps you to create more visually pleasing maps, as by enabling multiple layers and changing their opacities you can produce some nifty effects.

Map tiles

Let's take a short break now and talk about just a little bit of theory. It has been mentioned that OpenLayers works by requesting 'map tiles' from a backend map server, but I haven't really gone much into what that means. Nearly all layers work on this map tiling principle (except the Vector layer and the Image layer). So, what is it exactly and how does it work?

Think of how you might go about creating a web map from scratch—specifically, how would you handle the map image itself? You could go about it in two ways. First, you could just send back one giant image of a map. If the user zooms in, the server sends back an even bigger, more zoomed in image of a map. Using this strategy, you'd very quickly be sending over exponentially large image files every time the user zooms. This is why this method is not really practical.

Many images make up a map

The second way is that you break up the desired map image into a bunch of smaller images, or **map tiles**. So, no matter how far the user zooms in, the server only has to send over a relatively small amount of images. This sort of map tiling strategy is what nearly every web map does—Google Maps, Yahoo! Maps, most OpenLayers Layers, etc. When you request a new extent, OpenLayers asks for a new set of map images. Each map image is the same size (e.g., 256 x 256 pixels); this is referred to as the **tile size**, and can be specified when creating your map.

Let's take a look at an example of a basic OpenLayers map. In our example, when you're completely zoomed out, the entire visible area will fit in one map tile image.

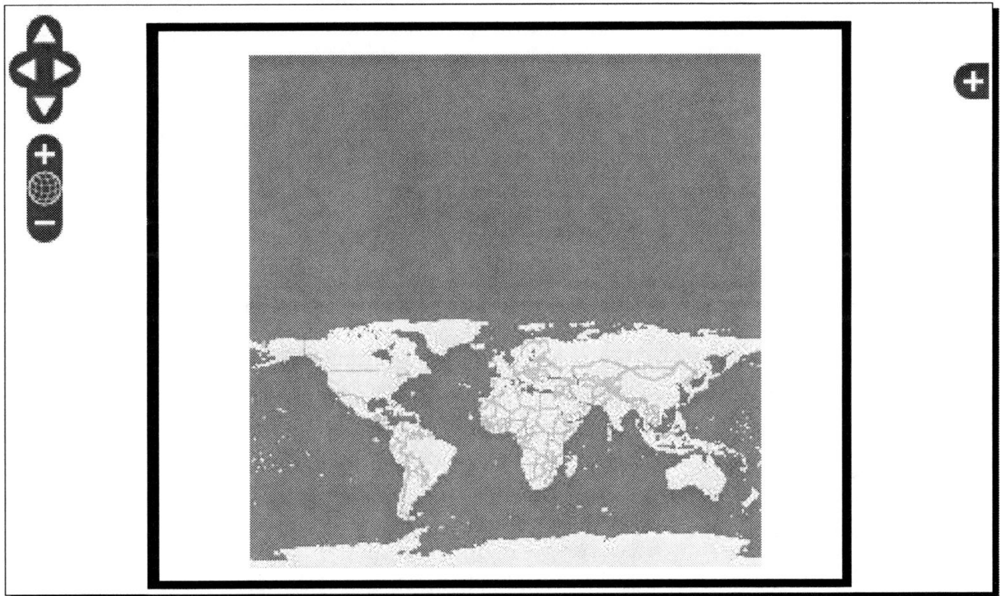

When the client asks for the map's max extent, only one map tile needs to be returned. OpenLayers will figure out what extents to ask the map server for. In this case, it only needs to ask for one map tile, because we're zoomed out so far that the entire world will fit in one map image.

At this point, you might be wondering if there is any benefit in breaking the images into tiles, as we're only getting back one image. However, when we zoom-in, it becomes more clear.

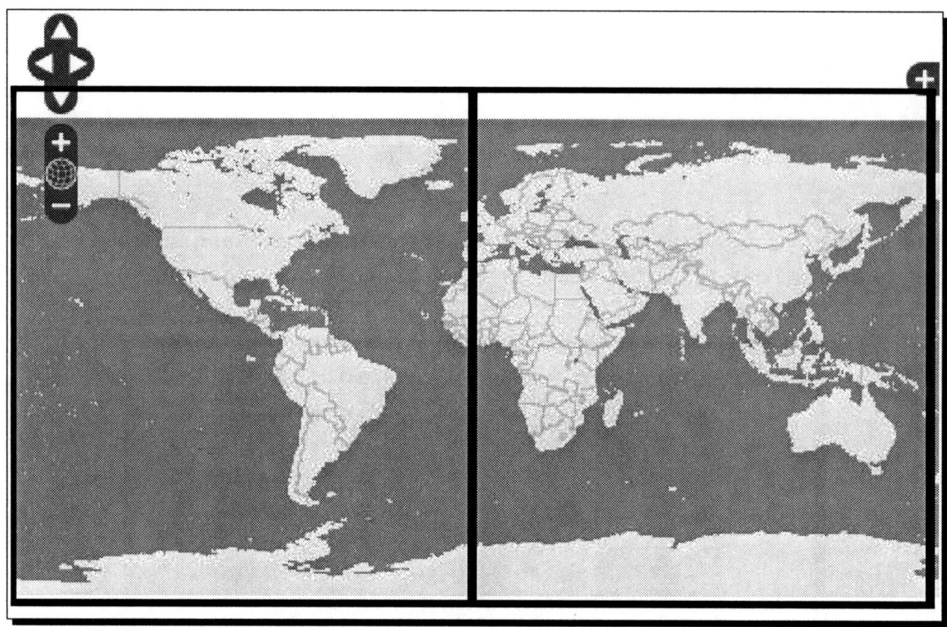

Now we've zoomed in once. OpenLayers has to figure out what the extent of your map is, and how many tiles it has to ask the map server for. OpenLayers calculates the extent for each tile, and then sends a request to the map server to get an image of the requested extent. So, in this example, OpenLayers determines that it needs to send two requests to the map server. Each request will result in a response of a map image, and then OpenLayers will piece the tiles together.

Keep in mind that the tile size is still the same as it was in the previous request. Your map only has one tile size, and in this case (and by default) it is `256 x 256` pixels. You can change the size of the tiles with the map's `tileSize` property, which we'll talk more about in Chapter 8 on the **Map** class. So what happens when we zoom in and move the map around a little bit?

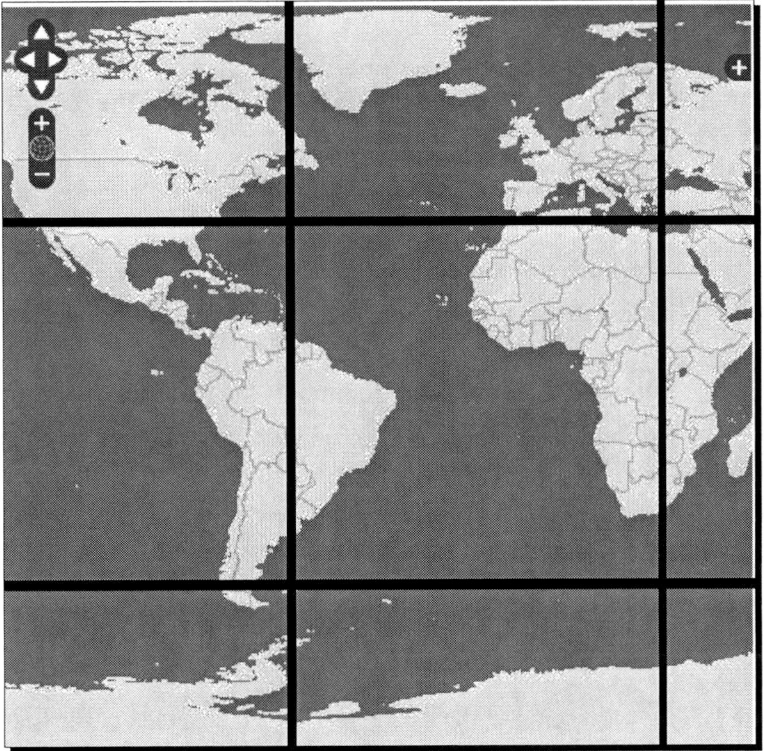

In this case, OpenLayers requests more tiles because the total map area is outside what you can see (called the **Viewport**). The tiles are all still 256 x 256 pixels, but now tiles lie outside of the map's visible range. Any time the user moves their map to a new area (by zooming or panning), OpenLayers figures out how many tiles it needs to get, the extent for each tile, and where to place them.

Available layer properties

Let's go over the properties available for OpenLayers version 2.9, as we'll be using them throughout the book. These properties can be used by any Layer class, as all Layer subclasses (such as the WMS and Google Maps Layer) inherit from them.

Data types

Before we talk about the layer properties, let's quickly go over the notation for the data types used. The curly brackets { } indicate the JavaScript data type the parameter expects. The data types are as follows:

- {`Array`}: An array of elements separated by commas and enclosed in brackets. For e.g.: `[1,2,3]`
- {`Boolean`}: Possible values are `true` or `false`.
- {`Float`}: Possible values are numbers that can contain a decimal point. For e.g.: `42.5`
- {`Integer`}: Possible values are whole numbers (no decimals). For e.g.: `42`
- {`Object`}: An anonymous object, key:value pairs separated by commas, enclosed in curly brackets. For e.g.: {`'answer': 42, 'question': null`}
- {`OpenLayers.`_______}: An object instantiated from an OpenLayers class. The blank could be any OpenLayers class. For e.g.: `new OpenLayers.Control.LayerSwitcher({});`
- {`String`}: Possible value is any string, indicated by enclosed quotes (either single quote, ', or double quote, "). For e.g.: `'This is a string'`

Now that we're familiar with some of the data types, let's take a look at the Layer properties available to us.

OpenLayers.Layer class properties

So far we've only been working with the WMS Layer class, but OpenLayers has many more Layer classes. The following properties apply to *all* layer classes. We can set these properties via the **options** argument when we create the layer, and we can access them in Firebug by simply calling `layer_object.property`.

The following is a table of layer properties available as of OpenLayers version 2.10. We will be using them throughout the book, and coming back to them often, so don't feel as if you need to memorize them right now. The latest properties can always be found in the OpenLayers Layer docs at `http://dev.openlayers.org/docs/files/OpenLayers/Layer-js.html`.

Property	Property Data Type	Description	Default Value
events	{OpenLayers.Event}	An OpenLayers event object. We can pass in an event object here that will call a function when an event, such as zooming in, occurs. We will talk more about events in a later chapter.	-
map	{OpenLayers.Map}	The map object that this layer belongs to. This is set automatically when the layer is added to the map via the `setMap()` function.	
isBaseLayer	{Boolean}	Determines if a layer is to act as a base layer.	false
alpha	{Boolean}	Specifies if the layer's images contain an alpha channel. This was originally designed to fix transparency issues in IE, but incurs a large performance hit. It is recommended that you do not use this.	false
displayIn LayerSwitcher	{Boolean}	Determines if the layer should be displayed in the layer switcher.	true
visibility	{Boolean}	Determines if the layer is visible on the map and enabled or disabled in the Layer Switcher control.	true
attribution	{String}	Text that is displayed when the Attribution control has been added to the map. By default, the attribution text appears in the bottom right and each layer's attribution is separated by a comma.	-
inRange	{Boolean}	Is either `True` or `False`, depending if the current map's resolution is within the layer's minimum and maximum range. This is set when the zoom level changes.	-
imageOffset	{OpenLayers.Pixel}	The displacement of the image tiles for layers with a gutter.	-

Property	Property Data Type	Description	Default Value
`options`	`{Object}`	Optional object whose properties will be set on the layer. Any of these layer properties can be defined in this options object. This is the same options object we've spent the past couple of pages discussing.	-
`eventListeners`	`{Object}`	Event listeners will be registered if this is set during the layer object's creation. We will discuss this in detail in Chapter 6.	-
`gutter`	`{Integer}`	Sometimes you may notice artifacts around the edges of tiles that the map requests. When you set the gutter value, OpenLayers will request tiles that are bigger than the normal tile size by two times the gutter value. So, if your default tile size was 256 x 256, and if you had a gutter value of 10 then OpenLayers would request tiles with a size of 276 x 276. Anything outside the normal tile though (256 x 256 in this case) is not shown, and to OpenLayers the tile size is still 256 x 256. This really only needs to be used when you encounter problems with artifacts near the edge of your tiles. Non-tiled layers always have a gutter value of zero.	0

Property	Property Data Type	Description	Default Value
`projection`	{`OpenLayers.Projection`} or {`String`}	This will override the default projection of the map if specified. You may also need to set the `maxExtent`, `maxResolution`, and units properties. If you pass in a string instead of a projection object, it will be converted to a projection object. Projections are used to display a three dimensional object (the earth) in two dimensions (on our map). Different projections use different coordinates and measurement units. We will cover projections in more detail in Chapter 4.	{`EPSG:4326`}
`units`	{`String`}	The units the map's layer is in. Possible values are `'degrees'` (or `'dd'`), `'m'`, `'ft'`, `'km'`, `'mi'`, or `'inches'`.	`'degrees'`
`scales`	{`Array`}	Contains the map scales, from highest to lowest values. The units property must also be set when using this. It is recommended that you use the resolutions property instead.	-
`resolutions`	{`Array`}	Contains an array of map resolutions (map units per pixel) from highest to lowest values. If this is not set, it will be calculated automatically based on other properties, such as `maxExtent`, `maxResolution`, etc.).	-

Property	Property Data Type	Description	Default Value
maxExtent	{OpenLayers.Bounds}	An OpenLayers.Bounds object consisting of min x, min y, max x, and max y values that specify the extent of the layer. Any coordinates outside this bounding box will not be displayed. If the displayOutsideMaxExtent property is set to false, tiles that fall outside these coordinates will simply not be requested.	-
maxResolution	{Float}	Sets the maximum resolution (the width or height, in map units, per pixel). Default max is 360 degrees/256 pixels. If you are not using a geographic projection, specify a different value.	-
numZoomLevels	{Float}	Specifies the number of zoom levels a layer has. The layer will not be displayed if the zoom level of the map is greater than this value.	16
minScale	{Float}	Specifies the minimum scale at which the layer will turn on.	-
MaxScale	{Float}	Specifies the maximum scale at which the layer will be shown. If the map scale is greater than this value, the layer will not be displayed.	-
displayOut sideMaxExtent	{Boolean}	Specifies if the map should request tiles that are completely outside of the layer's maxExtent property.	false
wrapDateLine	{Boolean}	This will cause the map to wrap around the date line. This allows you to continue dragging the map left/right forever, as the map is wrapped around onto itself.	-

Property	Property Data Type	Description	Default Value
`transitionEffect`	`{String}`	Specifies the transition effect to use when the map is panned or zoomed. Possible values at the time of writing are `null` (no effect) and '`resize`.'	`null`
`SUPPORTED_ TRANSITIONS`	`{Array}`	This is a constant—it does not change. It contains a list of support transition effects to use with the `transitionEffect` property.	-
`metadata`	`{Object}`	Allows you to store additional information about the layer. This does not have an effect on the layer itself.	-

Modifying layer properties

Now that you're familiar with a few more layer properties, try to modify the second example's code, passing in additional properties to the **options** object. Open up the previous example and use Firebug to access individual layer properties, for example, `map.layers[1].propertyName`. Play around by passing in different properties to the **options** object when creating the layer objects, and don't be afraid to break your code!

The OpenLayers.Layer class

So far, we've only been using the `OpenLayers.Layer.WMS` class in the examples. This has been the beginning of all our layer object instantiation code so far:

```
var wms = new OpenLayers.Layer.WMS(
```

Notice the period between Layer and WMS: `Layer.WMS`. This means that we're accessing the `WMS` subclass of the `Layer` superclass. What do I mean when I say this? Well, the `WMS` class is a subclass of the `Layer` class, so let's briefly refresh our knowledge about subclasses.

Subclasses

In Chapter 1, we mentioned **Subclasses**. Subclasses are, basically, classes that derive from some base class. This base class is called a **Superclass**. The Layer class is thus the **Superclass** of all Layer **subclasses** (Superclasses and Subclasses are still classes). Subclasses inherit all the properties of their superclass.

Layer Class—Sub and super classes

The `Layer` class is therefore the superclass from which all other Layer classes derive. The `Layer.WMS` layer class is different from the `Layer.Image` class, and each of those two classes has their own unique properties and functions. But both layers also share all the properties of their `Layer` superclass—so all those properties we discussed earlier apply to both classes.

Some Layer classes also inherit from multiple Layer class in a hierarchical way. For example, the `Layer.WMS` class inherits from the `Layer.Grid` class, which inherits from the `Layer` class.

Other layer types

OpenLayers supports a multitude of different Layer classes. As you may recall from Chapter 1, each Layer class is associated with a different map server back end. The `Layer.WMS` class is used to connect to a WMS map server, and the `Layer.Google` class is used to connect to the Google Maps service.

Because OpenLayers is such an actively developed framework, there are a few layer classes that are deprecated (not recommended to use anymore). Later versions of OpenLayers will deprecate more Layer classes, so we'll try to focus on the classes that should be around for a while. We won't be able to cover every Layer class, but we will discuss the common ones. The Layer classes which we don't mention below will not be covered in this book, either because they are deprecated or outside the scope of this book. Let's take a look.

Layer.ArcGIS93Rest

This is the class that allows us to interact with ArcGIS Server 9.3 via its REST interface. Interaction with the REST interface is handled by constructing requests with URLs, and is similar in concept to how GET requests work.

The structure to instantiate objects from this class is similar to `Layer.WMS`, as both inherit from the `Layer.Grid` class. ArcGIS Server is a third party, proprietary piece of software from ESRI, but OpenLayers provides excellent support for it. The OpenLayers documentation for the ArcGIS layer can be found at `http://dev.openlayers.org/docs/files/OpenLayers/Layer/ArcGIS93Rest-js.html`.

The documentation for ArcGIS Server's REST API can be found at `http://resources.esri.com/help/9.3/arcgisserver/apis/rest/index.html`.

Layer.ArcIMS

This layer class is similar to the ArcGIS93Rest class, and allows us to display data from ArcIMS Mapping Services. ArcIMS is another proprietary software product from ESRI. The documentation for this Layer class is at `http://dev.openlayers.org/docs/files/OpenLayers/Layer/ArcIMS-js.html`. More information about ArcIMS can be found at `http://www.esri.com/software/arcgis/arcims/index.html`.

Layer.Google

This layer allows us to interact with Google Maps via the Google Maps API. The documentation for this layer class is located at `http://dev.openlayers.org/docs/files/OpenLayers/Layer/Google-js.html`.

Time for Action – creating a Google Maps layer

Let's take a look at how to create a Google Maps layer.

1. From this point onward, I'm going to assume that when I say "create a new map" you will use the template from `http://vasir.net/openlayers_book/`, or create a copy of the example from Chapter 1 and remove the WMS layer calls (they both result in the same code). So, create a new map.

2. The first thing we'll need to do is add in a script tag to the `<head>` section that references the Google API library. This allows us to actually use the Google Maps library:

   ```
   <script src="http://maps.google.com/maps/api/js?sensor=false"></
   script>
   ```

3. Now, we'll need to create a Google Maps layer object. We won't pass in any additional settings, so the default settings will be used. By default, we'll see the Google 'Streets' Map (we could ask for the aerial imagery layer, the physical topology layer, etc—we'll cover this soon). Add the following in your `init` function:

   ```
   var google_map_layer = new OpenLayers.Layer.Google(
     'Google Map Layer',
     {}
   );
   ```

4. All we have to do now is add the layer to the map. Before you do this, make sure you've removed the existing line of code that adds the WMS layer to the map. We only want to have our map contain the `google_map_layer`.

   ```
   map.addLayer(google_map_layer);
   ```

You should see something like this:

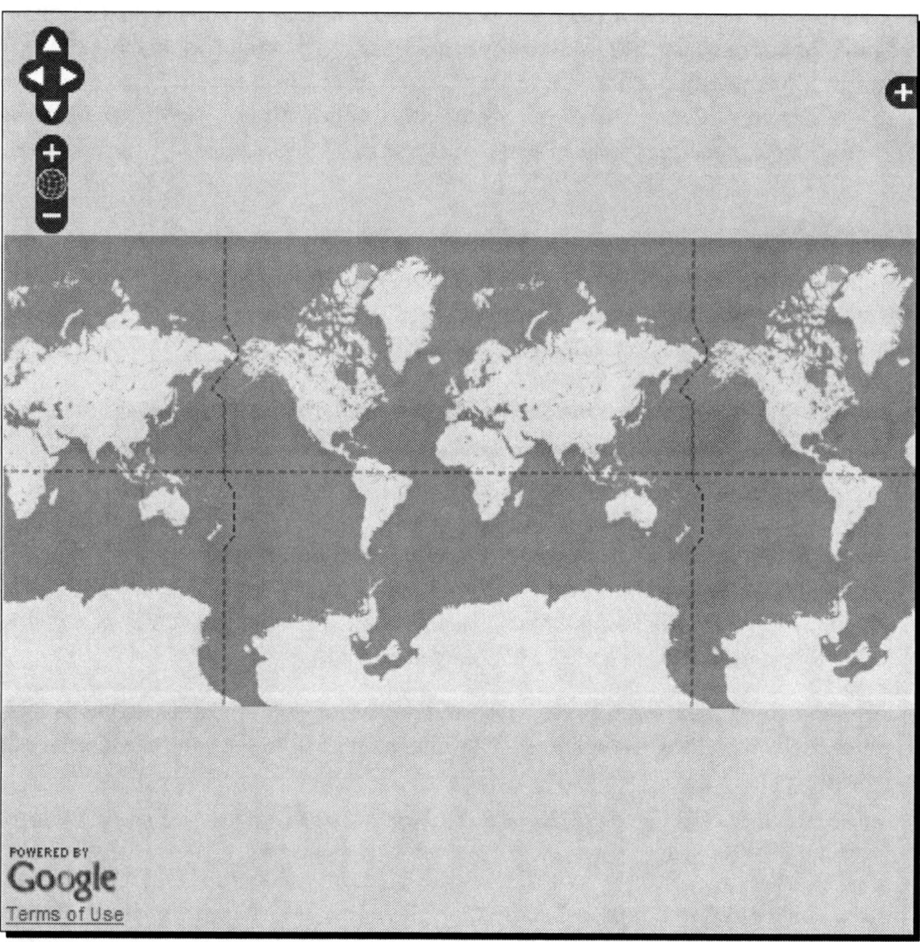

What Just Happened?

We just created a map with a single Google Maps layer object using the Google Maps API (version 3). The layer that Google is showing us is the default layer named `ROADMAP` (referred to also as the 'streets' map). We can change the type of layer we see by changing the `type` value in the layer's **options** object. The possible values we can set for the `type` key are:

- `google.maps.MapTypeId.ROADMAP` (the default)
- `google.maps.MapTypeId.TERRAIN`
- `google.maps.MapTypeId.HYBRID`
- `google.maps.MapTypeId.SATELLITE`

You'll notice that each type is preceded by `google.maps.MapTypeID.`, which must be present. For example, to specify that you wish to use the hybrid layer (satellite imagery combined with the `ROADMAP` layer), you could use:

```
var google_hybrid_layer = new OpenLayers.Layer.Google(
    "Google Hybrid",
    {type: google.maps.MapTypeId.HYBRID}
);
```

Because of the projections Google Maps and the other third party APIs use, it can be little tricky to get other layers to work with them—we'll talk about this more in Chapter 4 and Chapter 5. Briefly though, it has to do with the fact that these third party APIs use a projection called `EPSG:900913`, which uses a different coordinate system than `EPSG:4326` (the projection our WMS layers have been in so far). Because of this, the coordinates don't match up. So, we can't just place our WMS layer (which is in the `EPSG:4326` projection) on top of the Google Layer (which is in the `EPSG:900913` projection), as the coordinates are very different. In the next chapters, we'll address how to solve this issue.

The Google Maps Version 3 API can be found at `http://code.google.com/apis/maps/documentation/javascript/` and more information on possible Google Maps Layer types can be found at `http://code.google.com/apis/maps/documentation/javascript/overlays.html`.

Layer.Grid

This is a base class that many other layers, such as WMS, inherit from. We won't be using it explicitly, but it is important to know that it exists. It works, basically, by constructing a grid and placing tiles (map images) inside the grid. It uses the HTTPRequest class to communicate with a map server to get the tiles it needs to build the map.

Classes that inherit from it, such as WMS, work in a similar way. So, if you're familiar with how to use the WMS layer, you'll be familiar with how to use nearly any class that inherits from the `Layer.Grid` class. The documentation for this class is at `http://dev.openlayers.org/docs/files/OpenLayers/Layer/Grid-js.html`.

Layer.Image

This class allows us to use an image as a map layer. It's bit different than the other layer classes OpenLayers offers, because it doesn't strictly follow a client/server model. Once the initial request for the image is made, the client has the image and OpenLayers handles all further map interaction—no further requests are made to the server after the first request to get the image. There are no tiles, like with other raster (non vector, which is nearly every other layer class) layers. Instead, just a single image is used.

The original purpose (and one of the best uses) of this class is to use an image for the overview map control. But it can be used for many more things than just that—this class, a great example of OpenLayers can be used for other purposes than just mapping.

Time for Action – using the image layer

Let's use the image layer to create a sort of image viewer.

1. First we'll need to add an image layer. The image layer expects the `name` as the first parameter (like other layers), the URL of the image next, then an `{OpenLayers.Bounds}` object specifying bounds of the image, then an `{OpenLayers.Size}` object which contains Width, Height pixel dimensions, and finally an optional **options** object.

```
var image_layer = new OpenLayers.Layer.Image(
  'Wallpaper',
  'http://us.starcraft2.com/images/wallpapers/wall3/
wall3-1920x1200.jpg',
  new OpenLayers.Bounds(-180,-112.5,180,112.5),
  new OpenLayers.Size(1920,1200),
  {numZoomLevels:7, maxResolution:.625}
);
```

2. Let's create another image layer now. We'll set the opacity to 20 percent and make sure it's not a base layer by setting `isBaseLayer: false` in the **options** object. We'll also be using a different URL:

```
var image_layer_2 = new OpenLayers.Layer.Image(
  'Wallpaper 2',
  'http://us.starcraft2.com/images/wallpapers/wall6/
wall6-1920x1200.jpg',
  new OpenLayers.Bounds(-180,-112.5,180,112.5),
  new OpenLayers.Size(1920,1200),
  {numZoomLevels:7, maxResolution:.625, isBaseLayer:false,
opacity:0.2}
);
```

3. Finally, add the image layers to the map:

```
map.addLayers([image_layer, image_layer_2]);
```

You should see the following:

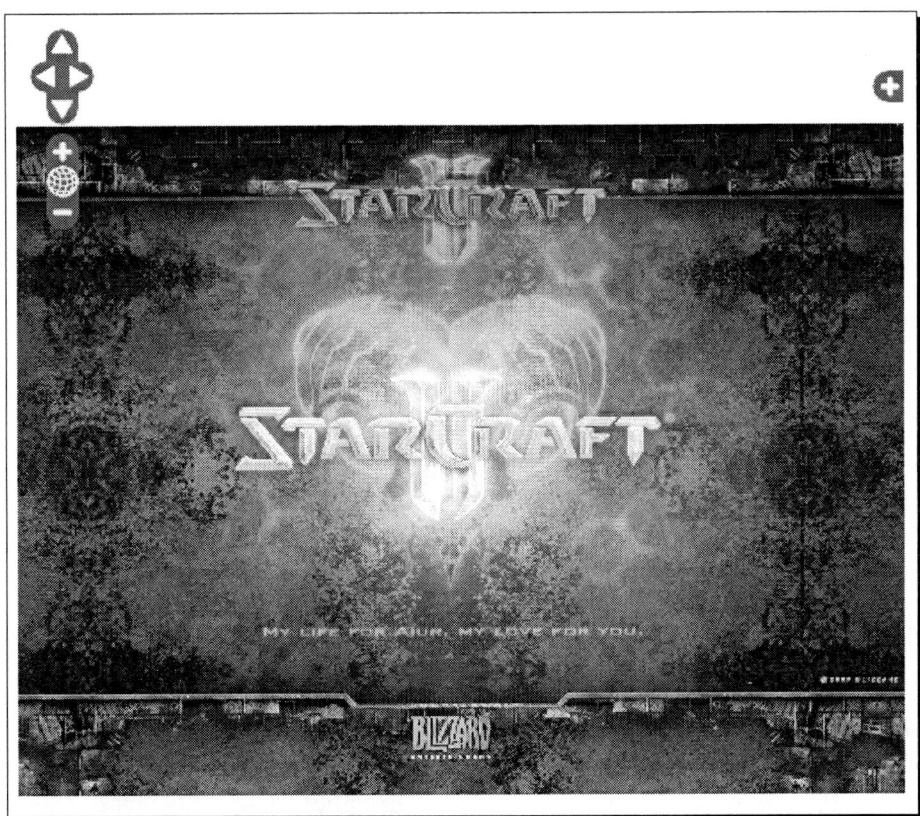

What Just Happened?

We just created an OpenLayers map that wasn't a map at all, but more of an image viewer. There are plenty of other uses for this though—you could overlay an image on top of a WMS layer, create a map from image layers consisting of high resolution scans of older printed maps, etc. The parameters required to create an image layer are:

Image layer parameters

- `name`: {String} Name of the layer.
- `url`: {String} URL of the image. Can be on your own computer/server, or an external server.

- `extent`: {OpenLayers.Bounds} The extent of the image.
- `size`: {OpenLayers.Size} The size of the image, in pixels.
- `options`: {Object} An anonymous object containing the layer property settings.

Let's take a look at our `image_layer` object's extent, size, and options arguments:

```
new OpenLayers.Bounds(-180,-112.5,180,112.5),
new OpenLayers.Size(1920,1200),
{numZoomLevels:7, maxResolution:.625}
```

The **extent** argument is an `{OpenLayers.Bounds}` object, which is created via `OpenLayers.Bounds(-180,-112.5,180,112.5)`. We pass in the min x, min y, max x, and max y values to create the bounding box. For images, you may have to play around with the values depending on your image's dimensions. The ratio of our image (1920/1200) is 1.6, so I've set the bounds to have a similar ratio (180 / 112.5 = 1.6).

The **size** argument, `new OpenLayers.Size(1920,1200)`, is an `{OpenLayers.Size}` object, and we pass in the width and height of the image.

For the next argument, the **options**, we pass in `{numZoomLevels:7, maxResolution:.625}`. The `numZoomLevels` property can be anything you'd like, but higher values may allow you to zoom in too far to the image. The value of `maxResolution` property is set to `.625`, which is a value I arrived at by dividing 1200/1920 (the width divided by the height)—just a rough calculation that, in case, makes the map look just about right. Documentation for this layer class is at `http://dev.openlayers.org/docs/files/OpenLayers/Layer/Image-js.html`.

Have a Go Hero – make your own image based maps

Using the previous example's code, find other high resolution images and create a similar 'image viewer' with them. Add as many layers as you'd like, and play around with the opacity setting to see how the image layers interact with each other.

Layer.MapGuide

This is the layer for the open source MapGuide platform. We won't be covering MapGuide in this book, but it is a popular project and, since it is free and open source, you're welcome to install it on your own computer. It behaves similar to the `Layer.WMS` class and has the same parameters. It also inherits from `Layer.Grid`. The documentation for this layer class can be found at `http://dev.openlayers.org/docs/files/OpenLayers/Layer/MapGuide-js.html`. More information on MapGuide can be found at `http://mapguide.osgeo.org/`.

Layer.TileCache

The TileCache layer allows you to interact with MetaCarta's TileCache, which is free open source software that caches WMS requests. TileCache provides enormous performance boosts because it caches requests to a WMS server. This means that once a request has been made, the response (the map image) is stored either on the server's hard drive or in memory and is immediately returned to the client.

The normal process of requesting a map image from a WMS server goes like this:

1. Client sends request to WMS server, asking for a specific part of the map.
2. WMS Server receives the request and generates an image based on the requested map extent.
3. WMS Server returns the rendered map image to the client.

The bottleneck is Step 2, the WMS server rendering the image based on the request. With caching (either through TileCache or by other means), the second step becomes a lot easier. With caching, the server only has to generate an image once, and then it saves it (in the hard drive or memory). So, instead of having to generate an image for every request, it simply grabs an image which it has *already* generated. This makes the request seem almost instantaneous, and most popular web maps use some form of caching—including Google Maps.

We will be discussing TileCache a little more in the last chapter, where we talk about deploying and using OpenLayers in a production environment. The documentation for this layer class is at `http://dev.openlayers.org/docs/files/OpenLayers/Layer/TileCache-js.html`. For more information on TileCache, head to `http://tilecache.org/`.

Layer.Vector

The vector layer is one of the more powerful features of OpenLayers. It allows us to draw points and polygons on the map, style them however we want, retrieve and use KML and other geo data formats, etc. The vector layer makes uses of **Protocols** (such as HTTP), **Formats** (such as KML), and **Strategies** (such as Clustering) to display and provide an interactive layer. The vector layer also allows us to create and edit vector features. In Chapter 9, our chapter on the Vector Layer class, we'll go into far more detail.

Layer.VirtualEarth

This layer allows us to interact with Microsoft's VirtualEarth API. It works in a similar way to the Google Layer, so we won't spend more time discussing it here. Chapter 6 will fully cover this layer class.

Layer.WFS

This is a class that is deprecated, so try to avoid using it, as it will soon no longer be supported. I wanted to explicitly mention it because it is on its way out, but I still see lots of code that uses it. **WFS** (**Web Feature Service**), allow us to interact with data that is stored on the server. If you would like to use WFS, the general procedure is to use the `Layer.Vector` class and use WFS as the format. We'll be covering this in detail in Chapter 9, our chapter on the Vector Layer class.

Layer.WMS

This is the Layer class we've been using throughout the book so far. It inherits from `Layer.Grid`, and is similar to other classes we've mentioned. WMS is a popular standard and the way we interact with it is similar to how we interact with other Layer classes. We will be using this class throughout the book, so you haven't seen the last of it. Layer class documentation can be found at `http://dev.openlayers.org/docs/files/OpenLayers/Layer/WMS-js.html`. More information and specifications of the WMS protocol can be found at `http://www.opengeospatial.org/standards/wms`.

Layer.Yahoo

This Layer class allows us to interact with the Yahoo! API. It works in a similar way to Layer.Google and Layer.VirtualEarth, and we'll be covering it in more detail in Chapter 6. Documentation for this layer class is at `http://dev.openlayers.org/docs/files/OpenLayers/Layer/Yahoo-js.html`. The Yahoo! Maps API can be found at `http://developer.yahoo.com/maps/`.

Accessing layer objects

The last topic to cover concerns the functions of the base Layer class. Before we do that though, let's go over how to access layer objects in Firebug. We'll be doing this often throughout the book, so it is quite important.

Time for Action – accessing map.layers

Let's jump in to using some of the Layer class functions.

1. Open up the second WMS example, **chapter3_ex2_options_config.html** in Firefox. We won't be editing the code yet.
2. Enable Firebug and go to the Console panel.

3. In the console, input and run this line of code:

```
map.layers;
```

4. You should then see a list of layers.

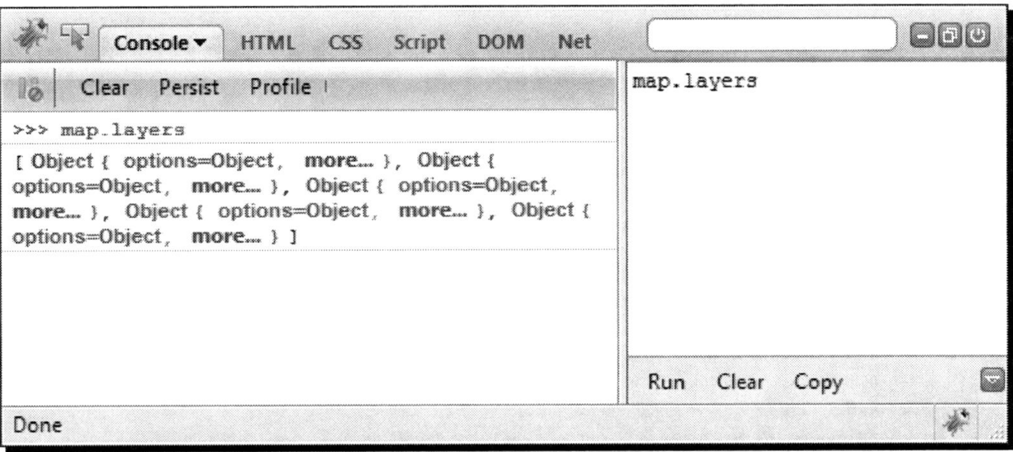

What Just Happened?

You just accessed the `layers` property of the global `map` object. This is a property of the map object that contains an array of all the layers in the map. The list is ordered by the way you add layers to the map, so the first item in the list corresponds to the first layer we added to the map, the `wms_layer_map` layer. Not only will Firebug list the layer objects, you can also access any one of them by clicking on them.

Time for Action – accessing layer objects in Firebug

Let's take a look at how to access an object in Firebug now.

Click on one of the items in the array of objects that was outputted from the previous *Time for Action* section. You should see something like this:

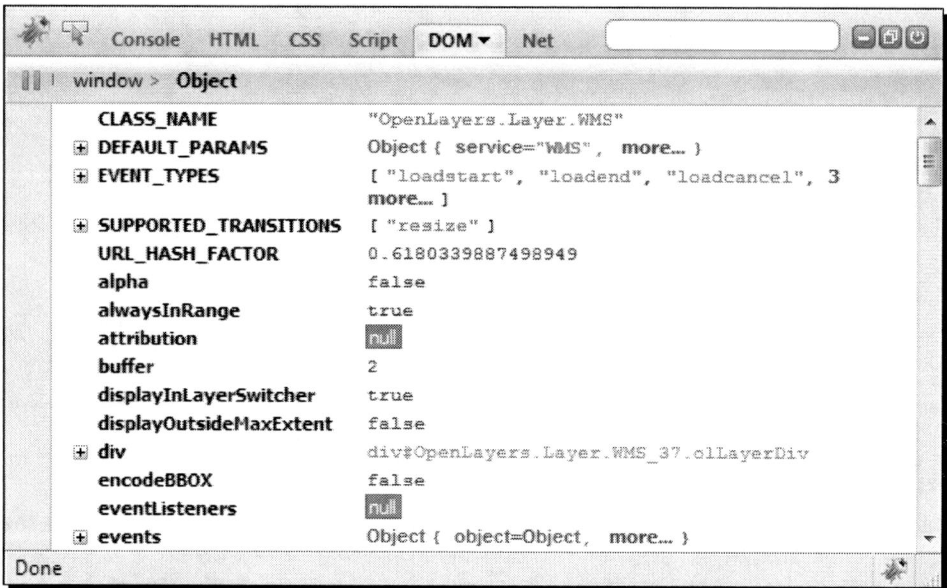

What Just Happened?

We just accessed our map's `wms_layer_map` layer object. What you see in the DOM panel is a listing of all the properties and functions that layer object contains. The DOM panel is one way we can access a layer object's properties. The DOM panel is a great way to get a quick look at all the properties and values of any object we wish to know more about. You'll notice some of the properties have not yet been mentioned; this is because some properties are specific to the `Layer.WMS` class, and is not included in the base `Layer` class.

Accessing layer properties

There are two common ways to access a layer object's properties.

map.layers

The first way is by accessing the layer object through the `map.layers` array, which we did in the previous example. Here, we are accessing the global map object, which was defined *outside* the `init()` function with `var map;`.

If we know the index of a layer object we wish to view, we can use `map.layers[n]` to access the layer object (where `n` is the index). For example, if we wanted to access the `wms_layer_map` layer object, we know it is the first layer added to the map so its index is 0 (because array start its index at 0), so we would type `map.layers[0]`. The next layer, `wms_layer_labels`, has an index of 1, and so on.

Accessing layers this way, however, is not advised. Adding a layer will change the array, as will deleting a layer. The best way to access layer objects is to store a reference to them, like we've been doing in all the examples (e.g., `var my_layer = new OpenLayers.Layer()`), as we'll go over now.

Storing references to layer objects

The second way is to define our layer objects as global variables, like how we did with our map object. So far, all our layer objects are defined *inside* the `init()` function, which means we can't access them or refer to them outside of the `init()` function. If we try to access the `wms_base_ground` layer object in Firebug, we will get an error because the `wms_layer_map` layer object is not a global variable as we are not 'inside' of the `init()` function in Firebug. This concept is referred to as `scope`.

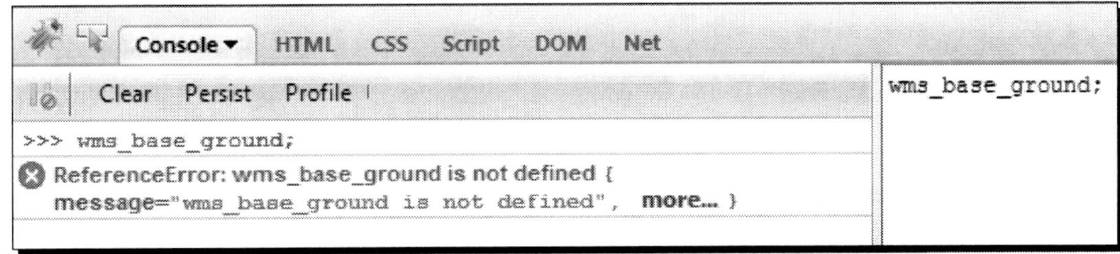

Let's look at our code to see how the map object is defined as a global variable.

```
var map;

function init() {
    //Setup our map object
    map = new OpenLayers.Map('map_element', {});

    // Setup our two layer objects
    var wms_layer_map = new OpenLayers.Layer.WMS( ...
```

When you specify `var`, you are basically saying 'create a new variable here'. Notice how we define `var map;` outside the `init()` function. Inside the `init()` function, we do not use `var` when we set `map` equal to the map object, because the map variable has *already* been created.

So, the process for making an object global is to:

1. Define the object/variable outside of the `init()` (or any function) with `var variable_name;`.
2. When you create the object inside the `init()` function, do not specify `var` when referring to `variable_name`.

Notice our code to create the `wms_layer_map` layer object: `var wms_layer_map = new OpenLayers.Layer.WMS(....)` Since we are using var inside the `init` function, the object is only now being created, and can only be referenced inside the `init` function. The `wms_layer_map` object will only be accessible inside the same scope that it was defined. In this case, since it was defined inside `init()`, we can only refer to it with the code that is inside the `init()` function. To define it globally to access it outside the function, we could do:

```
var map;
var wms_layer_map
function init(){
  map = new OpenLayers.Map ...
  wms_layer_map = new OpenLayers.Layer.WMS( ...
```

> Using global variables can make things easier, but try to avoid using them if possible. If you do use them, keep track of them and take care when naming them.

Pop Quiz – working with Variable Scope

Take a look at the following code. What will be the value of the variable `final`?

```
var a = 3;
//Create a function that will set a variable called 'b' equal to 5
function set_variable(){
  var b = 5;
}
//Call the function
set_variable()
final = a + b;
```

1. 8
2. 3
3. 5

4. There will be an error because the variable `b` cannot be accessed outside the `test` function.

Layer class methods

We've covered the properties of the base layer class and discussed most of the layer subclasses so far. The remaining topic to cover is the functions or methods of the base layer class. Since we'll be talking about the functions of the layer class, all layer subclasses inherit and use these functions. Before we get to the functions though, let's cover how to access layer objects in Firebug.

[What's the difference between a **function** and a **method**? A *method* is just a term for a *function* that is owned by an object or a class.]

Time for Action – defining a global layer object variable

Let's make the layer objects global variables access some properties of a layer, and call one of the layer's methods.

1. Make a copy of `chapter3_ex2_options_config.html`. Add the following lines right above the `init()` function:

```
var wms_layer_map, wms_state_lines, wms_labels, wms_water_depth,
wms_roads;
```

2. Inside your `init()` function, remove the `var` declaration before each of the layer object names. For example, the first line of your `wms_layer_map` definition should now look like this:

```
wms_layer_map = new OpenLayers.Layer.WMS(
```

3. Save the file (we'll refer to it as `chapter3_ex5_global_variables.html`).

4. Open it up in Firefox and enable the Firebug console.

5. In the console panel, input and run: `wms_layer_map;`. You should see some output like this:

```
Object { options=Object, more... }
```

6. Input and run the following command in Firebug:

```
wms_layer_map.name
```

7. Here we are directly accessing a property of the layer. You should see the layer's `name` property output:

   ```
   Base layer
   ```

8. Input and run the following command in Firebug:

   ```
   wms_layer_map.setVisibility(false);
   ```

9. Assuming you are at the full extent, you should no longer see the layer now, as you've just turned off the base layer's visibility.

What Just Happened?

We just made `wms_base_ground` a global variable, accessed a property of it, and called one of its methods. Any of the Layer class properties we talked about before can be accessed via `layer_object.property;`.

So, now that we're a bit more familiar with how to access layer properties and functions on the fly, let's go over the methods of the base layer class. Now, just like properties, most layer subclasses (e.g., `Layer.WMS`) have their own set of functions, but also inherit all the functions from the base layer class.

Layer class method definitions

All of the following functions can be called the same way we called the `setVisibility()` function; by calling `layer_object.function_name();`. Some methods require that you pass arguments into them. We won't cover all the functions of the base layer class, as some are either deprecated, found in the Map class function list, or outside the scope of this book.

The required arguments (if any) are listed under the parameters column.

Function	Description/Action	Parameters	Return Value
`setName( newName )`	Set a new name for the layer based on the passed in string. This will also update the display name for the layer in the layer switcher control, and may trigger a changelayer event.	`newName`: {`String`} The new name of the layer.	-

Function	Description/Action	Parameters	Return Value
`addOptions( options )`	Add additional options to the layer. The parameter behaves like the options parameter, and allows you to set properties on the layer.	`options:` {`Object`} An anonymous object containing key:value pairs of layer properties and values.	-
`redraw()`	Redraws the layer. Returns `true` if the layer was successfully redrawn or `false` if the layer could not be redrawn. You will need to call this while adding features to a vector layer, as we'll cover in Chapter 9.	-	{`Boolean`}
`getVisibility()`	Checks if the layer is visible or not. Returns `true` if the layer is visible, `false` if not.	-	{`Boolean`}
`SetVisibility( visibility )`	Sets the visibility to `true` or `false`, hide/ show the layer, and redraw it. The visibility determines if a layer should be shown or not.	`visibility:` {`Boolean`} `true` to show the layer, `false` to hide the layer.	-
`calculateInRange()`	Returns `true` or `false` if the layer can be displayed at the map's current resolution. If the `alwaysInRange` property is `true`, this will always return `true`.	-	{`Boolean`}
`setIsBaseLayer( is_base )`	Will turn the layer into a base layer if `true` is passed in and if `false` is passed in it will no longer make it a base layer.	`is_base:` {`Boolean`} Set to `true` to make layer a base layer, `false` to make it an overlay layer.	-

Function	Description/Action	Parameters	Return Value
`setOpacity( opacity )`	Sets the opacity of a layer based on the value passed in. The passed in `opacity` value is a float with valid values from `0` to `1`, with `0` being completely transparent and `1` being fully opaque. `0.5` would be 50 percent transparent.	`opacity`: `{Float}` Value of desired opacity.	-

Have a Go Hero – call some functions

Now that we've gone over some of the Layer class functions that we'll be making use of throughout this book, try calling them yourself. Open up Firefox, enable Firebug, and try calling some of the above functions on the layer objects (accessing the layer objects through either the `map.layers` array or the global layer objects themselves). Again, don't be afraid to experiment or break things!

Summary

In this chapter we talked about the Layer class. We covered the concept of layers and the differences between base layers and overlay layers. We went in depth with the WMS Layer class. We discussed the Layer class properties and methods and were introduced to various layer subclasses.

Whew! This was all likely a lot to take in. We covered a lot of Layer classes individually, but we have not yet made a map with different *types* of Layer classes. This is one of the things that OpenLayers excels at, and is what drives map 'mash ups.' To understand how to go about putting different layer classes together though, we'll need to have a basic understanding of projections—the topic of our next chapter.

4
Wrapping Our Heads Around Projections

When you look at a map, you are looking at a two dimensional representation of a three dimensional object (the earth). Because we are, essentially, 'losing' a dimension when we create a map, no map is a perfect representation of the earth. All maps have some distortion.

The distortion depends on what projection (a method of representing the earth's surface on a two dimensional plane) you use. In this chapter, we'll talk more about what projections are, why they're important, and how we use them in OpenLayers. We'll also cover some other fundamental geographic principles that will help make it easier to better understand OpenLayers.

In this chapter, we will cover:

- Concept of map projections
- Types of projections
- Longitude, latitude, and other geographic concepts
- OpenLayers projection class
- Transforming coordinates

Let's get started!

Map projections

No maps of the earth are truly perfect representations; all maps have some distortion. The reason for this is because they are attempting to represent a three dimensional object (an ellipsoid: the earth) in two dimensions (a plane: the map itself).

A **projection** is a representation of the entire, or parts of a, surface of a three dimensional sphere on a two dimensional plane (or other type of geometry).

Why on earth are Projections used?

Every map has some sort of projection—it is an inherent attribute of maps. Imagine unpeeling an orange and then flattening the peel out. Some kind of distortion will occur, and if you try to fully fit the peel into a square or rectangle (like a flat, two dimensional map), you'd have a very hard time.

To get the peel to fit perfectly onto a flat square or rectangle, you could try to stretch out certain parts of the peel or cut some pieces of the peel off and rearrange them. The same sort of idea applies while trying to create a map.

There are literately an infinite amount of possible map projections; an unlimited number of ways to represent a three dimensional surface in two dimensions, but none of them are totally distortion free.

So, if there are so many different map projections, how do we decide on what one to use? Is there a best one? The answer is no. The 'best' projection to use depends on the context in which you use your map, what you're looking at, and what characteristics you wish to preserve.

Projection characteristics

As a two dimensional representation is not without distortion, each projection makes a tradeoff between some characteristics. And as we lose a dimension when projecting the earth onto a map, we must make some sort of tradeoff between the characteristics we want to preserve. There are numerous characteristics, but for now let's focus on three of them.

Area

Area refers to the size of features on the map. Projections that preserve area are known as equal area projections (also known as equiareal, equivalent, or homolographic). A projection preserves area if, for example, an inch measured at different places on the map covers the same area. Because area remains the same, **angles**, **scales**, and **shapes** are distorted. This is what an equal area projected map may look like:

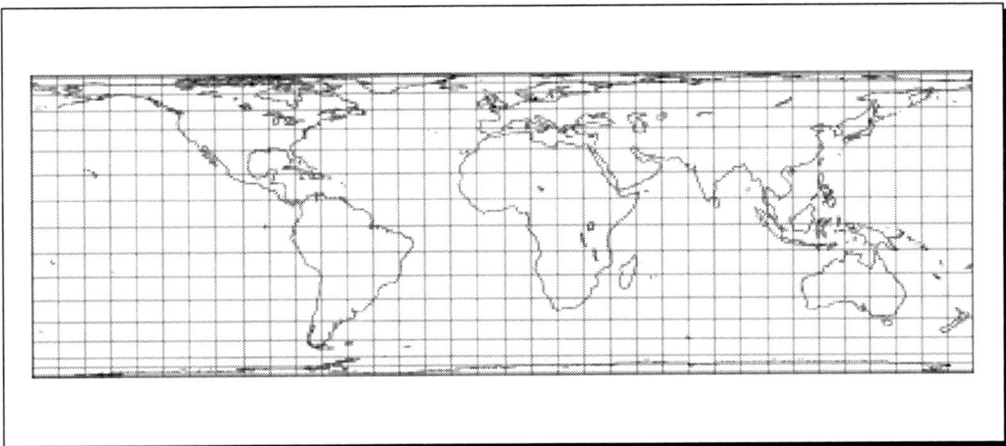

Scale

Scale is the ratio of the map's distance to the actual distance (e.g., one centimeter on the map may be equal to one hundred actual meters). All map projections show scale incorrectly at some areas throughout the map; no map can show the same scale throughout the map. There are parts of the map, however, where scale remains correct—the placement of these locations mitigates scale errors elsewhere. The deformation of scale also depends on the area being mapped. Projections are referred to as **equidistant** if they contain true scale between a point and every other point on the map.

Shape

Maps that preserve shape are known as **conformal** or **orthomorphic**. Shape means that relative angles to all points on a map are correct. Most maps that show the entire earth are conformal, such as the Mercator projection (used by Google Earth and other common web maps). Depending on the specific projection, areas throughout the map are generally distorted but may be correct in certain places. A map that is conformal cannot also be equal-area. The maps we've been using so far have been conformal.

Other characteristics

Projections have numerous other characteristics, such as bearing, distance, and direction. The key concept to take away here is that all projections preserve some characteristics at the expense of others. For instance, a map that preserves shape cannot completely preserve area.

There is no 'perfect' map projection. The usefulness of a projection depends on the context the map is being used in. A particular projection may excel for a certain task, e.g. navigation, but can be a poor choice for other purposes.

Types of projections

Projections are a way to represent three dimensions with two dimension surface. Projections are projected onto some geometric surface, three of the most common ones being a **plane**, **cone**, or **cylinder**.

Imagine a cylinder being wrapped around the earth, with the center of the cylinder's circumference touching the equator. Now, the earth is projected onto the surface of this cylinder, and if you cut the cylinder from top to bottom vertically and unwrap it, and lay it flat, you'd have a regular cylindrical projection:

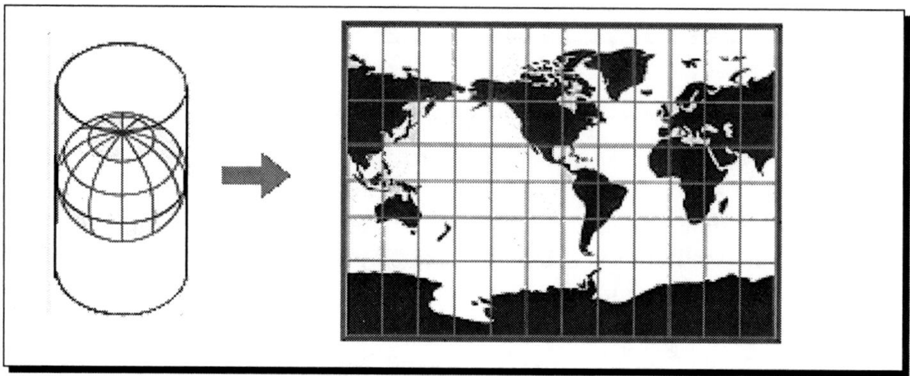

The **Mercator** projection is one type of projection. If you've never worked with projections before, there is a good chance that most of the maps you've seen were in this projection.

Because of its nature, there is heavy distortion near the ends of the poles. Looking at the previous screenshot, you can see that the cells get progressively larger, the closer you get to the North and South Poles. For example, Greenland looks larger than South America, but in reality it is about the size of Mexico. If area distortion is important in your map, you might consider using an **equal area** projection as we previously mentioned.

More information about projections can be found at the **USGS** (**US Geological Survey**) website at `http://egsc.usgs.gov/isb/pubs/MapProjections/projections.html`.

EPSG codes

As we mentioned, there are literally an infinite number of possible projections. So, it makes sense that there should be some universally agreed upon classification system that keeps track of projection information. There are many different classification systems, but OpenLayers uses **EPSG** codes. EPSG refers to the European Petroleum Survey Group, a scientific organization involved in oil exploration, which in 2005 was taken over by the OGP (**International Association of Oil and Gas Producers**).

For the purpose of OpenLayers, EPSG codes are referred to as:

```
EPSG:4326
```

The numbers (`4326` in this case) after `EPSG:` refer to the projection identification number. This projection, `EPSG:4326`, is the default projection which OpenLayers uses. It has been the projection used in all our examples so far, and uses the familiar Longitude/Latitude coordinate system, with coordinates that range from -180° to 180° (longitude) and -90° to 90° (latitude).

Time for Action – using different projection codes

Let's create a basic map using a different projection.

1. Using the template code, recreate your map object the following way. We'll be specifying the `projection` property, along with the `maxExtent`, `maxResolution`, and `units` properties. If we use a projection other than the default projection, we need to tell OpenLayers the type of coordinates to use, and setting the `maxExtent` is one way to do this. The projection we're going to use is `EPSG:900913`, a projection used by Google Maps and other third party APIs.

```
map = new OpenLayers.Map('map_element', {
 projection: 'EPSG:900913',
  maxExtent: new OpenLayers.Bounds(-20037508, -20037508,
    20037508, 20037508.34),
  maxResolution: 156543.0339,
  units: 'm'
});
```

2. Save the file, we'll refer to it as `chapter4_ex1.html`.

3. You should see something like the following:

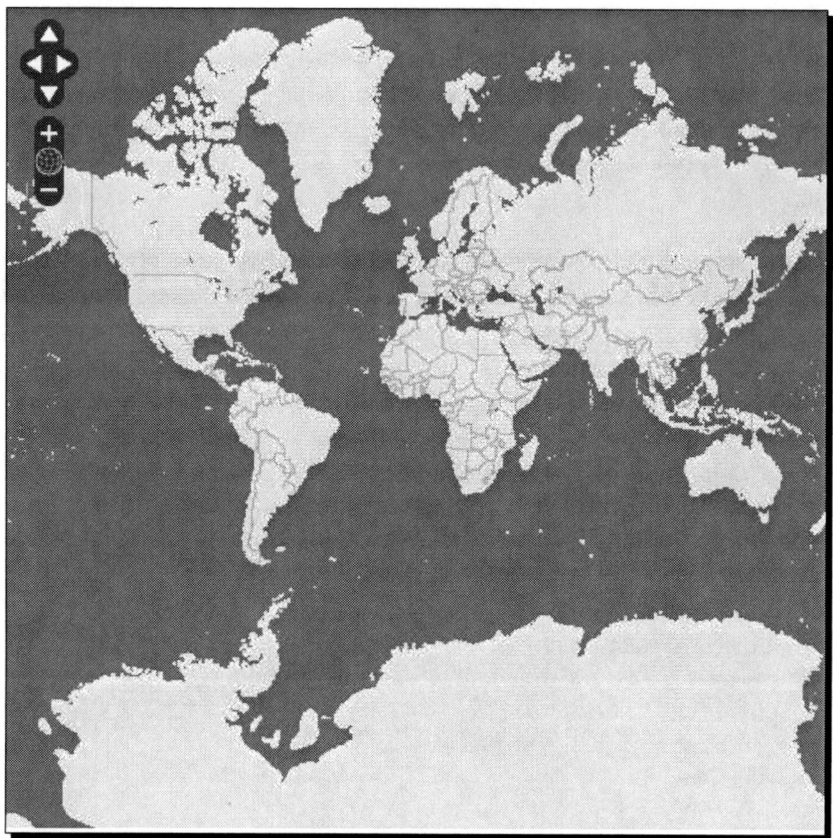

What Just Happened?

We just created map with the projection `EPSG:900913`. You'll notice that it looks quite a bit different than the maps we've made so far. This is because it is in a different projection.

Specifying a different projection

OpenLayers supports any projection, but if you want to use a projection other than `EPSG:4326`, you must specify the following three options:

- **maxExtent**: Default value is `-180,-90,180,90`
- **maxResolution**: Default value is `1.40625`
- **projection**: Default value is `EPSG:4326`

If you do not specify those options, the default values are used (all the other maps so far have been using the default values). You should also specify the `units` property, as we did with `units: 'm'`, depending on the units your projection uses.

The reason you must specify these properties is because different projections use different coordinates. In the above example, we set the maxExtent to:

```
maxExtent: new OpenLayers.Bounds(-20037508, -20037508,
           20037508, 20037508.34)
```

These values are much different than the default values—they are not longitude and latitude values. Instead, they use an x/y coordinate system, and to OpenLayers the longitude is the x value and latitude is the y value.

Pop Quiz – projections

Give some reasons why you might want to use a projection other than `EPSG:4326`. What areas would not be best suited for displaying the `EPSG:4326` projection?

Longitude/Latitude

Longitude and latitude are two terms most people are familiar with, even if they have limited geographic knowledge or get confused by the two. Let's take a look at the following screenshot and then go over these two terms.

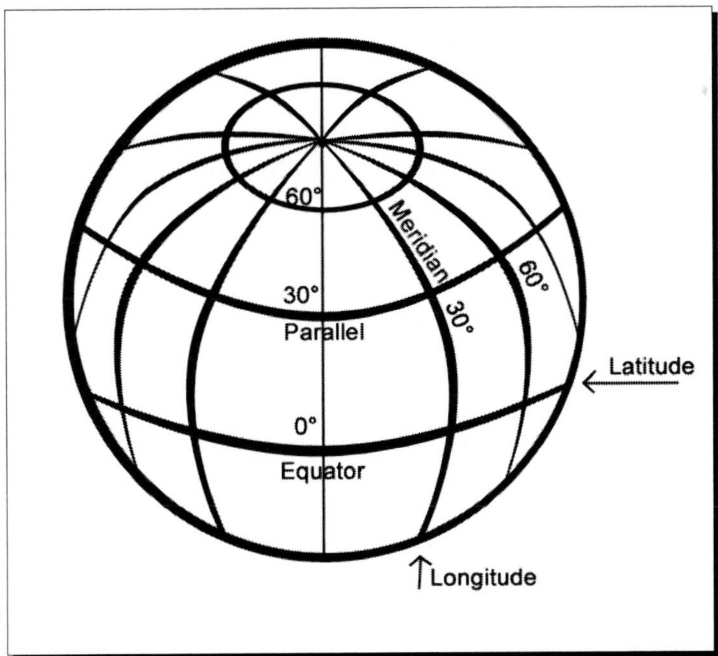

Latitude

Latitude lines are imaginary lines parallel to the equator, aptly known also as 'Parallels of Latitude'. Latitude is divided into 90 'degrees', or 90 spaces (or cells), above and below the equator. -90° is the South Pole, 0° would be the Equator, and 90° is the North Pole.

Each space, or cell, (from 42° to 43°, for example) is further divided into 60 minutes and each minute is divided into 60 seconds. The minutes and seconds terminology has little to do with time. In the context of mapping, they are just terms used for precision. The size of a degree of latitude is constant. Because they measure 'north to south', OpenLayers considers the **y** coordinate to be the latitude.

Longitude

Longitude lines are perpendicular to the lines of latitude. All lines of longitude, also known as meridians of longitude, intersect at the North Pole and South Pole, and unlike latitude, the length of each longitude line is the same. Longitude is divided into 360 'degrees', or spaces. Similar to latitude, each space is also divided into 60 minutes, and each minute is divided into 60 seconds.

As the space between longitude lines gets smaller, the closer you get to the poles the size of a degree of longitude changes. The closer you are to the poles, the shorter amount of time it would take you to walk around the earth.

With latitude, it makes sense to use the equator as 0°, but with longitude there is no spot better than another to start the 0° mark at. So, while this spot is really arbitrary, the Observatory of Greenwich, England is today universally considered to be 0° longitude. Because longitude measures east and west, OpenLayers considers the **x** coordinate to be longitude.

Time for Action – determining LonLat coordinates

Let's take a look at a couple of examples on coordinates from our previous maps.

1. Open up the final example from Chapter 1.
2. Pan around the map in any direction. Then, in Firebug, type:
   ```
   map.getCenter();
   ```
3. Depending on where you have panned, your output should read something like this:
   ```
   lon=-72.8125, lat=19.6875
   ```
4. Now, open up the example from the beginning of this chapter.
5. Pan around, and then in Firebug type:
   ```
   map.getCenter();
   ```

6. You should see something like:

```
lon=-9397474.0038099,lat=3595597.9798909
```

What Just Happened?

We just took a look at the longitude and latitude values for the center of the map in two different maps with different projections. When we call `map.getCenter()`, we get back an OpenLayers LonLat object.

In the first map, the max extent of the map was between -180° and 180° for longitude, and between -90° and 90° for latitude. These are the values used by the `EPSG: 4326`, and it is a longitude/latitude type of coordinate system. The values for longitude and latitude change in the second map because they are not in the same projection (they are in `EPSG:900913`).

OpenLayers projection class

So far, we've been talking about the abstract idea of a projection. Let's dive into OpenLayer's Projection class, `OpenLayers.Projection`, which is what we use to actually handle projections. The Projection class relies on an external library called Proj4js, which can be found at `http://proj4js.org`. First, we'll talk about what we can do without the proj4js library, and then talk about what we can do with it.

Creating a projection object

To instantiate an object from the Projection class, the code would look like the following:

```
my_proj = new OpenLayers.Projection('EPSG:4326', {});
```

Parameters

Let's take a look at the parameters for the **Projection** class.

- `projectionCode: {String}`: A string of identifying the **Well Known Identifier** (**WKID**) for the projection, such as an EPSG code in the form of `EPSG:4326`.
- `options:{Object}`: An optional object. For instantiating projection objects, it is very common to leave this out.

When creating a map and specifying the projection property, you can either pass in a projection object (like the one created above), or pass a string containing the projection code. This string, such as `EPSG:4326`, is also known as an **SRS code**. When passing in a code, like we've done with all our examples so far, OpenLayers automatically turns it into a projection object for you.

Functions

The Projection class has a number of methods, including:

Function	Description	Parameters
`getCode()`	Returns a {`String`} containing the projection code, e.g., `'EPSG:4326'`	-
`getUnits()`	Returns a {`String`} the `units` string for the projection, e.g., `'degrees'`. If the Proj4js library is not included on your page, this will return `null`.	-
`addTransform(from, to, method)`	Define a custom transformation function between two projections. This usually will not be necessary, especially if you are using Proj4js, unless you need to define a custom projection transformation.	`from:` {`String`} Source projection code `to:` {`String`} Destination projection code `method:`{`Function`} A function that transforms the source point to the destination point, leaving the original point unmodified.
`transform(point, source, destination)`	Calling this function will transform the passed in `point` from the passed in `source` projection to the passed in `destination` projection. You can also pass in an {`Object`} as long as it contains `x` and `y` properties. This function will transform the point in place, meaning that the point you passed in will be transformed. If you need a copy of the `point`, you should first make a clone of it before calling `transform()` by calling the point's `clone()` method.	`point:` {`Geometry.Point`} An object from the `OpenLayers.Geometry.Point` class, containing an x and y coordinate `source:`{`OpenLayers.Projection`} Projection object of the source projection `destination:`{`OpenLayers.Projection`} Projection object of the destination map projection.

Transforming projections

Transforming a point means you take a coordinate in one projection and turn it into a coordinate of another projection. Apart from transforming EPSG:4326 to EPSG:900913 and vice-versa, OpenLayers does not provide support for transforming other projections out of the box—to do transforms of other projections, you'll need to include Proj4js (which can be found at http://proj4js.org/).

In most scenarios, it is the job of the backend map server to handle projection transformations, but often it's useful or faster to do it on the client side (such as in the case of vector layer coordinate transformations). Let's take a look at how to transform EPSG:4326 to EPSG:900913 with OpenLayers.

Time for Action – coordinate transforms

Proj4js is not necessary for this example, as transforming between these two projections is possible without Proj4js.

1. Open up the previous example in Firefox. We won't be modifying any code, so any page which includes the OpenLayers library will be fine.

2. Open Firebug. In the console, create two projection objects:

```
var proj_4326 = new OpenLayers.Projection('EPSG:4326');
var proj_900913 = new OpenLayers.Projection('EPSG:900913');
```

3. Now let's create a **LonLat** object which will contain a point in EPSG:4326 coordinates.

```
var point_to_transform = new OpenLayers.LonLat(-79, 42);
```

4. And now let's transform it. We'll take it from EPSG:4326 (our source proj_4326 projection object) to EPSG:900913 (our destination proj_900913 projection object):

```
point_to_transform.transform(proj_4326, proj_900913);
```

5. Finally, we'll print the new value:

```
console.log(point_to_transform);
console.log(point_to_transform.lon, point_to_transform.lat)
```

6. Your output should read something like:

```
lon=-8794239.7714444,lat=5160979.4433314 { lon=-8794239.7714444,
more...}
-8794239.7714444 5160979.4433314
```

What Just Happened?

We just transformed a point in the `EPSG:4326` projection to a point in the `EPSG:900913` projection. Let's take a closer look at the `transform` method we called on the `point_to_transform` object.

```
point_to_transform.transform(proj_4326, proj_900913);
```

This will transform the original point from the `proj_4326` projection to the `proj_900913` projection. Notice, we aren't calling the `transform()` function of a projection object, but of a **LonLat** object. The `transform()` function's definition for an **OpenLayers.LonLat** object is as follows:

Function	Description	Parameters
`transform(source, dest)`	This function transforms a point in place, meaning that the original point will be transformed; hence the original value will be lost. If you need a copy of it, use the `.clone()` method first. It returns itself.	`source`: Source projection `dest`: Destination projection.

In this case, our source projection is in `EPSG:4326`, and our destination projection is in `EPSG:900913`. Keep in mind however, that `EPSG:4326` and `EPSG:900913` are the only two projections you can do transforms on with OpenLayers if you do not include the Proj4js library.

When creating your map, all your raster layers (image-based layers; nearly every layer except the vector and image layer) must be in the same projection as your map. You can do projection transformations with coordinates and the vector layer, but once OpenLayers gets back an image from a map server it cannot reproject the image itself (that's something the map server has to do).

The Proj4js library

The **Proj4js** library allows you to transform the coordinates from one coordinate system into another coordinate system. The Proj4js website is located at `http://proj4js.org`. By just including the Proj4js library on your page (like you do with OpenLayers), you can do more transforms within OpenLayers. Not all EPSG codes are supported, but there are many and if your desired code is not supported you can add a projection definition for it.

The site http://spatialreference.org contains Proj4js definitions for most of the EPSG codes.

Ideally, you should be using the same projection throughout your map, but there are times when you may want to display the coordinates in a different projection—such as with a vector layer. Let's take a look at how to setup the Proj4js library.

Time for Action – setting up Proj4js.org

This step is similar to the way we set up OpenLayers.

1. Download Proj4js from http://trac.osgeo.org/proj4js/wiki/Download. At the time of writing, the latest version was proj4js-1.0.1.zip, so go ahead and download it (or whichever the latest version is).

2. Extract it and copy the **proj4js** folder to your root code directory (the folder where your OpenLayers.js file is located).

3. Add the following line in the <head> section of your code **after** the OpenLayers library inclusion code.

```
<script type='text/javascript' src="proj4js/lib/
proj4js-combined.js"></script>
```

4. Now, open up the page and start Firebug. Type and run the following:

```
var test_proj = new Proj4js.Proj('EPSG:4325');
console.log(test_proj);
```

5. You should see output that looks like the following:

```
Object { srsCodeInput="EPSG:4325", more...}
```

What Just Happened?

We just included the Proj4js library and tested to see if it worked. If you received an error when you attempted to call new Proj4js.Proj() it means that the location of the **proj4js-combined.js** file was wrong. Ensure that the directories are set up properly (your example file should be in the same directory as the **proj4js** folder, and inside the **proj4js** folder should be a bunch of files and folders, including a lib folder that contains the **proj4js-combined.js** file).

Defining custom projections

Now that the Proj4js library is included, you can do transforms with more projections the same way we did in the previous example. Not all projections are defined; however, you are able to define them yourself, for example:

```
Proj4js.defs["EPSG:27563"] = "+title=LAMB sud france  +proj=lcc
+lat_1=44.1 +lat_0=44.1 +lon_0=0 +k_0=0.999877499 +x_0=600000
+y_0=200000 +a=6378249.2 +b=6356515 +towgs84=-168,-60,320,0,0,0,0
+pm=paris +units=m";
```

After that, you'd be able to use `EPSG:27563` for projection transformations just like you were able to use `EPSG:4326` and `EPSG:900913` from the earlier examples.

There are a number of already defined projections, and you can view them more extensively at `http://proj4js.org`. A more complete list (containing Proj4js definitions for nearly any EPSG code) can be found at `http://spatialreference.org/`.

Summary

In this chapter, we talked about projections. We covered what they are and the various different types of projections. Longitude, latitude, and other geographic concepts were also discussed. While we just scratched the surface of these pretty complex topics, you should have enough fundamental information to understand how to use projections.

We also talked about the **Projection** class, along with how to transform coordinates and use the **Proj4js** library. You'll often work with data in coordinate systems other than `EPSG:4326`, and knowing how to work with and transform data in other projections is important.

In the next chapter, we'll take a look at Google Maps and other third party APIs, and put some of our recently gained knowledge of projections to use.

5

Interacting with Third Party APIs

Web maps are very popular today, and are growing in popularity. After Google Maps was introduced, there was an explosion of interactive web maps. Google provides an API to interface with its mapping service, as do others now, and OpenLayers work well with most of them. Not only can we use these third party APIs with OpenLayers, we can also 'mashup' other layers on top of them.

In this chapter, we're going to learn:

- Concept of third party mapping APIs
- Using the layer classes for third party APIs: Google, Microsoft, and Yahoo!
- How to use OpenStreetMap
- Working with Spherical Mercator
- Combining different layer classes

Third party mapping APIs

Web based maps are commonplace today. The catalyst for the explosive growth of web maps was the introduction of Google Maps. Web maps existed before, but they were not quick or developer friendly. In June 2005, Google released an API for Google Maps which provided a front end client (the role OpenLayers plays) along with an access to the backend map server.

This allowed anyone to insert not just a Google Map on their site, but also allowed them to add in their own point data and manipulate the map in other ways. Google Maps grew in popularity, and other companies, such as Microsoft and Yahoo!, followed in their footsteps, creating their own web-mapping APIs.

Map mashups

The term **mashup** refers to an application that combines various different data sources and functionality together. A **map mashup** is a map that combines different layers and data. Third party mapping APIs, like Google and Yahoo! Maps, allow people to more easily create these 'map mashups'. For example, a map with a Google Maps base layer overlaid with markers that track places you've traveled to could be considered a map mashup.

OpenLayers did not introduce map mashups, but it allows us to create very powerful ones with ease. Combining a Google's Map layer, a WMS layer, and a Vector layer is pretty simple with OpenLayers.

OpenLayers and third party APIs

OpenLayers allows you to use third party mapping APIs inside your map application, letting you use their maps inside of yours. The main caveat is that, at the time of writing, the third party API map must be a base layer (but, as we discussed before, you can use as many base layers as you wish).

The three large commercial mapping APIs that OpenLayers can communicate with are **Google Maps**, **Yahoo! Maps**, and **Bing (Microsoft) Maps**. There is another free and open source API that OpenLayers works well with (and works in a similar manner to the previous three) called **OpenStreetMap**.

We'll first take a look at each of these four Layer classes, and then we'll go over how to combine them with other Layer classes.

Google Maps

The software behind Google Maps consists of a client and server. The client is what you use when you visit `http://maps.google.com`, and it communicates with the Google Maps backend servers. Google provides an API that lets you use their own client and backend server, but since OpenLayers is used as our client, we're only interested in interacting with Google's backend map server.

There may be legal restrictions depending on how you plan to use the Google Maps. Full restrictions can be found at `http://code.google.com/apis/maps/terms.html` and `http://www.google.com/intl/en_ALL/help/legalnotices_maps.html`.

In the previous chapters, we've set up the Google Layer using Version 3 (V3) of the Google Map API. Because Google Maps updates their API, OpenLayers must also update to accommodate any changes that are made. OpenLayers versions prior to 2.10 (the one this book is based on) use Version 2 (V2) of the Google Maps API. Google Maps V2 usage is deprecated however, so we will focus on using V3. From our perspective, our code doesn't change much—OpenLayers handles all the version specific functionality behind the scenes for us.

However, you are likely to encounter older OpenLayers maps made using Google Maps Version 2, so we will cover how to use both V2 and V3. Again, please use only V3 when making new maps, as V2 will eventually no longer be supported.

Differences between Google Maps version 2 and version 3

There are really only three things that you must do differently when going from Google Maps V3 to V2 (or vice versa):

1. The script tag you add in to reference the Google Maps library is different. You do not need to provide an API key with V3 of the Google Maps API.
2. The layer names used in the `type` property are different. For example, the 'terrain' layer in V3 is defined as `type: google.maps.MapTypeId.TERRAIN`, but in V2 it is `type: G_PHYSICAL_MAP`.
3. The layer is configured with spherical Mercator (we'll cover what this means shortly).

It is recommended you use V3 of the Google Maps API. The official Google Maps V3 documentation can be found at `http://code.google.com/apis/maps/documentation/javascript/`.

Official Google Maps API docs for V2 can be found at `http://code.google.com/apis/maps/documentation/javascript/v2/reference.html`.

Time for Action – using Goole Maps V3 (standard way)

Let's create a map using V3 of the Google Maps API. We've already done this in Chapter 3, so you should be somewhat familiar with it. This is the standard way to use the Google Maps Layer, and you should use this method unless you specifically need a layer type in V2 that V3 does not yet support.

With versions of OpenLayers prior to 2.10, accessing Google Maps V3 may not work.

1. Version 3 of the Google Maps API does not require an API key. However, you still must include the following in your `<head>` section, so OpenLayers knows where to look for the Google Maps API library. We'll be asking the map's API and specify that we want `v3.2` of the Google Maps API (you can leave the `&v=3.2` parameter if you'd like to let Google Maps provide the latest version for you automatically). Add this before your OpenLayers inclusion script:

```
<script
src="http://maps.google.com/maps/api/js?sensor=false&v=3.2"></
script>
```

2. Let's start by adding a hybrid layer to our map. The type property is in the form of `google.maps.MapTypeId.TYPE`, where `TYPE` in this case is `HYBRID`:

```
var google_hybrid = new OpenLayers.Layer.Google(
    "Google Hybrid",
    {type: google.maps.MapTypeId.HYBRID}
);
```

3. Now we'll add a physical (topographic type) layer:

```
var google_physical = new OpenLayers.Layer.Google(
    "Google Physical",
    {type: google.maps.MapTypeId.TERRAIN}
);
```

4. To add a satellite layer type:

```
var google_satellite = new OpenLayers.Layer.Google(
    "Google Satellite",
    {type: google.maps.MapTypeId.SATELLITE}
);
```

5. Now, we'll create a streets layer. If we do not pass in a layer type, the streets layer is used by default. If you wish to manually specify the type, the streets map type is `google.maps.MapTypeId.ROADMAP`.

```
var google_streets = new OpenLayers.Layer.Google(
    "Google Streets",
    {}
);
```

6. We'll add the layers to the map:

```
map.addLayers([google_hybrid,google_physical,google_satellite,
    google_streets]);
```

7. Finally, add a layer switcher control. You'll also notice that all the layers on the map that we've added are all base layers. By default, third party map API layers act as base layers.

```
map.addControl(new OpenLayers.Control.LayerSwitcher());
```

8. Open up the page. You should see something similar to this:

What Just Happened?

We just created a map using Google Maps API V3. We only needed to do two things:

1. Include the Google Maps V3 API with `<script src="http://maps.google.com/maps/api/js?sensor=false&v=3.2"></script>`. This lets OpenLayers access the Google Maps API.
2. Set the `type` property, such as `type: google.maps.MapTypeId.HYBRID`.

Including the Google Maps API enables OpenLayers to communicate with the Google Maps backend. Because we included the Google Maps API, we can use variables that are part of it. Specifically, the possible values for the `type` property come directly from the Google Maps API—for example, if we didn't include the API, we could not use `google.maps.MapTypeId.HYBRID`.

Notice that if you run `map.getCenter();` in Firebug, the center point we get back has very different coordinates than what we're used to—they aren't longitude/latitude values. This is because `sphericalMercator` is set for us automatically, so we can easily lay other layers, such as vector layers, on top of the third party map layer. Before we cover the reason for this (which is related to the other third party mapping APIs) let's go over the Google Map Layer class in more detail.

Creating a Google Map layer object

The format to create a Google Map layer object is the same for both V2 and V3 of the Google Maps API. The basic format for instantiating a Google Maps layer is:

```
var google_layer_object = new OpenLayers.Layer.Google(
    'Layer Name',
    {Properties}
);
```

The first argument, as with most Layer classes, is the layer's **name**. The second argument is a **properties** object. There are just a few Google Layer specific properties, so let's go over them.

Google layer properties

Because the Google Layer inherits from the base Layer class, you can use nearly any property that the Layer class provides—such as `numZoomLevels` or `maxExtent`. We'll cover just the properties that are specific to the Google Maps layer class. The possible values for the **type** attribute depend on the version of the Google Maps API used.

sphericalMercator {Boolean}

This property determines if the map should behave as a Mercator-projected map. Setting to `true` will allow us to use other layers, such as the Vector layer, with the actual map projection. Spherical Mercator is covered in more depth later in this chapter. When using V3 of the Google Map API, this property is automatically set to `true`. With V2, you will have manually set it to `true`. Example: `sphericalMercator: true`.

type {GmapType}

The `type` property specifies the Google Map layer type—what layer Google should give us. V2 and V3 of the Google Maps API have different possible values. Let's go over Version 3's values, and then take a look at Version 2's values.

V3 GMapType values

The standard, V3 way to refer to layer types is in the form of:

```
var google_layer_V3 = new OpenLayers.Layer.Google(
    'Google Maps V3 Layer',
    {type: google.maps.MapTypeId.TYPE}
);
```

To specify the layer type, we can simply change the `TYPE` property. The possible `TYPE` values can be one of the following:

Type	Description
`google.maps.MapTypeId.ROADMAP`	The default value, used if nothing is passed in. Shows the default street map (same as `G_NORMAL_MAP`).
`google.maps.MapTypeId.HYBRID`	Displays a map with a semi-transparent street layer overlaid on satellite imagery (same as `G_HYBRID_MAP`).
`google.maps.MapTypeId.SATELLITE`	Displays satellite imagery (same as `G_SATELLITE_MAP`).
`google.maps.MapTypeId.TERRAIN`	Displays a map with features such as terrain (same as `G_PHYSICAL_MAP`).

An up-to-date list of possible layer types can be found in the Google Maps API documentation at `http://code.google.com/apis/maps/documentation/javascript/maptypes.html#MapTypes`.

At the time of writing, the non-earth (moon, Mars, and sky) layers were not yet available from Google Maps.

V2 GMapType values

Version 2 of the Google Maps API provides various layers as well. Some of the layer types are even maps of other planets, but no extra work is required to view them inside the OpenLayers. To specify the map type for V2, use the following:

```
var google_layer_V2 = new OpenLayers.Layer.Google(
    'Google Maps V2 Layer',
    {type: TYPE}
);
```

The possible `TYPE` values are the following:

Type	Description
`G_NORMAL_MAP`	The default value. This is used if no GMapType is specified. This map type will display the normal street map.
`G_SATTELITE_MAP`	Displays satellite imagery.
`G_AERIAL_MAP`	Displays aerial photography.
`G_HYBRID_MAP`	Displays a map with a semi-transparent street layer overlaid on satellite imagery.
`G_AERIAL_HYBRID_MAP`	Displays a map with a semi-transparent street layer overlaid on aerial imagery.
`G_PHYSICAL_MAP`	Displays a map with features such as terrain.
`G_MOON_ELEVATION_MAP`	Displays a terrain map of the moon with altitude color coded.
`G_MOON_VISIBLE_MAP`	Displays photography taken from orbit around the moon.
`G_MARS_ELEVATION_MAP`	Displays a terrain map of Mars with altitude color coded.
`G_MARS_VISIBLE_MAP`	Displays photography taken from orbit around Mars.
`G_MARS_INFRARED_MAP`	Displays infrared imagery of Mars. Warm areas are bright and cooler areas are dark.
`G_SKY_VISIBLE`	Displays a map of the full celestial sphere.

To use any of these layer types, simply pass in the type name when creating the layer. Example: `type: G_NORMAL_MAP`.

The previous list was the supported layer types at time of writing, but current and up-to-date layer values can be found on the Google Maps V2 API docs at `http://code.google.com/apis/maps/documentation/javascript/v2/reference.html#GMapType`.

Time for Action – creating a Google Map layer with V2 (Deprecated)

Let's create a map with V2 of the Google Maps API. This is not the proper way to use the Google Maps layer, but I am including it because you are likely to come across a code that uses V2 of the API. Google Maps V2 also provides a few different layer types (like a moon layer) that V3 does not provide at the time of writing.

1. V2 of the Google Maps API requires you to register an API key, so grab one (for free) at `http://code.google.com/apis/maps/signup.html`. If you don't have a domain name, use `http://localhost`.

2. In the `<head>` section, *before* the OpenLayers script tag, include the following. Replace `YOUR_KEY` with the key generated from Step 1:

```
<script
src='http://maps.google.com/maps?file=api&amp;v=2&amp;key=YOUR_
KEY'></script>
```

3. Let's create some layers now. The format of the `type` attribute is slightly different with V2. We'll go over the possible layer type values right after this example. First, let's create some layers, starting with a 'hybrid' layer. The `type` value for the hybrid layer is `G_HYBRID_MAP`. We'll also specify 20 zoom levels with the `numZoomLevels` property. Different base layers can support different numbers of zoom levels:

```
//Create Google Map Layer objects
var google_hybrid = new OpenLayers.Layer.Google(
    "Google Hybrid",
    {type: G_HYBRID_MAP, numZoomLevels: 20}
);
```

4. Now let's create a 'physical' layer, which is a terrain/topology type of layer. The type is `G_PHYSICAL_MAP`, and we'll specify a different `numZoomLevels` property:

```
var google_physical = new OpenLayers.Layer.Google(
    "Google Physical",
    {type: G_PHYSICAL_MAP, numZoomLevels: 22}
);
```

5. We'll use the `G_SATELLITE_MAP` to create a satellite layer:

```
var google_satellite = new OpenLayers.Layer.Google(
    "Google Satellite",
    {type: G_SATELLITE_MAP}
);
```

6. If we don't pass in a `type`, the default 'streets map' layer will be used. This is the layer you'll see by default in Google Maps. If you wish to manually specify this layer type, it is called `G_NORMAL_MAP`.

```
var google_streets = new OpenLayers.Layer.Google(
    "Google Streets",
    {}
);
```

7. Now let's add a layer type that is not (at the time of writing) supported by V3 of the Google Maps API—a layer of Mars:

```
var google_mars = new OpenLayers.Layer.Google(
    "Google Mars",
    {type: G_MARS_VISIBLE_MAP}
);
```

8. Finally we just add the layers to the map:

```
map.addLayers([google_hybrid,google_physical,google_satellite,
  google_streets,google_mars]);
```

9. Take a look at your map. You should see something like this:

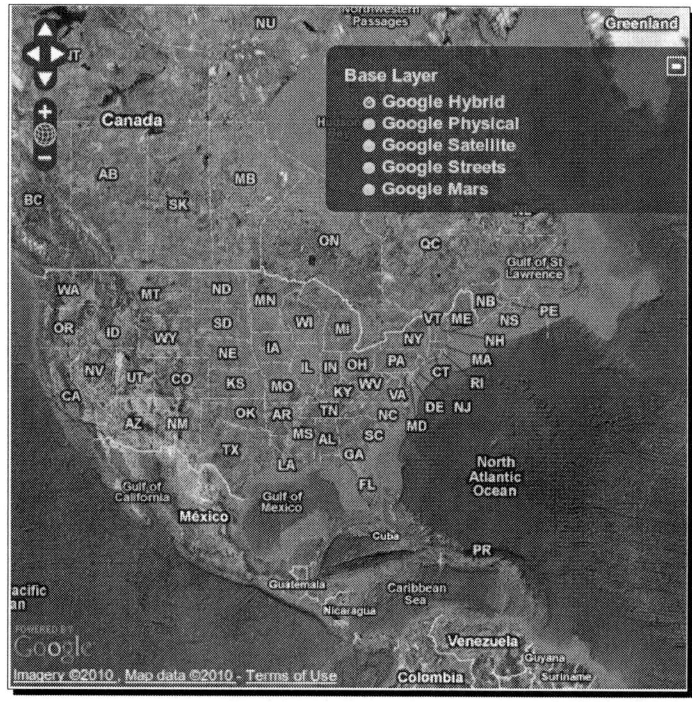

What Just Happened?

We just created a map using Google Maps V2 with a few of the possible Google Maps layer types. Because we're using a different version of the API here, you'll notice that our code is slightly different than it was when using the standard (V3) of the Google Maps API. Specifically, the `type` property is different because V2 of the API supports different layer types than Version 3 does.

Yahoo! Maps API

OpenLayers provides us with an easy way to interface with the Yahoo! mapping API as well. We work with it similar to how we work with the Google Maps Layer class. The official Yahoo! Maps API documentation can be found at `http://developer.yahoo.com/maps/`. Let's take a look!

Time for Action – using the Yahoo! Maps Layer

Let's create a map with the Yahoo! Maps Layer class.

1. In the `<head>` section, we need to reference the location of the Yahoo! Maps API. Add the following before the OpenLayers inclusion script tag:

```
<script
src="http://api.maps.yahoo.com/ajaxymap?v=3.0&appid=euzuro-
openlayers"></script>
```

2. Let's set up some Yahoo! layer objects now. Like the Google Maps Layer, we specify the type of the layer we want by setting the `type` property. Let's create a hybrid layer. The `type` property for Yahoo! layers start with `YAHOO_MAP_`, followed by a three character code:

```
var yahoo_hybrid = new OpenLayers.Layer.Yahoo(
  "Hybrid",
  {type: YAHOO_MAP_HYB, numZoomLevels: 24}
);
```

3. Now let's create a satellite layer type. The three character code for satellite is `SAT`. We'll also set a different amount of zoom levels to further illustrate how each base layer can have its own amount of zoom levels:

```
var yahoo_satellite = new OpenLayers.Layer.Yahoo(
  "Satellite",
  {type: YAHOO_MAP_SAT, numZoomLevels: 20}
);
```

4. Let's add a default layer next. If we don't pass a `type` in, the default value will be used, which is `YAHOO_MAP_REG`—a street-like map.

```
var yahoo_street = new OpenLayers.Layer.Yahoo(
  "Street",
  {}
);
```

5. Finally we just add the layers to the map:

```
map.addLayers([yahoo_hybrid, yahoo_satellite, yahoo_street]);
```

6. Open the page. You should see something like the following:

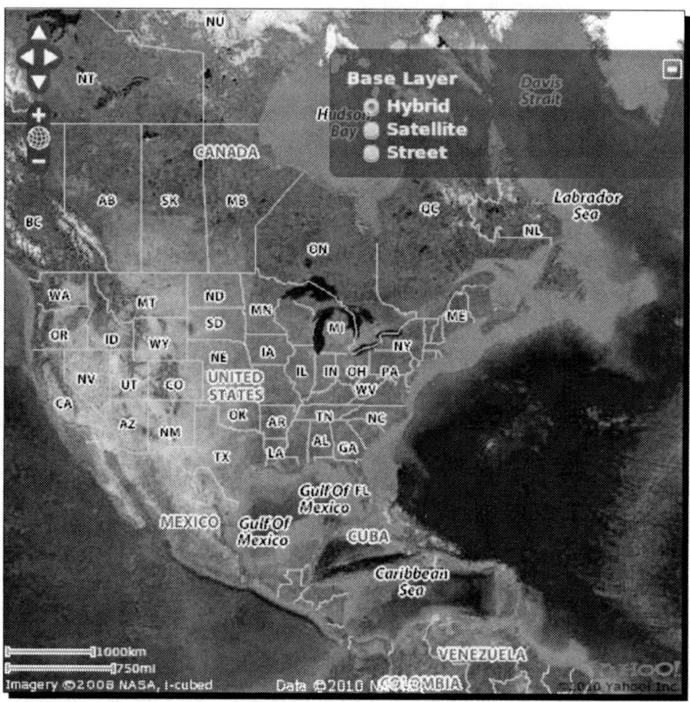

What Just Happened?

We just created a map with a Yahoo! Maps layer. Like the Google Maps layer, we need to include a link to the Yahoo! API—but we do not need an API key. We included the API with:

```
<script src="http://api.maps.yahoo.com/ajaxymap?v=3.0&appid=euzuro-
openlayers"></script>
```

Like the Google Maps API script, this script allows OpenLayers to communicate with the Yahoo! Maps API. It also provides us values to use for the `type` property.

Yahoo! Maps Layer class properties

Like the Google Maps, our main focus on this layer class will be on the `type` property. Let's go over the available `type` values.

Yahoo! Maps Layer types

At the time of writing there were three layer types the Yahoo! Maps API gives us access to:

Type	Description
`YAHOO_MAP_HYB`	Displays a hybrid map consisting of the satellite map overlaid with the regular street map.
`YAHOO_MAP_SAT`	Displays satellite photography.
`YAHOO_MAP_REG`	Displays a street map. This is the default type value, so if `type` is not passed in this will be used.

Microsoft's mapping API

Microsoft provides an interface to their mapping services as well. Their mapping service previously was referred to as Virtual Earth, but they have since re-branded it as **Bing Maps**. Hence, in OpenLayers, the Layer Class is called VirtualEarth, and we use it the same way we've created Google and Yahoo! layers. The official Microsoft documentation can be found at `http://msdn.microsoft.com/en-us/library/dd877180.aspx`.

Time for Action – creating a Bing/Virtual Earth Layer

1. Include a reference to the Microsoft Mapping API in your `<head>` section, before the OpenLayers inclusion script:

```
<script
src="http://ecn.dev.virtualearth.net/mapcontrol/mapcontrol.
ashx?v=6.2&mkt=en-us"></script>
```

2. Let's set up some layer objects now. We specify the `type` property like in the previous examples. For this layer, the type is prefixed by `VEMapStyle.`, which stands for 'Virtual Earth Map Style'. Let's create a 'shaded' layer, which in this case is the street/road layer with shaded elevation:

```
var ve_shaded = new OpenLayers.Layer.VirtualEarth(
  "Shaded",
  {type: VEMapStyle.Shaded}
);
```

3. We'll add an aerial (satellite imagery) layer now:

```
var ve_aerial = new OpenLayers.Layer.VirtualEarth(
  "Aerial",
  {type: VEMapStyle.Aerial}
);
```

4. Now, let's create a default layer. If we don't pass in a `type`, the `VEMapStyle.Road` layer will be used. It is similar to the shaded layer, but without the shading. We'll also use another property called `animationEnabled`, which we'll set to `false`. By default, this property is set to `true` and controls whether or not a zooming animation will be applied to the layer (this animation is a Virtual Earth layer specific property):

```
var ve_road = new OpenLayers.Layer.VirtualEarth(
    "Road",
    {animationEnabled: false}
);
```

5. Let's add a hybrid layer:

```
var ve_hybrid = new OpenLayers.Layer.VirtualEarth(
  "Hybrid",
  {type: VEMapStyle.Hybrid}
);
```

6. Finally, add the layer objects to the map:

```
map.addLayers([ve_shaded, ve_aerial, ve_road, ve_hybrid]);
```

7. You should see something like the following:

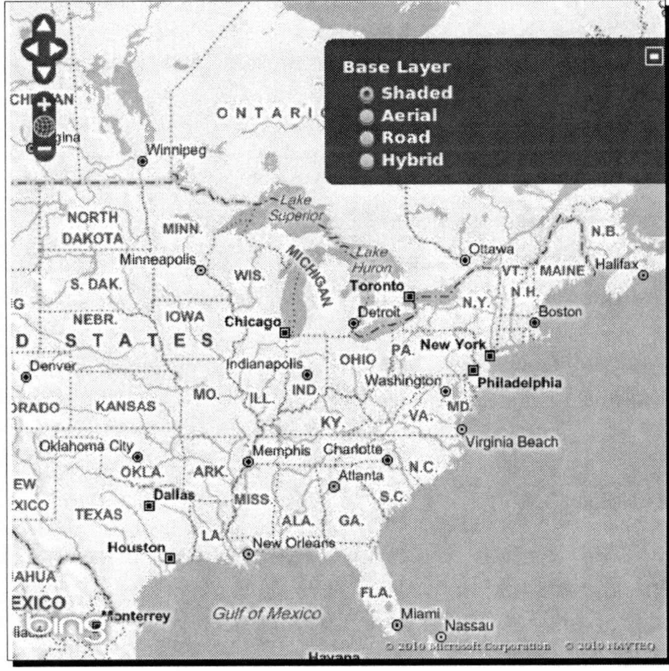

What Just Happened?

We just made a map using the Microsoft Virtual Earth/Bing API. It works similar to how the Google and Yahoo! Maps API work—by providing a script tag to the Microsoft mapping API. We can communicate with Microsoft's map server and use different `type` values. Let's go over the properties, as there is a new one the other third party layer classes do not provide.

VirtualEarth layer class properties

Like the previous layers, the `type` property controls what layers we get back from the map server. However, there is a unique `animationEnabled` property that we can use with the VirtualEarth layer. Let's take a look at it:

Property	Data Type	Description
`animationEnabled`	`{Boolean}`	This property determines if panning/zooming animations should be enabled. By default, the value is `true`. If it is `false`, the animations will be the same as the other layers' animations. If you look at the Road layer from the previous example, you can see the difference with this property set to `false`.

Possible type values

The possible values for the `type` property, at the time of writing, are the following.

Type	Description
`VEMapStyle.Shaded`	Displays a shaded street/road map, showing elevations.
`VEMapStyle.Aerial`	Displays aerial (satellite) imagery.
`VEMapStyle.Road`	Displays a road map.
`VEMapStyle.Hybrid`	Displays an aerial layer overlaid with a road map.

Let's cover one more layer type before we start combining different layers together—the **OpenStreetMap** Layer.

OpenStreetMap

OpenStreetMap (or **OSM**) is a free, wiki-style, map of the world driven by user contributed content. You are able to use your own OSM tiles or ones provided through the OpenStreetMap servers. Unlike the previous third party APIs, there is no `type` property to specify for this layer.

Setting up an OpenStreetMap service and tiles yourself is not too difficult, but it is outside the scope of this book (visit `http://wiki.openstreetmap.org/wiki/OpenLayers_Simple_Example` for more information on this). Accessing OSM with OpenLayers, however, isn't.

More information about OpenStreetMap can be found at `http://www.openstreetmap.org/`.

Time for Action – creating an OpenStreetMap Layer

1. For the OpenStreetMap layer, we do not need to include a script; we can access it outside of the box.

2. This will be pretty simple. We just need to create an OSM layer object:

```
var osm_layer = new OpenLayers.Layer.OSM(
    'OpenStreetMap Layer'
);
```

3. Then, we just add the layer object to the map. Even though we're only passing in one layer object, we'll use the `addLayers` function to keep our code consistent:

```
map.addLayers([osm_layer]);
```

4. You should see something like this:

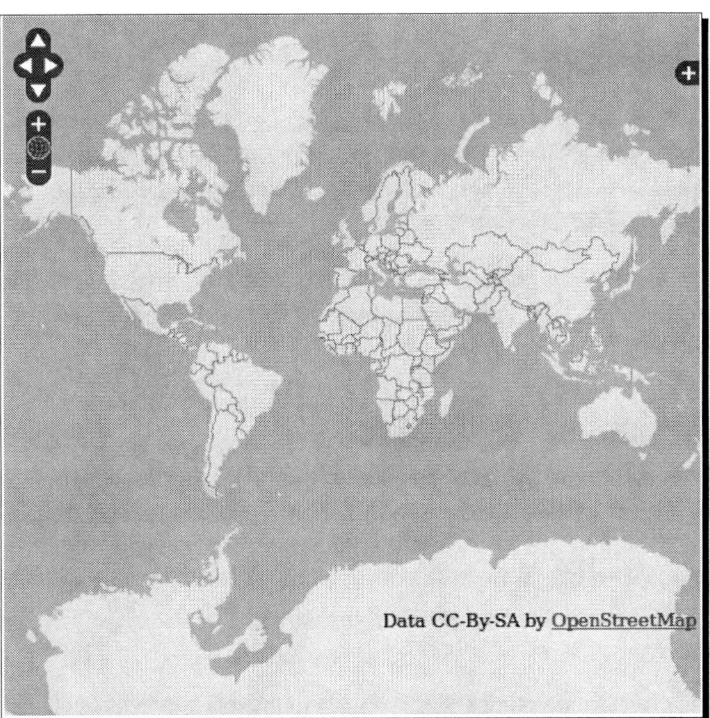

What Just Happened?

The map we just created is showing an OpenStreetMap layer. Unlike the previous layers, we did not have to provide an API key or link to OSM specific files—OpenLayers knows about it already. Another thing that separates the OpenStreetMap layer from the other third party map layers is that the OSM layer has no `type` property.

Accessing your own OSM tiles

The above code uses the publicly available OSM tiles, but it is easy to point it at your own tiles. To do so, create the layer in this format:

```
var osm_layer = new OpenLayers.Layer.OSM(
  'My OSM Layer',
  'http://URL_TO_TILES/${z}/${x}/${y}.png',
```

```
        {}
    );
```

To use this, you would replace `URL_TO_TILES` with the server hosting your OSM tiles. The `${z}`, `${x}`, `${y}` are variables which OpenLayers will replace with the appropriate values to reference specific map tiles.

Spherical Mercator

Let's talk about **Spherical Mercator**. I've made a couple of references to it throughout this chapter, but what is it? It is a term used to refer to the projection that many commercial, third party mapping APIs use. We need to use Spherical Mercator to properly overlay data and layers on top of third party map layers.

All the APIs we've used in this chapter so far (Google, Yahoo!, VirtualEarth/Bing, and OSM) are in the Spherical Mercator projection—a projection that treats the earth as a sphere (as opposed to an ellipsoid).

Spherical Mercator—EPSG code

The official EPSG code for the projection is currently `EPSG:3857`, but when the code was established it was referred to as `EPSG:900913`. This `EPSG:900913` code can still be used in OpenLayers, as the `EPSG:3857` code is identical to it. Google was one of the (if not the) first to publish maps with this projection—notice how 900913 resembles 'gOOglE' (with a backwards 'E' for 3).

You may also see other EPSG codes that represent the same Spherical Mercator projection. For example, ArcGIS version 9.3 uses the code `EPSG:102113`, and you may also encounter the standard `EPSG:3785`. These all refer to the same 'Spherical Mercator' projection and can be used interchangeably.

So, what does this mean for us? Well, when we use these third party APIs, we use coordinates that don't look like Lon/Lat coordinates (they are x, y in meters). Because the earth is treated as a sphere in the Spherical Mercator projection, calculations are affected and data from other sources may not match up perfectly with it if we don't re-project our data.

We need to set up Spherical Mercator before we can add in other layer classes and have them line up correctly, so let's take a look.

Time for Action – using Spherical Mercator

Let's set up a map using Spherical Mercator with a Yahoo! Maps Layer. When using the Google Maps Layer (V3), the `sphericalMercator` property is set to `true` automatically, so you do not need to do anything extra. However, explicitly specifying it is a good idea when working with other layers that are not in the Spherical Mercator projection.

1. Since we'll use the Virtual Earth layer type, we need to make sure to include the Microsoft Mapping API:

```
<script
src="http://ecn.dev.virtualearth.net/mapcontrol/mapcontrol.
ashx?v=6.2&mkt=en-us"></script>
```

2. The first step is to specify the `maxExtent`, `maxResolution`, `units`, and `projection` properties when creating our map object. If you'll remember from the previous chapter, these are the properties we must set when we specify a map projection other than the default `EPSG:4326` projection. We'll also set the `displayProjection` property to an `EPSG:4326` projection object. This `displayProjection` property specifies what projection various controls, such as the `MousePosition` control, display coordinates in. For the `EPSG: 900913` projection, (-)`128 * 156543.0339` is the max extent.

```
map = new OpenLayers.Map('map_element',{
  maxExtent: new OpenLayers.Bounds(
      -128 * 156543.0339,
      -128 * 156543.0339,
      128 * 156543.0339,
      128 * 156543.0339),
  maxResolution: 156543.0339,
  units: 'm',
  projection: new OpenLayers.Projection('EPSG:900913'),
  displayProjection: new OpenLayers.Projection("EPSG:4326"),
});
```

3. Now, we'll create a Microsoft Virtual Earth (Bing) map layer object. This time, we'll specify `sphericalMercator: true` so the layer is properly projected to the projection:

```
var ve_road = new OpenLayers.Layer.VirtualEarth(
    "Road",
    {sphericalMercator:true}
);
```

4. Open the map, and in Firebug run the command:

   ```
   map.getProjection();
   ```

5. You should see the following output:

   ```
   "EPSG:900913"
   ```

What Just Happened?

We just set up a map using a Yahoo! Maps Layer with Spherical Mercator enabled on it. When using a different projection, we have to specify some properties (as we talked about in the previous chapter). Let's briefly go over the properties relevant to the `EPSG:900913`, the Spherical Mercator, projection.

Map properties with Spherical Mercator layers

Because we're working in a different projection, we have to tell OpenLayers some things about the map so it knows how to set it up. Let's take a look at the map properties which we set in the code above.

maxExtent

The first property we pass in to the map properties is:

```
maxExtent: new OpenLayers.Bounds(
    -128 * 156543.0339,
    -128 * 156543.0339,
    128 * 156543.0339,
    128 * 156543.0339),
```

The `maxExtent` property tells OpenLayers the maximum boundaries of the map. The four numbers represent the minimum x, the minimum y, the maximum x, and the maximum y coordinates. The numbers we use here are the coordinates for the extent of the world in `EPSP:900913`—quite different from Longitude/Latitude coordinates. Without specifying the `maxExtent`, our map would not display properly since OpenLayers would not know what the boundaries of the world are.

maxResolution

This property sets the maxResolution of the map, which is based on fitting the map's extent into 256 pixels. This is a `{Float}` data type. For example,

```
maxResolution: 156543.0339,
```

More information about this property can be found in Chapter 8, the chapter about the Map Class.

units

This specifies that the map is in meters. It is a `{String}` data type.

```
units: 'm',
```

By default, the `units` property is set to `degrees`. Since Spherical Mercator is a projection that uses meters, we need to specify it here.

projection

Here we set the map's projection to be `ESPG:900913`, i.e., the Spherical Mercator projection:

```
projection: new OpenLayers.Projection('EPSG:900913'),
```

If we wish to work with Longitude/Latitude, or other layer types in a different projection, we need to transform the coordinates from `EPSG:900913` to the appropriate other projection. Once we start to use a third party map API, we're stuck using the Spherical Mercator projection.

Using Google Maps and other layers

Getting other layers to play nicely with these third party layers involve three things, two of which we've already done:

1. Set up the correct map projection properties.
2. Make sure `sphericalMercator` is set to `true` on the third party map layer.
3. Ensure all raster layers (any non-Vector or Image layer), such as WMS, are in the map's projection. In this case, we'll need to make sure we ask our WMS server for map tiles in the `EPSG:900913` projection.

Using what we learned so far, let's make a mashup. We'll use a Google Maps layer as the base layer, and WMS and Vector layers as overlay layers.

Time For Action – creating your first mashup

Let's make a map 'mashup' that consists of a Google Map layer, a WMS layer, and a Vector layer.

1. First, we need to add the Google Maps V3 script API tag in the `<head>` section:

```
<script src="http://maps.google.com/maps/api/
js?sensor=false&v=3.2"></script
>
```

2. Now, set up your map object with the proper projection info, like in the previous example:

```
map = new OpenLayers.Map('map_element',{
  maxExtent: new OpenLayers.Bounds(
  -128 * 156543.0339,
  -128 * 156543.0339,
  128 * 156543.0339,
  128 * 156543.0339),
  maxResolution: 156543.0339,
  units: 'm',
  projection: new OpenLayers.Projection('EPSG:900913'),
  displayProjection: new OpenLayers.Projection("EPSG:4326"),
});
```

3. Now let's create a Google Maps layer. Because we are using V3 of the API, we do *not* need to specify `sphericalMercator: true` because it is set to `true` automatically.

```
var google_streets = new OpenLayers.Layer.Google(
  "Google Streets",
  {numZoomLevels: 20}
);
```

4. We'll create our WMS layer now and specify that we want the `basic` and various label layers back from the WMS server. We'll also set the opacity to `.7`, or 70 percent opaque, and set `isBaseLayer: false` so we're sure it will be an overlay layer. Now, we are not specifying a `projection` property on the layer because our layer will inherit the projection of the map object. All layers (with the exception of the Vector layer) should be in the same projection as your map. The WMS server we're using *does* support the `EPSG:900913` projection, so we'll get back proper map tiles. If the WMS service does not support this projection, we wouldn't be able to use it—we'll talk about this more after the example. Go ahead and create the WMS layer:

```
var wms_layer = new OpenLayers.Layer.WMS(
```

```
    'OpenLayers WMS',
    'http://vmap0.tiles.osgeo.org/wms/vmap0',
    {layers: 'basic,clabel,ctylabel,statelabel', transparent: true},
    {isBaseLayer: false,
    opacity: .7}
);
```

5. Now let's add a Vector layer. It will be in the `EPSG:900913` projection as well, since it inherits the projection from the map object. We could, however, specify a different projection for the vector layer and re-project vector data on the fly (we can't do this on raster layers, like the WMS layer)—but we'll save this topic for Chapter 9, our Vector layer chapter. Create the vector layer object:

```
var vector_layer = new OpenLayers.Layer.Vector(
  'Editable Vectors');
```

6. We'll add an **EditingToolbar** control now, which lets us add points and polygons to a vector layer via a toolbar that will appear in the upper right corner of the map (by default). When creating the control object, we simply pass in the vector layer object we wish the control to use:

```
//Add a vector editing control
map.addControl(new
OpenLayers.Control.EditingToolbar(vector_layer));
```

7. Finally, we just need to add the layers to the map.

```
map.addLayers([google_streets, wms_layer, vector_layer]);
```

8. Open up your map now. You can add points and polygons to the vector layer via the **EditingToolbar** control in the top right corner:

What Just Happened?

We just created a map using Google Maps, WMS, and Vector layers. We also have an **EditingToolbar** control hooked up to the vector layer object, which will let us create points and polygons in the vector layer. Any points or polygons (also called **features**) we create will be in the map's projection, `EPSG:900913`, and line up with the Google Map layer below it.

WMS with Spherical Mercator/third party map layers

We also have a WMS layer, set to be an overlay layer. To use a WMS service on top of a Google Maps layer (or any other third party map layer), the WMS service must support the `EPSG:900913` projection. The WMS service we used, `http://vmap0.tiles.osgeo.org/wms/vmap0`, does support this projection so the map tile images properly lined up with the Google Maps layer. If a WMS service does not support the `EPSG:900913` projection, the map tile images would not properly line up.

> To find out what projections a WMS service supports, you can make a `getCapabilities` request to the server. To make this request, specify the `request`, `service`, and `version` properties in the URL. For example, `http://wmsserver/?request=GetCapabilities&service=WMS&version=1.1.1`.

Summary

In this chapter, we talked about what third party mapping APIs are and how to use them. We learned how to use the Google, Yahoo!, and Microsoft mapping APIs, along with the OpenStreetMaps API. We also discussed Spherical Mercator and demonstrated how to use it. Finally, we created a map 'mashup', mixing various different layer types together.

The next chapter will focus on another part of OpenLayers—the **Control** class. This is another thing that sets OpenLayers apart from other mapping libraries. With it, we're able to interact with our map, add tons of additional functionality, and even create our own custom controls.

6
Taking Control of Controls

So far, we've taken for granted that the map will move when we drag it. Or that we can just click a layer in the layer switcher and it will turn on or off. Or that we can zoom in and out. We haven't yet talked much about what actually is behind the map interaction or how it works.

Simply put, the OpenLayers Control class is what makes our maps interactive. There are many built in controls, each with their own unique functions. But, not only do you have a large number of pre-made controls at your disposal, you also have the ability to easily create your own controls.

In this chapter, we'll cover:

- What controls are
- Adding controls to a map
- The Control class and its subclasses
- Using panels to add controls outside of the map
- Creating custom controls

What are controls?

Controls allow us to interact with our map. They also allow us to display extra information, such as displaying a scale bar with the **ScaleLine** control. Some controls do not have a visual appearance, such as the **ArgParser** control, but others do, such as the **OverviewMap** control. You can have as many controls on your map as you'd like. There are even some cases where you may not want any controls—such as embedding an unmovable map in a page, or showing a static map for printing.

Using controls in OpenLayers

Most controls are added directly to the map, such as the **Navigation** control. Others are added to the map, but can also be placed in a `<div>` tag outside the map—like the overview map control.

Other controls act similar to buttons which can be clicked or toggled on and off. These types of controls can be placed inside of a **panel**, which can also be placed outside the map.

Furthermore, we can even create our own controls and place them directly in the map or inside of a panel. We'll cover all this and more, so let's get started with how to add controls to your map.

Adding controls to your map

There are two methods for adding controls to a map.

1. Pass in a JavaScript array of OpenLayers Control objects when you instantiate the map object.
2. Add controls to the map object after it has been created by calling either of the two map functions `addControl()`, passing in a single control object, or `addControls()`, passing in an array of control objects.

When you create your map, four control objects are added automatically. These four controls are:

- `OpenLayers.Control.Navigation`: Responsible for handling map interaction from mouse events, such as dragging the mouse, zooming with the scroll bar, and double-clicking.
- `OpenLayers.Control.PanZoom`: Adds a Pan/Zoom bar to the top left hand side of the map. Contains up/down/left/right arrows for panning, and zoom in, zoom out, and zoom to maximum map extent buttons for zooming.

- `OpenLayers.Control.ArgParser`: Allows the map to zoom to a specific location and turn on/off layers based on the URL that you call the map with. In other words, when you use the `OpenLayers.Control.Permalink` control to generate a URL, the `ArgParser` control will parse the URL and manipulate the map based on the parameters embedded in the URL. We'll cover both controls in detail later in this chapter.
- `OpenLayers.Control.Attribution`: This control will add attributions from layers to the map if any attributions are passed into the layer object.

Since these controls are added without us explicitly adding them, how do we opt to not include them? The simplest way is to pass in an empty array to the `controls` property when we instantiate a map object.

Time for Action – creating a map with no controls

Without controls, our map will not be interactive. This is sometimes exactly what you want, such as when displaying a map on a printer friendly page.

1. First, we'll need to create our map object and pass in an empty array to the `controls` property:

```
map = new OpenLayers.Map('map_element', {
  controls: []
});
```

2. Now, no controls will be added to the map unless you manually call `addControl` or `addControls`. Let's create and add a WMS layer to our map:

```
var wms_layer = new OpenLayers.Layer.WMS(
  'WMS Layer Title',
  'http://vmap0.tiles.osgeo.org/wms/vmap0',
  {layers: 'basic'},
  {}
);
map.addLayer(wms_layer);
```

3. Make sure you also set the extent—as stated in previous chapters, this step will be implied in all future examples:

```
if(!map.getCenter()){
  map.zoomToMaxExtent();
}
```

4. Open up the page. You should see a map with no controls, and you won't be able to pan around or zoom in since the map has no controls, as shown below:

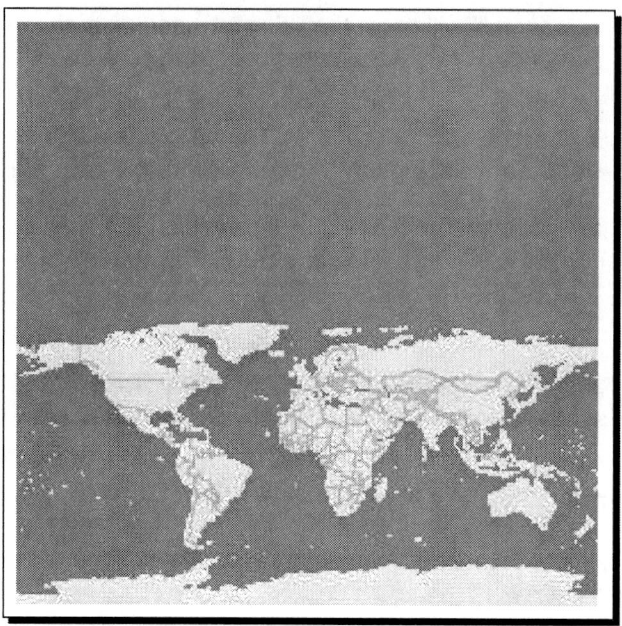

What Just Happened?

We just created a map without any controls. Users cannot interact with the map—they can see it, but they cannot navigate or change it. By passing in an empty array when we instantiated our `map` object via `controls: []`, we overrode the four controls that are added to the map by default.

Time for Action – adding controls to a map

There are tons of other controls that OpenLayers provides that aren't passed in by default but are still very useful. Let's take a look at some of them and how to add them to our map. After we cover how to do this, we'll go over each Control class in more detail.

1. What we'll do now is create an array of control objects that we'll pass in when creating our map object. Let's create a **NavigationControl** object first. This way, we'll be able to reference the control anywhere in our code easily. Next, we'll create a JavaScript array that will contain the `navigation_control` object we created; along with four other control objects we'll immediately instantiate. So, the first thing we'll need to do inside our `init()` function is to create an array of control objects:

```
var navigation_control = new OpenLayers.Control.Navigation({});
```

```
var controls_array = [
  navigation_control,
  new OpenLayers.Control.PanZoomBar({}),
  new OpenLayers.Control.LayerSwitcher({}),
  new OpenLayers.Control.Permalink(),
  new OpenLayers.Control.MousePosition({})
];
```

2. Now we'll create the `map` object and pass in the array of controls we just made:

```
map = new OpenLayers.Map('map_element', {
  controls: controls_array
});
```

3. Create and add a WMS layer like in the previous example. If I ask you to create a WMS layer in future examples in this chapter, I'll be referring to this block of code.

```
var wms_layer = new OpenLayers.Layer.WMS(
  'WMS Layer Title',
  'http://vmap0.tiles.osgeo.org/wms/vmap0',
  {layers: 'basic'},
  {}
);

map.addLayer(wms_layer);
```

4. Passing in an array of control objects when creating our `map` object is one way to add controls, but as you know we can also call `addControl` or `addControls`. Let's call `addControl` and pass in an object that will be instantiated on the fly—we won't create a variable to reference it.

```
map.addControl(new OpenLayers.Control.ScaleLine());
```

5. Let's make an overview map control object. We'll instantiate it and save a reference to it by using a variable, then add it to the map by passing it into an array and calling `addControls`. We'll also pass in a **KeyboardDefaults** control which we will instantiate in the `addControls` itself. Both ways work—passing in a reference to a control object, or instantiating an object in the method call:

```
var overview_map = new OpenLayers.Control.OverviewMap();
map.addControls([
  overview_map,
  new OpenLayers.Control.KeyboardDefaults()
]);
```

6. Open up the page. You should see something similar to this:

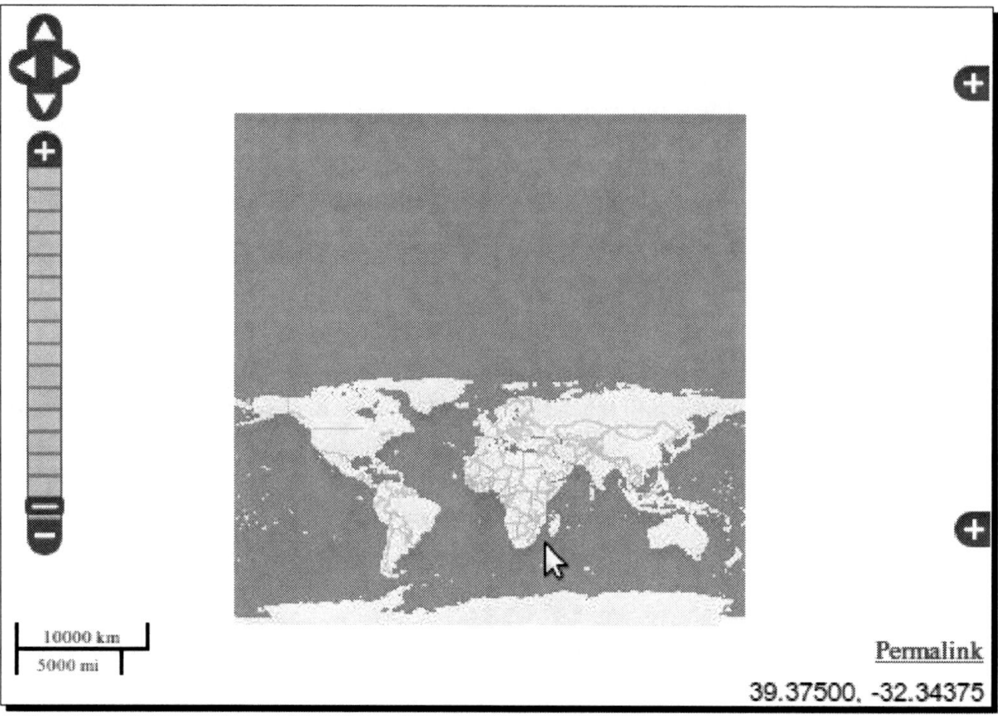

What Just Happened?

We added various controls to our map by passing in an array of control objects when constructing the map object, and by calling `map.addControl` and `map.addControls`. These two functions take in control object(s) and add them to the map, which also causes the `map.control` array to get updated.

Have a go hero – add controls

Add and remove various controls and see if you can determine which controls are which. Take a look at the **Control** class documentation at `http://dev.openlayers.org/docs/files/OpenLayers/Control-js.html` to see a list of all available control classes (we'll cover each one soon) and try adding different controls to your map.

Use `map.removeControl()` and pass in a control object you wish to remove. You can either use the variable name, or a less eloquent method of accessing the `controls` array itself, e.g.:

```
map.removeControls(map.controls[2]);
```

Doing it this way should make it clear why creating variables is a much better way to instantiate control/layer objects, as it makes it much easier to access the right object. Another downside to using the `controls` array itself is that removing a control will affect the index of all other controls, so there can be a lot of guesswork involved as to what control you're actually removing. So, in short, avoid removing controls this way if you can.

Adding controls by passing in an array of controls

The first way to specify controls for your map is to pass them in as an array when the map object is instantiated. Passing in an array of control objects when creating your map object is the preferred way to add controls—it keeps all your control objects in one place, making your code a little easier to read and maintain.

In the above example, we created an array that held five control objects, four of which were instantiated in the array itself:

```
var navigation_control = new OpenLayers.Control.Navigation({});
var controls_array = [
  navigation_control,
  new OpenLayers.Control.PanZoomBar({}),
  new OpenLayers.Control.LayerSwitcher({}),
  new OpenLayers.Control.Permalink(),
  new OpenLayers.Control.MousePosition({})
];
```

As we've mentioned before, it's best to create a reference to an object (be it a control or a layer object) before adding it to your map. We created the `navigation_control` object outside an array, so we can easily access it just by referring to it.

To access the other controls, we'd have to either call `controls_array[index]` or `map.controls[index]`, where `index` is the index of the control you wish to access. You should try to avoid this method if possible, as the array may change, throwing off the index. Furthermore, accessing controls by index like this affects your code's readability, as it's not immediately obvious which control object you're trying to access.

Adding controls to map with addControl() and addControls()

There are cases where you might want to dynamically add controls to your map after it has been created. To do so, we can use either the `addControl()` method of our map object and pass in a single control object, or we can use `addControls()` and pass in an array of objects.

In the example above, we called `addControl` and passed in a **ScaleLine** control object, which we instantiated on the fly:

```
map.addControl(new OpenLayers.Control.ScaleLine({}));
```

We also used `addControls` by passing in a control object that has already been instantiated and an object which we created in the function call itself:

```
var overview_map = new OpenLayers.Control.OverviewMap();
map.addControls([
  overview_map,
  new OpenLayers.Control.KeyboardDefaults()
]);
```

Whichever method of adding controls you use, you should try to keep all your control related code together. The bulk of the time you spend programming will be spent in reading your code and not writing it. Your code will be much easier for you to read and maintain if you organize it. There is no 'right' way to go about organizing your code, but keeping related things (like code blocks related to controls) grouped together is a good rule of thumb.

Removing controls

So, we know how to add controls, but how about removing them? There are two common ways to do this:

- Call `map.removeControl(map.controls[x]);` where `x` is the index of the control you wish to remove. As we stated before, removing controls this way is discouraged because it is not clear which control is actually being removed.
- Another way is to call `map.removeControl(control_object);` where `control_object` is a reference to a control object you've already instantiated. Be sure to keep in mind, if you define an object with `var` inside a function, you won't be able to access it outside the function.

Now that we're familiar with how to add and remove controls, let's get into the **Control** class itself and take a look at various different types of controls.

OpenLayers.Control class

As we saw in the previous example, there are quite a few controls available to us. The **Control** class is similar in nature to the **Layer** class—there is a base **Control** class which all other control subclasses inherit from. Because most controls provide completely different functionality from one another, the base **Control** class does not contain a lot of properties.

The official, up to date documentation for this class can be found at `http://dev.openlayers.org/docs/files/OpenLayers/Control-js.html`.

OpenLayers.Control properties

Like properties of other classes, you can specify these properties when instantiating your control object. There are a few properties of the base **OpenLayers.Control** class, which are inherited by all other Control classes:

Name	Type	Description
autoActivate	`{Boolean}`	Set the control to activate when added to the map. Default value is `false`.
div	`{HTML Element}`	Many controls support the ability to be placed in a div outside the map. (This does not work for all controls, however.) An example call would look like: `{div: document.getElementById('my_control_div') }`
id	`{String}`	This specifies the ID of the HTML element that will be assigned to the control.
eventListeners	`{Object}`	This object specifies event listeners to register. Events are covered later in this chapter.
displayClass	`{String}`	Specifies the CSS class that the control will receive. By default, controls receive a class name made up of `OlControl` plus the control name, e.g. `OlControlNavToolBar`. We cover this in more detail in Chapter 7 on styling controls.
title	`{String}`	The title you set here will be displayed in a tooltip (or other places, when appropriate).
type	`{Number}`	Specifies the *type* of control, which is related to how the control functions. Used in various cases, such as when working with buttons or panels. We cover this later in the chapter, on the section on panels.

OpenLayers.Control functions

There are a few functions that all control subclasses inherit that we should take a look at.

Name	Description
`destroy()`	This will perform any clean up actions (such as removing any events attached to the control) and then remove the control from the map. Since the control is removed from the map, it also will no longer show up when accessing `map.controls`.

Name	Description
`moveTo(location)`	This function takes in a single parameter, `location`, an **OpenLayers.Pixel** object, and will move the control to the passed in pixel coordinate (in the order of x coordinate, y coordinate). This function will only really affect controls which have a visible component. An example call might be: `control_object.moveTo(new OpenLayers.Pixel(200,100));` which would move the control to the x, y, position of 200, 100 inside of the map. The origin is the top left of the map, so it would move 200 pixels to the right and 100 pixels down.
`activate()`	Calling this function will activate the control and its event handler (if one is set). Returns `true` if control was successfully activated and `false` if it was already active.
`deactivate()`	Deactivates the control and any associated event handlers. The behavior of this will vary among controls. Returns `true` if control was successfully deactivated and `false` if it was already inactive.
`draw()`	This function initializes the control. You will rarely have to call this, as it is usually called automatically. There may, however, be cases where you may want to issue the call manually. It returns a `{DOMElement}` which is a reference to the div containing the control (if one exists).

OpenLayers.Control subclasses

OpenLayers provides a lot of different types of controls, and an up to date list can always be found at `http://dev.openlayers.org/docs/files/OpenLayers/Control-js.html`. Some controls are deprecated, and should not be used, so we will not cover controls that will not be supported in OpenLayers version 3.0 or greater.

Some properties and functions of some controls are mainly for advanced users and are outside the scope of this book, so we won't cover them all. Some other controls are used in accordance only with the **Vector** Layer class—so we'll get to those in Chapter 9. However, that still leaves us a lot to cover here now, so let's get started!

OpenLayers.Control.ArgParser

As we mentioned earlier, this is a control added to the map by default. It is aptly named; it parses the arguments passed in via the URL. For example, when appending `?zoom=0&lat=0&lon=0&layers=B` to the URL of your map, the **ArgParser** control will parse the variables (i.e., `zoom=0`, `lat=0`, `lon=0`, and `layers=B`).

This control will then manipulate the map based on the parameters—it would zoom the map to level 0, set the lat and lon to 0, and turn on a certain layer. The **ArgParser** control does not handle the generation of these URL parameters. It is usually used in accordance with the **Permalink** control. The **Permalink** control, as we'll see soon, is the control that actually generates the URL.

Example Call: `var argparser_control = new OpenLayers.Control.ArgParser();`

OpenLayers.Control.Permalink

The **Permalink** control will create an HTML link element (an anchor, an `<a>`, element) at the bottom right of the map. The link has a URL embedded with the current map's longitude, latitude, zoom values, and layer information (e.g., which layers are turned on).

When visiting a page from one of these generated URLs, the URL is read in by the **ArgParser** control we just discussed. Anytime the map is updated (zooming, panning, turning layers on/off, etc.) the permalink URL changes to reflect the map's current state.

Example Call: `var permalink_control = new OpenLayers.Control.Permalink();`

When using the **Permalink** control, an **ArgParser** control will be automatically added to the map.

OpenLayers.Control.Attribution

This is another control added to your map by default. It will display layer attributions on the map (if you specify the attribution property for the layers). A layer attribution is just some string that will be displayed on your map with this control. You can also specify the separator by setting the `separator` property, which will separate the attributions for each layer. For this control to be useful, you must specify the `attribution` property of layers that you want to show attributions for.

Attribution properties

Name	Type	Description	Default Value
separator	`{String}`	Separator used between layer attribution text.	`', '`
div	`{HTML Element}`	HTML Element to place this control in. Example: `document.getElementById('map_control_div');`	

Time for Action – using attributions

Let's take a look at the attribution control in action.

1. To make the **Attribution** control useful, we must specify an `attribution` property on our layer objects. So, let's create a WMS layer with this property set to `'Base WMS Layer'`:

```
var wms_base = new OpenLayers.Layer.WMS(
  'OpenLayers WMS',
  'http://vmap0.tiles.osgeo.org/wms/vmap0',
  {layers: 'basic'},
  {attribution: 'Base WMS layer'}
);
```

2. Now, let's add another layer and set the `attribution` text to `'State Boundary'`.

```
var wms_state_lines = new OpenLayers.Layer.WMS(
  'State Line Layer',
  'http://vmap0.tiles.osgeo.org/wms/vmap0',
  {layers: 'stateboundary'},
  {attribution: 'State Boundary', isBaseLayer: false,
   opacity: .2}
);
```

3. Finally, add the layers to the map:

```
map.addLayers([wms_base, wms_state_lines]);
```

4. You should see something like the following, with the layer attribution text at the bottom right hand of the map:

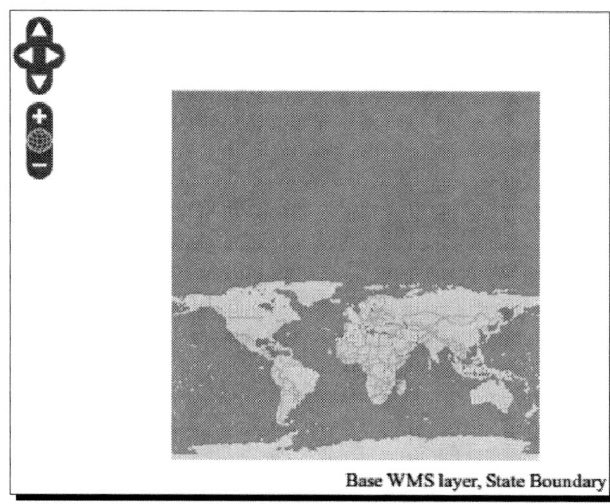

What Just Happened?

You just used the attribution control with two layers containing an `attribution` property. The text on the bottom right of the map shows the current active layers' attribution text. Let's continue going over more of the built in control classes.

OpenLayers.Control.EditingToolbar

The **EditingToolbar** control is a panel composed of tools that allow drawing and editing of vector features. It required a vector layer to be present in your map. We will cover this control, and how to use it, in much detail in Chapter 9.

OpenLayers.Control.Graticule

This will display lines of longitude and latitude (or whichever measurements your projection is) on your map. Unlike some of the other controls, this control has quite a few properties that we can set to change the way it behaves. This is what our map looks like after adding the Graticule control with the default parameters:

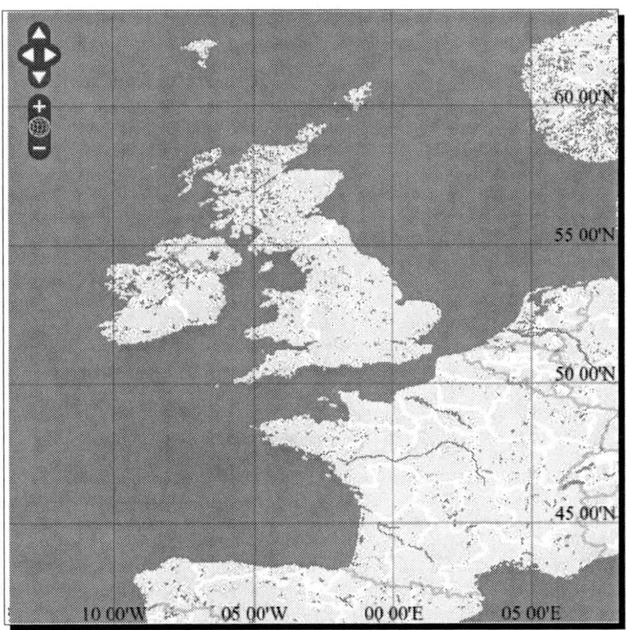

Let's go over the properties of the **Graticule** control.

Graticule properties

Name	Type	Description	Default Value
intervals	`{Float {Array}}`	An array of floats of possible graticule widths, in degrees. The different widths will be used depending on the current map zoom levels. Example: `intervals: [50,30,15,7,4,2,1,.5]`	`[45,30,20,10,5,2,1,0.5,0.2,0.1,0.05,0.01,0.005,0.002,0.001]`
displayInLayerSwitcher	`{Boolean}`	If set to `true`, the graticule control will be displayed in the layer switcher.	`true`
visible	`{Boolean}`	Determines if the graticule control should be visible or not.	`true`
numPoints	`{Integer}`	Specifies the number of points to use in each of the graticule lines.	`50`
targetSize	`{Integer}`	Determines the maximum size of the grid in pixels on the map.	`200`
layerName	`{String}`	Specifies the layer name that will be displayed in the LayerSwitcher control.	`null`
labeled	`{Boolean}`	Determines if the graticule lines should be labeled.	`true`
labelFormat	`{String}`	The format of the coordinates the labels will display in. Possible values, for example, would be `'d'`, `'dm'`, or `'dms'`, which represent 'degree', 'minutes', and 'seconds', which determine how precise the coordinates will be displayed in.	`'dm'`
lineSymbolizer	{Symbolizer}	Specifies the **symbolizer** to be used to render the lines. A symbolizer specifies style information. In Chapter 10, we will discuss symbolizers and how to use them in detail.	
labelSymbolizer	{Symbolizer}	The symbolizer used to render labels, which controls the label style. Chapter 10 discusses symbolizers (objects that define style) in detail.	

OpenLayers.Control.KeyboardDefaults

This control adds panning and zooming functionality, controlled by the keyboard. By pressing the arrow keys, plus/minus keys, or home keys, the map will be moved or zoomed. There is one relevant property we should take a look at.

KeyboardDefaults properties

Name	Type	Description	Default Value
slideFactor	`{Integer}`	Sets the amount of pixels to slide the map by.	`75`

OpenLayers.Control.LayerSwitcher

This control will create a layer list that allows you to turn on/off map layers. By default, it creates a toggle-able window in the map, but you can pass in a div HTML element and the layer list will be created in it.

LayerSwitcher properties

Name	Type	Description	Default Value
ascending	`{Boolean}`	Changes the order the layers are displayed.	`true`
roundedCorner	`{Boolean}`	Specifies if rounded corners should be created for the layer switcher window.	`true`
div	`{HTML Element}`	If specified, the HTML Element to place this control in. If you use this, you should set the `roundedCorner` property to `false`, otherwise, rounded corners will be created inside the target div. Example: `document.getElementById('map_control_div');`	`null`

LayerSwitcher functions

There are a couple of functions we can manually call to show or hide the **LayerSwitcher** control.

- **minimizeControl()**: When called, it will minimize the layer switcher control. Especially useful if you want to programmatically hide the layer switcher control.
- **maximizeControl()**: Shows the layer switcher control; it essentially does the opposite of `mimizeControl()`.

OpenLayers.Control.MousePosition

This control displays the longitude and latitude of where the mouse is currently located. By default, the control displays the position on the bottom right hand side of the map.

MousePosition properties

Name	Type	Description	Default Value
prefix	`{String}`	The string that will be added to the beginning of the coordinate text.	`''`
suffix	`{String}`	The string that will be added after the coordinate text.	`''`
emptyString	`{String}`	Text that will be displayed instead of the coordinates if the mouse is moved outside of the map. By default, when the mouse is moved outside of the map the last known coordinates will remain displayed.	`null`
separator	`{String}`	The string that will be placed in between the longitude and latitude.	`','`
numDigits	`{Integer}`	Specifies the numbers of digits after the decimal point (i.e., precision), of the coordinate displayed.	`5`

Name	Type	Description	Default Value
displayProjection	{OpenLayers.Projection}	Controls what projection the coordinates will be displayed in. Any projection other than EPSG:4326 or EPSG:900913 will require the Proj4js library to properly re-project the coordinates. If this property is not set, the map's projection will be used.	
div	{HTML Element}	If specified, the HTML Element to place this control in.	

OpenLayers.Control.Navigation

The **Navigation** control is one of the four controls added by default to your map. This control handles map navigation via mouse input, such as dragging the map and scrolling to zoom in. Let's take a look at a couple of the properties.

Navigation properties

Name	Type	Description	Default Value
documentDrag	{Boolean}	Determines whether the map should be allowed to be dragged when the mouse exits the map viewport (i.e., the map HTML div element).	false
handleRightClicks	{Boolean}	If set to turn, the map will intercept right clicks. On a double right click, the map will zoom out.	false
zoomWheel	{Boolean}	Specifies if the mouse scroll wheel will make the map zoom in.	true
autoActivate	{Boolean}	Determines whether the control should be activated when it is added to the map. It can be useful when adding this control to a panel.	true

OpenLayers.Control.NavigationHistory

The **NavigationHistory** control stores information about, as you could guess, map navigation. It is actually a control that creates two children controls called `next` and `previous`. You do not need to access these child controls directly, you should usually only use the methods of the **NavigationHistory** control object itself. By calling the `nextTrigger()` or `previousTrigger()` functions, you can go forwards or backwards (if possible) through your navigation history.

NavigationHistory properties

Name	Type	Description	Default Value
limit	`{Integer}`	Specifies the limit of history states to store.	`50`
nextStack	`{Array}`	Contains an array of next history states. Not used when instantiating an object.	
previousStack	`{Array}`	Contains an array of previous history states. Not used when instantiating an object.	

NavigationHistory functions

There are two functions we can call to access the navigation history.

- nextTrigger(): This function will call the child `next` control's trigger() function (which can also be called via `nav_history_control.next.trigger()`). If there is a next position, it will move the map to the next position on the position stack.
- previousTrigger(): This function will call the child `previous` control's trigger() function (which can also be called via `nav_history_control.previous.trigger()`). If there is a previous position, it will move the map to the previous position on the position stack.

Time for Action – using the NavigationHistory control

Let's use the **NavigationHistory** control's `nextTrigger` and `previousTrigger` methods to go through our navigation history.

1. Open up the previous examples and enable Firebug. We're going to create a **NavigationHistory** control object and add it to the map via the console. Enter and run the following code:

```
var nav_history_control = new
OpenLayers.Control.NavigationHistory();
map.addControl(nav_history_control);
```

2. Pan and zoom around the map. Each time you update the map, the **NavigationHistory** control stores information about your actions. Then, in Firebug, issue the following command:

```
nav_history_control.previousTrigger();
```

3. You should see the map return to the previous zoom level and coordinate. Now, let's return to where we were by calling:

```
nav_history_control.nextTrigger();
```

What Just Happened?

We just created and added a **NavigationHistory** control to the map, then called `previousTrigger()` and `nextTigger()` methods.

OpenLayers.Control.NavToolbar

OpenLayer's **NavToolbar** control creates a toolbar of navigation control buttons. It contains two buttons by default—one for panning, and one for zooming. The panning mode allows you to pan around the map like in the **Navigation** control; while the zoom control lets you select an extent to zoom to. This control comes in handy especially if you wish to provide additional custom functionality to your map.

OpenLayers.Control.OverviewMap

The **OverviewMap** control creates a toggle-able window at the bottom right side of your map that displays a smaller, zoomed out map containing a draggable rectangle that represents your current position on the map (i.e., an overview map). As you zoom in on the map itself, the overview map will update accordingly (although, you can turn this behavior off by setting the `numZoomLevels` property in the `mapOptions` property).

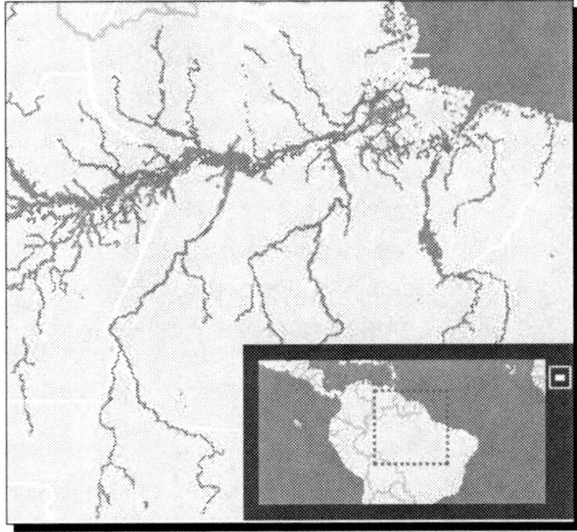

It's likely that you're familiar with this tool, and many people expect it to be on a web map as Google, Bing, etc. all have similar controls—so including it may be a good idea, depending on your application. There are a few configuration options we should cover.

OverviewMap properties

Name	Type	Description	Default Value
size	`{OpenLayers.Size}`	Sets the size of the overview map, in pixels, in the format of width, height. An example call would be: `size: new OpenLayers.Size(300,300)`. This will increase the size of the overview map itself, but the actual div element the overview map resides in is specified with CSS.	`new OpenLayers.Size(180, 90)`
layers	`{Array {OpenLayers.Layer}}`	Specifies an array of layers from the map to be used in the overview map. If none are added here, by default the base layer will be used in the overview map.	Uses the map base layer by default.
minRectSize	`{Integer}`	This property determines what the minimum width or height, in pixels, of the extent rectangle can be before it will be replaced with the value of the `minRectDisplayClass`. The larger the number, the bigger the extent rectangle will be before it gets replaced. This property can be used in accordance with the `minRatio` and `maxRatio` properties to provide a more custom behavior of the overview map control.	`15`

Name	Type	Description	Default Value
minRect DisplayClass	{String}	This specifies the name of the class that the extent rectangle will use when the `minRectSize` value is reached. We'll talk about control styling in much more detail in the next chapter on Styling Map Controls.	`'RectReplacement'`
minRatio	{Float}	This property will help determine when to zoom out the overview map. This ratio is calculated by dividing the overview map's resolution with the base map's resolution. The default value is `8`. This means that if the resolution of the overview map is less than 8 times the resolution of your main map, the overview map will zoom out.	`8`
maxRatio	{Float}	This property helps in determining when to zoom the overview map in. The same principle applies here as above. The default value is `32`, meaning, if the resolution of the overview map is greater than 32 times the resolution of the main map, the overview map will zoom in.	`32`

Name	Type	Description	Default Value
mapOptions	`{Object}`	This is an object just like the options property of the map object. It is an anonymous object that can contain the same options the map can contain. Setting some of these options can be very useful, especially the `numZoomLevels` property. For example, `mapOptions: {numZoomLevels: 1}` will cause the overview map never to zoom in or out, staying at the max extent.	`{}`
autoPan	`{Boolean}`	This property determines whether to automatically pan the overview map to keep the extent rectangle in the middle. Setting this value to `true` will mimic the behavior of the overview map in Google Maps.	`false`
div	`{HTML Element}`	If specified, the HTML Element to place this control in. If not specified, the **OverviewMap** control goes in the bottom right hand of the map.	

OverviewMap functions

- **minimizeControl()**: When called, it will minimize the layer switcher control. It is especially useful if you want to programmatically hide the layer switcher control.
- **maximizeControl()**: It shows the layer switcher control, it essentially does the opposite of `minimizeControl()`.

OpenLayers.Control.PanPanel

This control adds a pan panel to the top left hand side of the map. It contains four images: up, left, right, and down arrows. Clicking on an arrow will pan the map in the arrow's direction.

PanPanel properties

Name	Type	Description	Default Value
slideFactor	`{Integer}`	Similar to the **KeyboardDefault** control, it sets the amount of pixels to slide by.	`50`

OpenLayers.Control.PanZoom

This is another one of the four controls added to your map by default. It adds a **PanPanel** and **ZoomPanel** control to the top left side of the map. It contains the `slideFactor` property that the **PanPanel** has. Other than this property, there are no more properties to cover for this control.

OpenLayers.Control.PanZoomBar

This control is similar to the **PanZoom** control; however, it also adds a zoom bar with a slider which you can move up and down to specify the zoom level. There are just a couple properties we'll take a look at.

PanZoomBar properties

Name	Type	Description	Default Value
zoomWorldIcon	`{Boolean}`	Specifies whether the zoom to max extent world icon should be displayed. If set to `false`, the icon will be hidden.	`true`
div	`{HTML Element}`	If specified, the HTML Element to place this control in.	

OpenLayers.Control.Scale

When using this control, your map will display the current map scale as a ratio (for example Scale = 1:443M) placed in the bottom right hand side of the map by default. There is only one relevant property we should take a look at.

Scale properties

Name	Type	Description	Default Value
geodesic	{`Boolean`}	Determines if geodesic measurement should be used. This value should be changed to `true` if your map's projection is `EPSG:900913`. When set to `true`, the scale is calculated from the horizontal size of the pixel to the center of the map.	`false`

OpenLayers.Control.ScaleLine

The **ScaleLine** control adds a line representing scale to the bottom left hand side of your map. It will show the scale using both km and mi, or m and ft when zoomed in (by default). By specifying different property values, we can change this behavior; let's take a look.

ScaleLine properties

Name	Type	Description	Default Value
maxWidth	{`Integer`}	Controls the maximum width of the scale line, in pixels.	`100`
topOutUnits	{`String`}	Specifies the units to zoom on the top bar of the scale line when the map is zoomed out.	`km` (kilometers)
topInUnits	{`String`}	Specifies the units to zoom on the top bar of the scale line when the map is zoomed in.	`m` (meters)
bottomOutUnits	{`String`}	Specifies the units to zoom on the bottom bar of the scale line when the map is zoomed out.	`mi` (miles)
bottomInUnits	{`String`}	Specifies the units to zoom on the bottom bar of the scale line when the map is zoomed in.	`ft` (feet)
geodesic	{`Boolean`}	Determines if geodesic measurement should be used. This value should be changed to `true` if your map's projection is `EPSG:900913`.	`false`
div	{`HTML Element`}	If specified, the HTML Element to place this control in.	

OpenLayers.Control.ZoomPanel

The **ZoomPanel** control will add a zoom panel to the top left of the map. It contains **ZoomIn**, **ZoomOut**, and **ZoomToMaxExtent** controls which are activated by clicking on the corresponding icons. It is part of the **PanZoom** control that is added to the map by default. That's it for our overview on the available built in controls! Let's move on to another related topic—**Panels**.

Panels

So far, we've covered the most common controls, ones that we'll be using throughout the book. There is another type of control that we have not yet discussed—the **panel** control. It is a container, a control that allows us to add and group together other controls inside of a (you guessed it) panel. We have, in fact, encountered the panel control to some degree with a few of the controls we've discussed. The **PanPanel** and **ZoomPanel** controls are actually panels which contain other controls.

Control types

With a panel, each control is represented by an icon (which can be styled anyway you wish). When the icon is clicked, the `activateControl` method of that control is called. Remembering to call `activateControl` is very important—most controls will not activate by themselves (we'll cover this in more detail soon). Some of the controls we've encountered can be placed inside a panel, as we'll see in a moment.

Each control in a panel has one of the three 'types':

- `OpenLayers.Control.TYPE_BUTTON`: This is a button type control, which acts like a button—when it is clicked, some event gets fired off. An example control of this type is the **ZoomIn** and **ZoomOut** buttons we encountered in the **ZoomPanel** Control.
- `OpenLayers.Control.TYPE_TOGGLE`: Controls like this are activated by a click and turned off by another click. Turning on one of these controls will not affect other controls, and you can have as many toggle controls as you would like in the same panel.
- `OpenLayers.Control.TYPE_TOOL`: This type of control is like the toggle control above, but only *one* tool type control can be active at a time. For instance, the **ZoomBox** control is one of the controls of this type.

Let's take a look at how to create a panel and see how we add controls to it.

Time for Action – using Panels

In this example, we're going to demonstrate how to create and use the Panel class. We'll create a panel control object that will be placed in a div outside the map, and then add control objects to the panel. We're going to place the panel in a div element outside of the map. We'll first create an HTML `<div>` element to contain our panel. Add a new div after the map div like this:

```
<div id='panel_div'></div>
```

1. Now, we need to create a panel control object. We're going to first create a **Navigation** control object, as it will act as the 'default control' for the panel, which means it will be the control activated by default. Then, we'll create our panel object and place it inside of the previously created `panel_div` HTML element. Add a WMS layer to the `init()` function and place the following code after the `map.addLayer()` call.

   ```
   var navigation_control = new OpenLayers.Control.Navigation();
   var control_panel = new OpenLayers.Control.Panel({
     div: document.getElementById('panel_div'),
     defaultControl: navigation_control
   });
   ```

2. Let's add some controls to it. The **Panel** control has a method called `addControls` which takes in an array of control objects. Let's add a **ZoomBox** and **ZoomToMaxExtent** control. Take note that we pass in `navigation_control`, an already instantiated object, instead of instantiating a **Navigation** control object on the fly. This `navigation_control` object is the same control object that the `defaultControl` property points to. If we just instantiated a Navigation control object here, the `defaultControl` property would be pointing to a different control object. Creating the navigation control object outside this array ensures that we use the same object.

   ```
   control_panel.addControls([
     navigation_control,
     new OpenLayers.Control.ZoomBox(),
     new OpenLayers.Control.ZoomToMaxExtent()
   ])
   ```

3. Now that we have created our panel, we just need to add it to the map. The panel control has a property called `autoActivate` which will activate the panel control when it is added to the map. By default, it is set to `true`. Panels must be activated to be used, so if you set this property to `false` you must call the panel's `activate()` method. Similarly, if you wanted a control other than the `defaultControl` to be activated by default, you would call the panels' `activateControl()` method and pass in the desired control.

```
map.addControl(control_panel);
```

4. There's just one more thing left to do. If you open up the page now, you probably won't see anything in the panel. This is because the controls do not yet have any style associated with them. We'll fully cover the rationale behind this, along with how to customize control styles, in the next chapter—but for now, just put the following CSS `<style>` tag in the `<head>` section of your page (outside of the `<script>` tag):

```
<style type='text/css'>
    /*Navigation Control*/
    #panel_div .olControlNavigationItemActive {
      background: #226699 url('http://dev.openlayers.org/releases/
OpenLayers-2.9.1/theme/default/img/pan_on.png');
      width:  22px;
      height: 22px;
    }
    #panel_div .olControlNavigationItemInactive {
      background: #996622 url('http://dev.openlayers.org/releases/
OpenLayers-2.9.1/theme/default/img/pan_off.png');
      width:  22px;
      height: 22px;
    }

    /*Zoom Box Control*/
    #panel_div .olControlZoomBoxItemInactive {
      width:  22px;
      height: 22px;
      background:#999933 url('http://dev.openlayers.org/releases/
OpenLayers-2.9.1/img/drag-rectangle-off.png');
    }
    #panel_div .olControlZoomBoxItemActive {
      width:  22px;
      height: 22px;
      background:#999966 url('http://dev.openlayers.org/releases/
OpenLayers-2.9.1/img/drag-rectangle-on.png');
    }
```

```
    /*Zoom to Max Extent Control*/
    #panel_div .olControlZoomToMaxExtentItemInactive {
      width:  18px;
      height: 18px;
      background:#333399 url('http://dev.openlayers.org/releases/
OpenLayers-2.9.1/img/zoom-world-mini.png');
    }
</style>
```

5. Open up the page now and you should see something like the following:

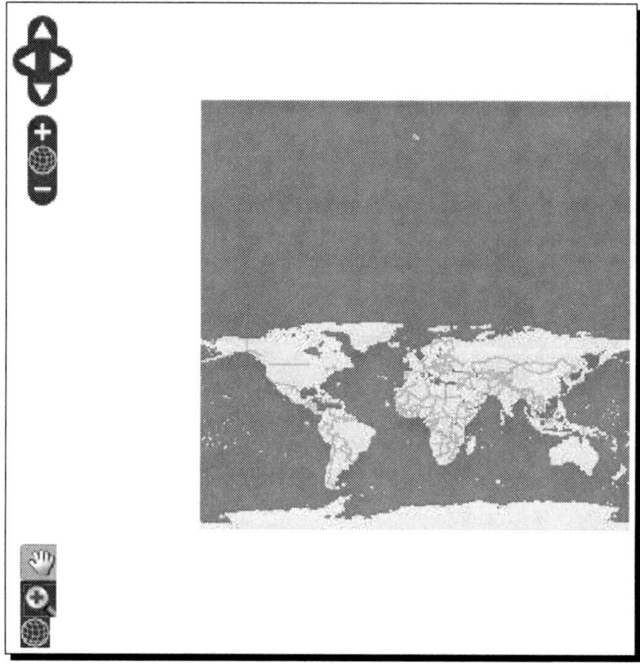

What Just Happened?

We just created a panel and placed three controls inside. By clicking on one of the buttons in the panel, you activate the control (specifically, the `activateControl` method is called). When creating controls inside the panels that you wish to activate programmatically, you must call the `activateControl` method of the panel, passing in the desired control object. If you click on the **ZoomBox** control button, you'll notice that the Navigation control gets deactivated—only one of these controls can be active at a time.

> Since the panel control is a control object that gets added to the map, the panel control is available in the `map.controls` array. The same is true for controls that are added to panels.

Pop Quiz – zoomBox control type

Which type of control is the ZoomBox Control?

1. TYPE_BUTTON
2. TYPE_TOGGLE
3. TYPE_TOOL
4. The Navigation Control does not have a control type
5. TYPE_I_DONT_KNOW

Hint: If you're not sure, take a look at the ZoomBox control object's `type` property.

OpenLayers.Control.Panel

As we saw in the previous example, we're able to create a panel and place the panel inside of a `<div>` element outside the map. If we do not specify the `div` property, the panel will be added directly to the map. The panel we made was pretty simple, but even creating more advanced panels isn't too difficult.

Before we start getting too fancy though, let's go over the properties and methods of the panel class so we know what we're working with.

Panel properties

Name	Type	Description	Default Value
controls	{Array {OpenLayers. Control}}	Specifies an array of control objects that get added to the panel. As in the previous example, you can either instantiate objects in the call itself (via new `OpenLayers.Control`) or use a previously created object. When you create a panel, you need to either use this property to specify the controls the panel receives, or use the panel's `addControls` method. Example: `controls: [new OpenLayers.Control.Navigation(), new OpenLayers.Control. ZoomBox()]`	[]
autoActivate	{Boolean}	Determines if the panel should be activated when it is added to the map. If this is not set to `true`, you must call the panel's `activate()` method before you use the panel.	true
defaultControl	{OpenLayers. Control}	Specifies the default control to be activated. This should point to a control that the panel will or does own. Like in the example above, you should pass in a control object that has already been instantiated. If you instantiate an object when specifying the value, instead of passing in an already created one, nothing will happen because the default control would be pointing to a different object than one owned by the panel. Example: `defaultControl: my_control_object`	null
saveState	{Boolean}	If this property is `true`, then the active state of the controls inside the panel (i.e., their state) will be saved if the panel is deactivated, and restored if it is activated. It will also override the `defaultControl` property (if set) after the first activation, restoring whatever controls were active instead.	false

Panel functions

The Panel class has just two functions that we need to know about for now.

- **Activate()**: This function will activate the panel control itself. By default, the `autoActivate` property is set to `true` and this function will be called automatically. However, if the panel is not activated by default, you must call this function to use the panel.
- **activateControl({OpenLayers.Control})**: This function will activate the passed in control. The control passed in must be a control that belongs to the panel. This is the function that gets called when a control inside the panel is clicked on by a user. If you wish to manually activate a control, you will call this function.

Now what?

Whew! We've covered the majority of controls OpenLayers offers and we've gone over how to use a panel. There's been a lot to take in, but don't feel overwhelmed. One of the reasons we covered so much is so that we can refer back to this chapter later if we need a refresher on how to use a control or what we can do with one.

So, now that we're done with the nitty gritty details, let's move on to something a little bit more complex.

Creating our own controls

You're familiar (or perhaps fed up) with control descriptions by now. Let's make things a little more interesting and create our own control. Here's the plan:

1. Quickly talk about the Button Control class.
2. Create a Button control with custom functionality.
3. Add the button to a panel.
4. Viola! You just created your own custom control.

So, before we talk about creating a custom button, let's go over the **Button** subclass that we didn't cover in the section above, which we'll use to create our custom controls.

OpenLayers.Control.Button

There's not much to cover here really, as we've been over the base control class. There are two properties we need to discuss however—the `type` and `displayClass` property. We'll use these two properties when creating our own custom control.

Button properties

Name	Type	Description	Default Value
type	{Integer}	This is an integer which represents the type of control this button is. This is part of what we discussed earlier—the button types. `OpenLayers.Control.TYPE_BUTTON` is represented by a `1`, `OpenLayers.Contro.lTYPE_TOGGLE` is represented by a `2`, and `OpenLayers.Control.TYPE_TOOL` is represented by a `3`. By default, as this is a `OpenLayers.Control.TYPE_BUTTON` control, the value is `1`. However, by changing the value of this property you can change its control type. You can specify the type by either using the {`Integer`} number (such as `2`), or use the built in constant name. The constant name starts with `OpenLayers.Control` and is followed by the control type (such as `OpenLayers.Control.TYPE_BUTTON`). Both methods accomplish the same thing, but using the constant name is cleaner and easier to read.	`1` (or `OpenLayers.Control.TYPE_BUTTON`)
displayClass	{String}	This string will specify the name of the CSS class the button will be assigned. An example would be `'olControlMyButton'`. Whatever class you specify, OpenLayers automatically adds in `'ItemInactive'` at the end of it. If it is a toggle-able button, then `'ItemActive'` will be added to the end when the button is active. We'll cover this in great detail in the next chapter. If this property is not defined, it will get the default value of `'olControlButtonItem'` (with `'Inactive'` or `'Active'` added at the end).	`olControlButtonItemInactive`

Button functions

There is also only one function we need to go over. One of the main uses of this function is that we usually pass it in when we instantiate the button object.

- **trigger()**: This function is called when the control button is clicked (assuming it is an `OpenLayers.Control.TYPE_BUTTON` control). If we don't define it when creating our button (or define it after the button is created), nothing will happen when we click on our button. When passing in this as a property while creating your button object, a function return code (a function's name) should be passed in and not an actual function. So, to define this on instantiation, create a function outside the `new OpenLayers.Control.Button` call and then refer to that function's name as the trigger. For example,

```
var my_func = function(){ alert( 'Stop clicking me'); }
var my_button = new OpenLayers.Control.Button({ trigger: my_func
});
```

Creating a custom button

You know a bit more about the **Button** class now, so let's put that knowledge to use. We'll create a fairly simple custom button (of control type `TYPE_BUTTON`) that will update the base layer's opacity and zoom the map to a random spot. We'll cover the few basic things that should be included when creating a button:

- Specifying the button's `displayClass` to give it style (optional)
- Creating a function and setting it as the trigger function
- Adding the button a panel, and then adding that panel to a map

Time for Action – creating a simple button

Let's create a simple button that has a CSS class and contains a trigger function that does a little something when we click on it.

1. Create a new page using the map template from Chapter 1. We'll be creating a button and a panel to place the button in (although, this time, the panel will be inside the map).

2. Before we create our button, let's create a function that will be called when we click on the button via the `trigger` function. We're actually going to create a variable and assign a function to it—this is one of the things that makes JavaScript pretty powerful. Let's make the function change the map's layer opacity and zoom to a random coordinate. Inside the `init()` function, add a WMS layer and after the `map.addLayer(wms);` call, add the following. It will generate a random coordinate, set the map's center to it, and change the WMS layer's opacity:

```
var custom_button_func = function(){
  //Get a random coordinate from -90 to 90
  var random_lon = Math.floor(Math.random() * 360) - 180;
  var random_lat = Math.floor(Math.random() * 180) - 90;

    if(map.layers[0].opacity === 1){
        //If the layer opacity is 1 (fully opaque), then change it
and zoom
        map.layers[0].setOpacity(.5);
        map.setCenter(new OpenLayers.LonLat(random_lon,
random_lat), 3);
    }
    else{
        //If the layer opacity is anything but 1, change it and
zoom
        map.layers[0].setOpacity(1);
        map.setCenter(new OpenLayers.LonLat(random_lon,
random_lat), 3);
    }
};
```

3. Now let's create our button control object. We're going to assign it a CSS class and set the `trigger` to be the `custom_button_func` we just created. So, when the button is clicked, `custom_button_func` function will be called. Notice how we just passed in the *name* of the function (also known as the function's return code) and we don't use parenthesis like we normally do when we call a function.

```
var my_button = new OpenLayers.Control.Button({
  displayClass: 'olControlCustomButton',
  trigger: custom_button_func
});
```

4. Let's create a panel that will store the newly created button. We won't pass in a div, so it will be added straight into the map.

```
        var control_panel = new OpenLayers.Control.Panel({});
```

5. We've got our panel made, so now we need to add our custom button to it. Even though we only have one control, we still must call `addControls` as there is not a singular `addControl` method of the Panel class.

```
control_panel.addControls([
    custom_button
])
```

6. Almost there! Now, let's add the panel to the map:

```
map.addControl(control_panel);
```

7. Now, by default, the panel will appear in the top left corner of the map. We could change this via CSS, but let's stick to what we've covered so far and use the `moveTo` function, moving the panel 450 pixels to the right (the origin is the top left of the map).

```
control_panel.moveTo(new OpenLayers.Pixel(450,0));
```

8. One last thing, if we view the map right now, we wouldn't see our button. This is because we have assigned it a custom CSS class, but we have not yet defined the class. So, let's add the following to the `<head>` section, before the `<script>` tags. Even though our `displayClass` was set to `olControlCustomButton`, we must define `olControlCustomButtonItemInactive`, as that's the actual class name OpenLayers generates for the inactive state of the button.

```
<style type='text/css'>
    /*Custom Button*/
    .olControlCustomButtonItemInactive {
        background:#22dd22;
        border:5px solid #202020;
        cursor: pointer;
        height: 28px;
        width:  28px;
    }
</style>
```

9. OK. Take a look at the map. You should see a big honking ugly button on the top right hand side of the map:

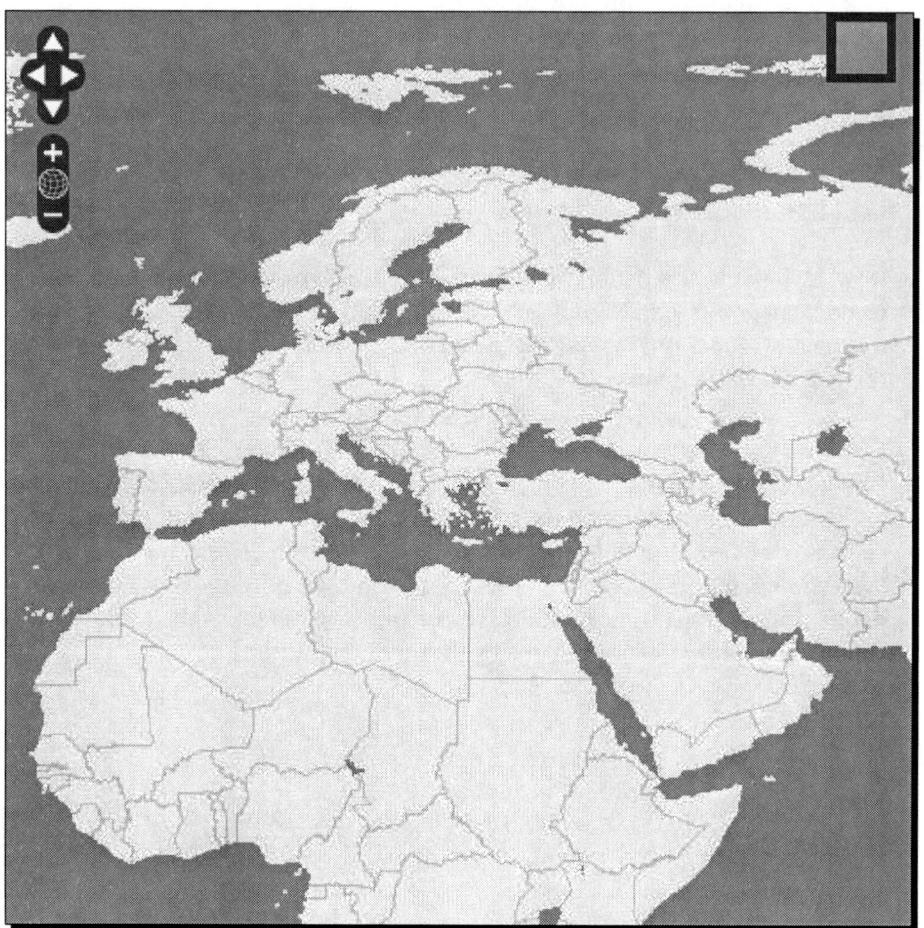

What Just Happened?

We just created a fairly simple button control that will change the map's opacity and center location when clicked. In the next chapter, we'll talk more about how to use CSS to make it look like a button instead of an ugly green box. Before we finish up this chapter though, let's go over one more thing—creating a custom button that has a different control type than the `TYPE_BUTTON` control we just made.

Other control types

So, with the previous example, we created a button control whose type was `TYPE_BUTTON`. It works like we expect and should work, but what if we wanted it to be toggle-able? We know, from earlier in the chapter, that there are `TYPE_TOOL` and `TYPE_TOGGLE` button types, and we mentioned how we could assign a button to be one of those types.

Process for creating other button control types

While there are a few different ways to achieve this, the process basically boils down to the following:

- Create a control object (either by extending the base Control class—a more advanced technique, or by creating a Button control) and specify the `type`
- Specify functions that will get called when certain events occur (e.g., when the control is activated)

To keep things simple and accomplish this, we're going create a **Button** control like we did in the previous example. Then, we'll specify `eventHandlers` that will call functions when the control is activated. But what's an event?

Events

An **event** basically means what it sounds like—something happening. Really, all user input is an event—a key press, a mouse click, etc. are all events.

Using JavaScript, we're able to access user generated events, such as a mouse click, and do things when an event occurs. Events are what drive the interaction in OpenLayers—when you drag the map, you are actually issuing a mouse event that OpenLayers interprets and then updates the map accordingly.

OpenLayers has its own **Event** class which makes interacting with events easier, and even enables us to create our own custom events. We won't get much into that right now, but we should briefly talk about something known as event handlers.

Event listeners and handlers

If you understood the previous paragraphs, then you may be able to guess what an event handler (and listener) is. In essence, an **event listener** is something that listens for events, and an **event handler** is something that responds to an event.

Consider the button control we created in the previous example. The control will wait for someone to click on it—this is the event listener. When the button is clicked, the `trigger` function is called—this is the event handler. So, in OpenLayers, **event listeners** are used to add **event handler** functions to certain event types (such as clicks or mouse overs).

Custom events

While user created events give us plenty to work with, life is easier if we can work with events other than just mouse clicks and key presses. If we can interact with events that are fired off not by the user, but by the map itself, then we can do a whole lot of more interesting and neat things. And of course, we wouldn't be building this concept up if OpenLayers didn't provide us with the ability to do so.

While we won't be creating our own custom events here, we will be working with custom events. When you click on a `TYPE_TOGGLE` control button, a custom event called `activate` is fired. In turn, if we want to call some function when that happens, we can assign an `eventHandler` to the `activate` event. We'll go over exactly this when we create a more advanced custom control.

Creating a TYPE_TOGGLE control

Now it's time to create some more custom controls with `TYPE_TOGGLE` and `TYPE_TOOL`. Two things need to happen for us to do this—we must create the control object, and then we have to assign functions that get called when the control is activated (i.e., an event handler). The previous section on events was used to provide an explanation for the theory behind events, but don't worry if you're a little confused. We're going to clarify, through code, what we will talk about. Let's get to it!

Time for Action – creating a custom TYPE_TOGGLE control

We're going to create a `TYPE_TOGGLE` control button. We'll actually be using events in two ways. We'll use events to call a function when the control is activated/deactivated (i.e., toggled). This activated/deactivated concept is important, as we cannot use controls if they are not activated.

When the toggle control is activated, the `activate()` function that gets called will add an event handler to the map. The map event handler will look for a click event and upon a click will call a function which updates the base layer's opacity. When the control is deactivated, the `deactivate()` function that gets called will remove the map event handler.

1. Open up the previous example. We'll be using that as the basis for this example. We don't really need to change anything there, so let's go ahead and start creating our buttons!

2. First, we're going to create the function that will randomly change the map's base layer's opacity when the map is clicked. This will only happen when our toggle control is active. Right before the `map.addControl(control_panel);` line, insert the following:

```
//Function that the map will call when the map is clicked (only
when
//  the toggle button is active though)
var map_event_function = function(){
    map.layers[0].setOpacity(Math.random());
}
```

3. Before we create a `TYPE_TOGGLE` button, we need to create two functions: one that will get called when it is activated and one called when it is deactivated. This is similar to what we did in the previous example. Let's do that, right after the previous code:

```
//Create a function for the toggle button
var toggle_button_activate_func = function(){
    //Attach the map_event_function to the map
    map.events.register('click', map, map_event_function);
}

var toggle_button_deactivate_func = function(){
    //Remove the map_event_function from the map
    map.events.unregister('click', map, map_event_function);

    //Restore the layer's opacity
    map.layers[0].setOpacity(1);
}
```

4. Now, we need to create the toggle control itself. The format is similar to before, but we'll be using a couple different properties. Because this is a toggle control, we won't use a trigger function. Instead, we'll add two event listeners—one for the activate event, and another for the deactivate event. We'll also set the type to `OpenLayers.Control.TYPE_TOGGLE` (the `TYPE_TOGGLE` type—we could also set the type to `2` to accomplish the same thing, but it's much more readable to use the built in constant name). Add the following on the next line:

```
//Create the toggle button object
var custom_toggle_button = new OpenLayers.Control.Button({
    displayClass: 'olControlCustomButtonToggle',
    eventListeners: {
        'activate': toggle_button_activate_func,
        'deactivate': toggle_button_deactivate_func
    },
```

```
        type: OpenLayers.Control.TYPE_TOGGLE
    })
```

5. You can probably guess the next part—add the control to the panel. Easy enough!

```
control_panel.addControls([custom_toggle_button]);
```

6. Now, just make sure the `control_panel` is added to the map:

```
map.addControl(control_panel);
```

7. Lastly, we just need to add the appropriate CSS classes. We gave our toggle control the class of `olControlCustomButtonToggle`, so we'll need to add the appropriate classes. Because this is a toggle control, there are actually two CSS classes we need—one for active, and another for inactive. Add the following inside the `<style>` tag in the `<head>` section:

```
/*Custom Toggle Button*/

.olControlCustomButtonToggleItemActive {
    background:#336699;
    border:5px solid #202020;
    cursor: pointer;
    height: 28px;
    width:  28px;
}
.olControlCustomButtonToggleItemInactive {
    background:#003366;
    border:5px solid #202020;
    cursor: pointer;
    height: 28px;
    width:  28px;
}
```

8. All done! When you click the newly created control, the `activate()` event is fired, and since we added an event listener for it the appropriate `toggle_button_activate_func` is called. It will add an event handler to the map that will wait for a click. When the mouse click event fires, the base layer's opacity will be set to some random value between `0` (fully transparent) and `1` (fully opaque). Then, when the toggle control is clicked again, it will be deactivated and the layer will return to full opaqueness.

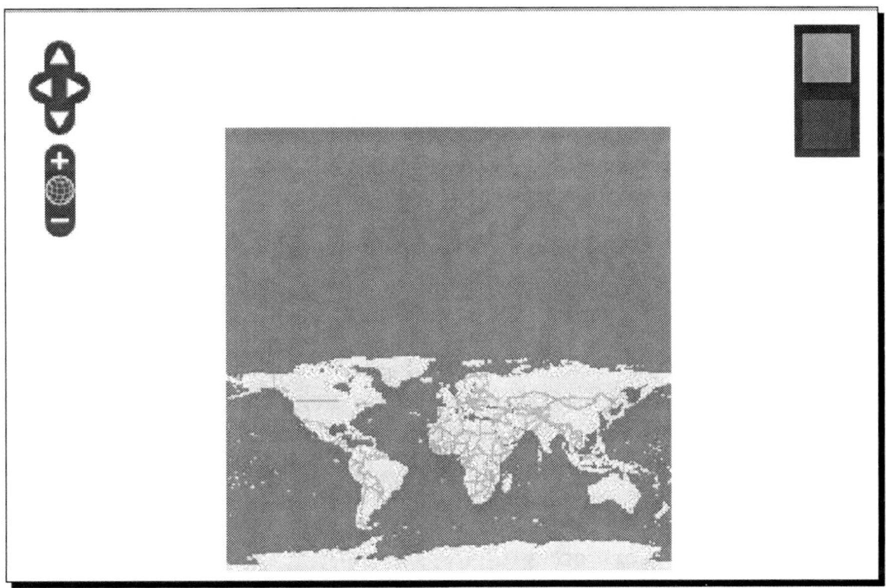

What Just Happened?

You probably have a good idea now of how the controls we just made work. Just as a quick recap, the following happens:

1. The `custom_toggle_button` toggle control waits for the `activate` or `deactivate` events to be fired (these are custom OpenLayers events, not general JavaScript events like a mouse click). This is done by registering the events with `map.events.register`.
2. When the `custom_toggle_button` control is clicked (which toggles it on), the `activate control` event is detected and the corresponding `toggle_button_activate_func` function gets called.
3. The `toggle_button_activate_func` function that gets called then adds an event listener to the map (with `map.events.register` again).
4. This event listener will wait for a `click` (a mouse click, a general JavaScript event) and then fire off the `map_event_function` every time a click is received.
5. When the `custom_toggle_button` control button receives a `deactivate` event (i.e., it is clicked and toggled off), the corresponding `toggle_button_deactivate_func` function is called.
6. The `toggle_button_deactivate_func` function removes the previously added map event listener with `map.events.unregister`. Therefore, the listener is gone and mouse clicks on the map will no longer cause the `map_event_function` to be fired off.

And that's about it!

When using panels and controls inside panels, make sure that the controls get activated via `activate()` or the panels' `activateControl()` methods. The control cannot be used if a control is not activated (or cannot be activated by the user by clicking on the control, for example).

Summary

We covered a good deal in this chapter. We talked about the idea behind controls and how they are used in OpenLayers. We then demonstrated how to add controls to a map. We covered the Control class and its various subclasses in depth. We also went over how to set up panels and how to add controls to them. To finish the chapter, we provided an introduction to events and learned how to create our own custom controls.

Even though we've been pretty thorough in this chapter, there's still more to learn about controls—such as how to style them. In Chapter 9, on the Vector layer class, we'll go over some Vector layer specific controls we neglected. This chapter was likely a lot to take in, but the next chapter will be a bit shorter. We'll discuss styling controls using CSS, and we'll make controls that actually look like they should be clicked, not just big green and blue squares.

7
Styling Controls

So far, we've seen how we can customize nearly everything offered by OpenLayers—Layers, Controls, etc. However, we haven't been too concerned with the actual appearance of the interface of our maps.

OpenLayers provides pretty good looking default controls, so you may not find it necessary to change them. Like nearly everything else in OpenLayers though, changing the style and images used by the Control class is easy.

We talked about the Control class in the last chapter, and in this chapter we'll explore how OpenLayers applies styles to controls and how to go about customizing controls.

In this chapter we'll:

- Talk about what CSS is and what purpose it serves
- Discuss how HTML uses CSS
- Go over how OpenLayers uses CSS
- Cover the naming schemes OpenLayers uses for controls
- Give controls some custom styles

Let's dive in!

What is CSS?

CSS is an acronym for **Cascading Style Sheets**. It is a type of markup language used to specify the appearance of HTML elements. CSS is actually quite simple, and if you've been able to follow along up to this point in the book, you will have absolutely no problem at all with CSS. Before we get into it a little more, let's talk a little bit about how CSS works.

Ideas behind CSS and HTML

HTML, **CSS**, and **JavaScript** serve three distinct purposes.

- **HTML** is used, as we've seen, to create the structure and *content* of a webpage
- **CSS**, on the other hand, is used to control the site's *presentation*, or how the page should look
- **JavaScript**, as we've seen throughout the book, is used to handle the *logic* behind the site

So, when you make a site you will have at least three discrete things to consider—the HTML behind it, the CSS that styles the HTML, and the **JavaScript** that handles any logic or user interaction. For now, we'll focus on HTML and CSS.

Ideally, HTML, CSS, and JavaScript should not mix (i.e., you shouldn't use style tags, or tags like `<center>`, in your HTML). Your HTML pages should link to external JavaScript and CSS files, especially in a production environment. One advantage of following this principle is that if you want to change the way your website looks, you only have to edit the CSS in one place (the external file) instead of on every page. The disadvantage is that it is slightly easier and faster to edit things if everything is contained inside the same HTML file; that's why we've been doing it this way so far.

But how do we edit the CSS and what does this even mean?

Editing CSS

If you're familiar with CSS, feel free to skip the next few pages and go directly to the second section on *How OpenLayers uses CSS*. If you aren't, don't fret! It's quite easy.

CSS isn't a programming language; in fact, you already are familiar with how it is structured. Let's look at the 'template' code for applying a CSS style:

```
element {
  property: value;
  property-two: value;
}
```

Looks familiar? It's essentially what an anonymous object in JavaScript looks like. The main difference is that a semi colon (`;`) is required at the end of each line (not a comma).

> You'll notice we also have `property: value` (key: value pairs). There are many different possible properties and values. We'll cover common ones later in this chapter, but a full list can be found at `http://www.w3schools.com/css/css_reference.asp`.

The other difference, you'll notice, is that there is something called an `element` in front of the brackets. This refers to a single (or multiple) HTML element—either by **tag name**, **class name**, or **ID**. Multiple elements are separated by a comma.

HTML elements

So far, we've talked just a little bit about elements in HTML. Every <tag> in your HTML page is an element (e.g., `<div id='my_div'>This div is an element</div>`). Now, to use CSS, we have to have a way to refer to the element(s) we want to give a style to. This is the `element` part of the CSS code outline above.

> The **DOM** (**Document Object Model**) is a way to represent objects (such as these elements) that are in your page. We won't go into much depth about it now, but if you are interested in learning more then `http://w3schools.com/dom/default.asp` is a great resource.

HTML—IDs and classes

We can refer to specific elements in two primary ways: via an ID or class name(s).

HTML IDs

Every HTML element can have a single **ID**. The ID is unique, and no elements should share the same ID. For example,

```
<div id='map_element'></div>
```

With this code, we're creating a `div` element with an ID of 'map'—no other element (be it a `div` or otherwise) should have the same ID. So, IDs are very useful when we want to refer to one specific element. We've used the ID property to specify the div that our maps should appear in (via `<div id='map_element'></div>` and specifying `map_element` when instantiating our map object).

HTML classes

There is another way to refer to elements, via **class names**. Classes in HTML have little in common with the classes you're used to from JavaScript. The only things you really need to know about classes in HTML is that, unlike an ID, class names can be used multiple times (that's primarily what they're designed for) and an element can have multiple class names (separated by a single space).

So, what does this look like in HTML?

```
<div id='some_div' class='some_class_1'></div>
<div id='some_other_div' class='some_class1 some_class2'></div>
```

Here, we have two different div elements, each with different IDs. However, both elements share the class `some_class1` and will receive whatever properties that class contains. The second div will also inherit any properties that the class `some_class` contains.

Styling HTML elements with CSS

Now that we know how HTML uses classes and IDs, we can learn how to use them with CSS. Specifically, how do we refer to the `element` in our CSS code? There are three ways to specify an element in CSS:

- **Element Type**: Specifying the name of an element alone will apply the style to *all* elements of that type. For example:

  ```
  div {
    color: #ff0000;
  }
  ```

  This would apply the color `#ff0000` (red) to *all* div elements.

- **Element ID**: Specifying the ID will cause the style to be applied only to the element with the specified ID. To do this, place an octothorpe (a hash or pound sign, `#`) in front of the desired ID. For example:

  ```
  #map_element {
    height:500px;
    width:500px;
  }
  ```

- **Element Class Name**: Specifying the class name will cause the style to be applied to all elements that have the desired class name. To do this, place a period in front of the class name. For example:

  ```
  .some_class1 {
    color:#0000ff;
  }
  ```

Using CSS in your code

So we know how to refer to elements now, but how do we use CSS in our HTML? There are three ways to go about this:

- **Including an external CSS file**: This is the preferred way to add CSS to our HTML pages, as we only need to change the style in one place if we need to make changes. It works similar in principle to how including an external JavaScript file works—we basically point to an external CSS file, and the page will read it in. To do this, we place a `<link>` tag in the `<head>` section of our HTML page. For example:

  ```
  <link rel='stylesheet' href='style.css' />
  ```

  The `rel` attribute specifies the link is a stylesheet, and the `href` specifies the location of the `.css` file itself.

- **Including the CSS in a <style> tag in the <head> tag**: This is another way to specify CSS, but is the least desirable way to go about it, as we'll have to update it on every page if we want to change some style. However, when working with only one file this isn't too much of an issue and this is why we've been doing it this way throughout the book so far. In the `<head>` tag, you can add a `<style>` tag, which will contain all your CSS definitions. Everything inside the `<style>` tag is interpreted as CSS code, similar to how code inside a `<script>` tag is considered as JavaScript code.

- **Including "in line" CSS definitions as style attributes on elements**: We've seen this in the previous chapters. Everything inside the quotes of the style attribute is considered CSS code. An example would be:

  ```
  <div id='map_element' style='height:500px; width:500;'></div>
  ```

For those familiar with the `<link>` tag, you may notice that we have only included the `rel` and `href` attributes. We do not need to specify the `type` attribute in HTML5, the current version of HTML at the time of writing.

Time for Action – using external CSS files

Let's create a simple page using an external CSS style sheet file (a `.css` file), making use of IDs and classes.

1. Create a new, empty HTML file. We'll just make a basic HTML5 page with a few `<div>` tags to demonstrate CSS inheritance. We'll also include a `<link>` tag that will reference a CSS file created in the next step, which contains all our CSS code.

2. First, we'll need to start the HTML page with a `DOCTYPE` tag that tells browsers this is an HTML5 standard page. Then, we'll need an `html` tag and a `head` tag, which contains some meta information (such as a `title` tag), and our JavaScript and CSS file links.

```
<!DOCTYPE html>
<html lang='en'>
<head>
    <meta charset='utf-8' />
    <link rel='stylesheet' href='ex1_style.css' />
    <title>Ugly_Webpage_01</title>
</head>
```

3. Now, we'll need to create a `body` tag which will contain our page's actual content. We'll also put in some `div` tags, which act as content blocks. Each `div` element will have a unique ID. Each div will also have at least one class. Classes can be used by multiple elements, and you can apply multiple classes to an element by separating the class name with a space:

```
<body>
    <div id='title' class='background_green'>
        Hello world!
    </div>
    <div id='content' class='background_green align_left'>
        The cake is a lie.
        <div id='message' class='align_left'>
            Hello, world.
        </div>
    </div>
</body>
</html>
```

4. Create a file called `ex1_style.css` and put in the following code. We'll specify a `background` and text `color` property for the `body` tag. Because elements inherit style from their parent element, every single element will also receive these two properties (but they can be overwritten):

```
body {
    background:#ffffff;
    color:#000000;
}
```

5. Let's specify styles for elements by IDs, which we'll designate with a # sign. IDs are used to specify a single element. This will cause the element that has the specified ID to be styled; however, we will define it. We'll also specify styles for classes by using a period (.). In CSS, classes are used to apply styles to multiple elements:

```
#title {
    font-size:1.5em;
    font-variant: small-caps;
}
#content {
    background:#ababab;
    color:#f0f0f0;
    font-weight:bold;
    text-align:right;
}
    #message {
        background:#336699;
    }
.background_green {
    background: #22dd22;
}
.align_left {
    text-align:left;
}
```

6. You should see something like this:

What Just Happened?

We've demonstrated what we've been talking about so far in this chapter, including an external CSS file and using IDs and class names to reference elements. You might be wondering why some styles got applied and others did not. Let's quickly go over why that happens, and then move onwards to learn about how OpenLayers uses CSS.

In CSS, you can use /* to begin a comment, and */ to end it. For example, `/* This is a comment */`

Have a Go Hero – view HTML and CSS in Firebug

Open up Firebug and go to any website. Firebug will automatically build an HTML tree and populate the **Style** tab with the site's style information. Poke around and try changing values with Firebug, and you'll be able to immediately see the site's appearance change based on the styles you apply with Firebug.

Cascading Style Sheets—Inheritance

CSS uses inheritance in a similar way our classes in JavaScript do. With CSS, child elements can inherit properties of their parent elements, as well as override them. So, as in the example above, our body element had a text color (the `color` property) of black (`#000000`). This means that any element inside the `body` element (which is, practically, every HTML element on the page) will receive the `color:#000000` property unless overwritten.

This is a situation where the 'cascading' part of CSS comes in. Styles 'cascade' downwards, so the properties found in the child element (the 'bottom' most elements) will override properties which it inherits from its parents (the elements above it).

Order of inheritance

When trying to determine which style an element will receive, any styles from the class name will overwrite base element styles, and any styles from the ID will overwrite class styles. Take a look at the following code:

```
<div id='my_element' class='random_class'> Some text </div>
<style>
  .random_class { #00ff00; }
  #my_element { color: #ff0000; }
  div { color: #000000; }
</style>
```

In this code, the element will have a final color of `#ff0000`. The base element (the `div` style) will be overwritten by the `.random_class` class style, and then the class style will be overwritten by the `#my_element` ID style. So, the order of importance is ID > class > base element type.

Using the `!important` statement after the value of a property will ensure that the property is not overwritten by any of its children. If however, one of the children contains an `!important` statement on that property, then it will be overwritten.

Referencing elements

One very useful thing we can do with CSS is to use the inheritance we just talked about. More specifically, we can write:

```
#my_element div {
  background: #2222ff;
}
```

This will apply a background color only to `div` elements that are children of `#my_element`. This nesting can be as deep as you'd like—just separate elements by a space. This, for example:

```
#my_element #my_inner_element .random_class a {
  font-weight: bold;
}
```

This would be applied to all `a` elements (an anchor tag, specified by `<a>`) inside all elements with a class of `random_class` inside an element with an ID of `my_inner_element` inside of an element with the ID `my_element`. If we want to apply the same style to multiple elements, we have to simply specify the elements and place a comma in between them:

```
#my_element1, #my_element2, .random_class {
  color:#cdcdcd;
}
```

Alright, we've covered the basics behind CSS and HTML element referencing, so let's see how OpenLayers uses CSS.

Pop Quiz – how to reference elements

Take a look at the following code. Try to think of at least three different ways you could reference the `inner_most` span element. Hint—think of ways to access it with inheritance as well.

```
<div id='outter_div'>
  <p class='paragraph_style'>
    <div id='middle_div'>
      <span id='inner_most'>

      </span>
    </div>
  </p>
</div>
```

OpenLayers and CSS

OpenLayers applies class names and IDs to most every HTML element it creates, so customizing your map's UI is quite easy once we know how it generates class names and IDs. Before we talk about how to override styles though, we need to know where the style files themselves are.

Styling OpenLayers—using themes

In OpenLayers, themes are used to control the appearance of your UI elements. A theme is comprised of a CSS file and any related user interface images. OpenLayers applies a lot of styles to your map by default, using a theme called `default`. Creating your own theme is easy though.

If you want to create custom UI styles for your map, you'll essentially need to either create a 'theme folder' which will contain a CSS file and images for your UI controls to use (e.g., pan arrow images), or manually overwrite certain default styles. The theme folder can be anywhere you'd like, just keep in mind what its path is when referencing it in your HTML file.

To use your own theme, you just need to do three things:

1. After including OpenLayers in your page, add a link to your CSS file which includes your customized map styles.
2. You must tell OpenLayers where to find the images you use for your map. To do this, specify the location of the folder your images are in (your theme folder) by adding the follow to your JavaScript code. The path is relative to the location of the file containing the JavaScript code:

   ```
   OpenLayers.ImgPath = 'path/to/your/theme_folder/';
   ```

3. Specify the location of your theme folder when creating your map object via the `theme` property. The path is relative to the location of the file containing the JavaScript code. For example:

   ```
     var map = new OpenLayers.Map('map_element', {theme:
   'theme_folder'});
   ```

Creating your own themes

Now we know how to use themes, but how do we create a theme? Well, the answer for that is simple—we just create a CSS file, some images, and create a folder that will house them. The images will go in a folder called **img** inside your theme folder. Then, we just tell OpenLayers to use that theme. The expected structure of the theme folder may change with later versions of OpenLayers, so the best way to figure what images are provided by default (and their names) is to look in the default theme folder. You can find it in the **theme | default** folder of your downloaded OpenLayers folder.

But the bigger question is how do we refer to the user interface elements? The answer lies in knowing how OpenLayers generates class names and IDs for the elements it creates.

OpenLayers—class names and IDs

To style an element, you must refer to it. If we want to refer to a specific div, we need to know its **class** and/or it's **ID**. OpenLayers generates class names and IDs, so we need to just know how the names are generated. The most common way is to style your controls using the generated class names.

Generated class names

The class names that OpenLayers generates for your controls follow the form of

```
.olControlControlNameExtra
```

This means that `.olControl` is always at the beginning of the class name, and `ControlName` is the name of the control class itself. The `Extra` refers to any additional descriptions or elements of the control (such as '`Inactive`' and '`Active`' added after many controls, especially button controls).

So, for instance, if we wanted to style the scale control line control, we would refer to it as

```
.olControlScaleLine
```

As we've encountered before, for button type controls we add '`Inactive`' or '`Active`' at the end. Other controls, such as the **OverviewMap** control, also contain an `OverviewMapElement` class name—the `element` refers to the generated HTML container of the overview control. There are other similar cases, such as the **LayerSwitcher** control. A quick way to figure out the class name of an element is to use Firebug to inspect your page and find the element.

We'll go over the class names of common controls soon, but first let's talk about another way to reference your control elements: by ID.

Generated IDs

Referring to control elements by class name is the preferred way of styling controls, but styling by ID is also possible. There are two ways to accomplish this:

- **Wrong way**: Using the generated ID. The ID is generated in the form of `OpenLayers.Control.ControlName_XX` where `XX` is a number that is assigned based on various things, such as control order. The number is likely to change based on how you make your map. So, if you use it in your style declarations and the ID changes, then the style will no longer be applied.
- **Right way**: Passing in an ID when creating the control and referring to it - in other words, when you create a new control, pass the `id` property with some string value which you will use as the element's ID. This way, we don't have to worry about the generated `XX` numbers changing, and we can be sure what the ID will be.

Alright, so we know how to refer to elements now, and how OpenLayers generates class names and IDs, so let's take a look at an example to solidify the concepts.

Time for Action – styling controls

Let's work with styling some OpenLayers controls. We won't be creating a theme here; instead, we'll just link to an external CSS file which will overwrite the default styles of the elements we wish to style.

1. Let's start off with creating a new page. We're going to also put all our custom styles in a file called **control_style.css**. So, whenever we add a style, be sure to put it in the **control_style.css**. Also, make sure to include the CSS file in the `<head>` section with:

```
<link rel='stylesheet' href='control_style.css' />
```

2. Now, let's create our map object. We'll specify the controls array when we instantiate it since we do not want the **PanZoombar** control in this example. We also are *not* using a custom theme (we are just overriding styles with the external CSS file), but if we were we would specify the `theme` property as well.

```
map = new OpenLayers.Map('map_element', {
  controls: [new OpenLayers.Control.Navigation()]
});
```

3. Alright, let's create some controls. We'll go over each control individually so we can see all the steps involved. First, let's create a **ScaleLine** control. In our JavaScript code, use the following to create a default **ScaleLine** control object:

```
map.addControl(new OpenLayers.Control.ScaleLine());
```

4. Now, let's apply some style to it. Because we haven't passed in a class name or ID, we'll use the class name that gets automatically generated. This is a standard control that does not have any 'active' or 'inactive' states, so we can just use the name generated by default, `olControlScaleLine`. In your `control_style.css` file, add the following:

```
.olControlScaleLine {
    background: #777777;
    color:#ffffff;
}
```

5. Most controls can be styled by just using their main class name (i.e., `.olControlControlName`). Other controls, such as buttons and controls with active/inactive states have additional class names. This is a good thing—you usually want a button to have a different style when it's clicked. Let's use the NavToolbar control—in your JavaScript code, input the following:

```
map.addControl(new OpenLayers.Control.NavToolbar());
```

6. Now, let's style the **NavToolbar** control. We have to style two things—the **NavToolbar** control itself (which is actually a panel) and the Inactive/Active states of the buttons it contains. The **NavToolbar** control also contains a **ZoomBox** control, which we'll need to style as well. It also contains Inactive/Active states that we'll need to style.

   By default, the buttons have a `left` and `top` property. We'll replace those values with `0` and add the `!important` value, which will make sure our newly set values are not overwritten. In your CSS file, add:

```
.olControlNavToolbar {
  top: 0;
}
.olControlNavigationItemInactive {
  background: #787878 !important;
  border: 2px solid #232323;
  cursor: pointer;
  left:0 !important;
  top:0 !important;
}
.olControlNavigationItemActive {
  background: #dedede !important;
  border: 2px solid #787878;
  cursor: pointer;
  left:0 !important;
  top:0 !important;
}
```

```
.olControlZoomBoxItemInactive {
  background: #336699 !important;
  border: 2px solid #232323;
  cursor: pointer;
  left:0 !important;
  top:0 !important;
}
.olControlZoomBoxItemActive {
  background: #77aadd !important;
  border: 2px solid #5588aa;
  cursor: pointer;
  left:0 !important;
  top:0 !important;
}
```

7. Let's create an **OverviewMap** control. In your JavaScript code, add the following:

```
map.addControl(new OpenLayers.Control.OverviewMap());
```

8. Now, let's style it. This is a control comprised of a few different elements, but they all have class names, so we can style it however we'd like. We'll style the background of the overview map when it's opened (via `.olControlOverviewMap`), the extent rectangle on the overview map, and the location of the minimize/maximize buttons. Add this to your CSS:

```
.olControlOverviewMapMaximizeButton,
.olControlOverviewMapMinimizeButton{
    bottom:0 !important;
}

.olControlOverviewMapElement {
    background: #cdcdcd !important;
}
.olControlOverviewMapExtentRectangle {
    background:rgba(60,90,120,.7);
    border:2px dashed #22dd22 !important;
}
```

9. Open up your map, move around, and look at your controls. You should see something like this:

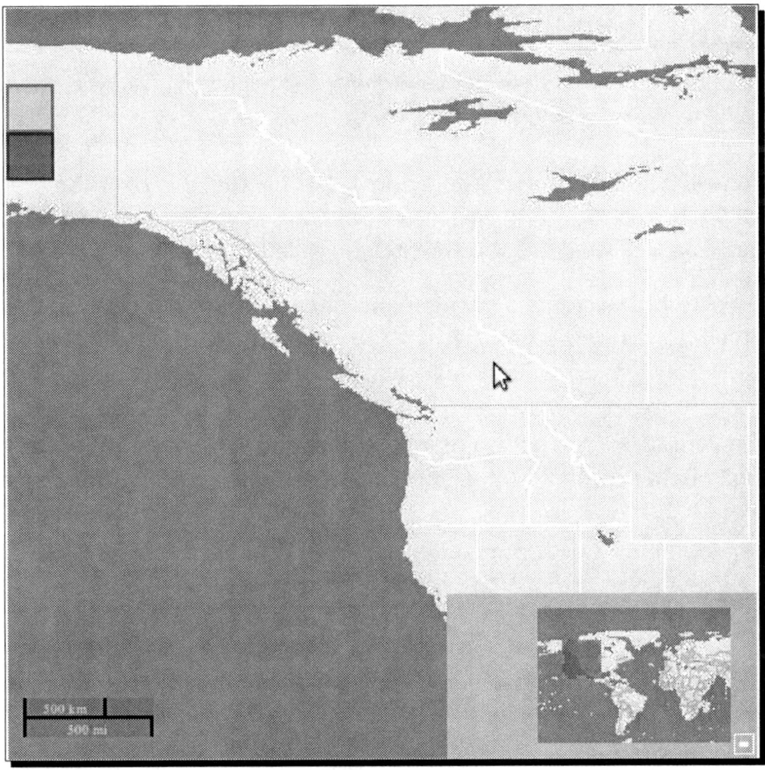

What Just Happened?

We made a few controls and added styles to them. We applied styles in the following three different ways:

- Styling the controls themselves based on their class name (e.g., `olControlScaleLine`)
- Styling button controls (their Inactive and Active states)
- Styling various other elements created by the control

It may not always be immediately obvious what class names to use to refer to a control, but it is always possible to figure it out. One of the quickest and easiest ways to do so is to use Firebug (or other web development tools) to inspect your page's generated HTML and look for elements that have the control's name in the class name.

Time for Action – styling the LayerSwitcher control

Let's take a look now at how to style the **LayerSwitcher** control. Unlike the previous example, we'll place this control in a div element outside the map.

1. Start a new page. We'll link to an external CSS file that will override the base **LayerSwitcher** control style, like in the previous example. Include a `<link>` tag that references a file called **ex3_layerswitcher_style.css**, which we'll create soon.

2. Next, we'll need to create a div element that will house our control. Create a div tag after the `map_element` div:

```
<div id='layer_switcher_control'></div>
```

3. Now, in your JavaScript code, create the map and WMS layer object as normal. Add a **LayerSwitcher** control, and pass in the `layer_switcher_control` element as the `div` property:

```
map.addControl(new OpenLayers.Control.LayerSwitcher({
  div: document.getElementById('layer_switcher_control')
}));
```

4. Now, if you open up the map you should see the map with the layer switcher control beneath it:

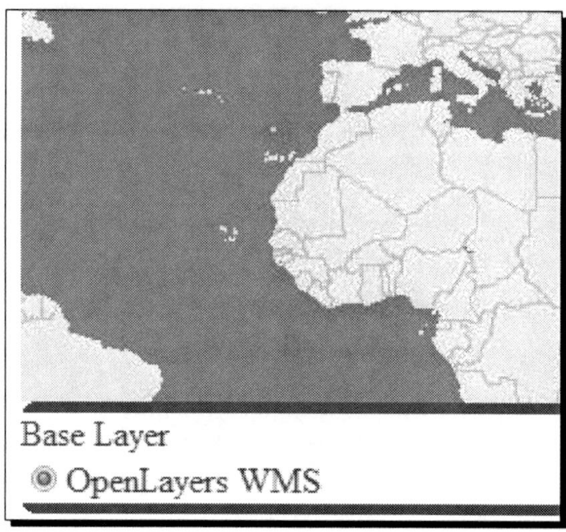

5. By default, it looks pretty plain. It also has a border with rounded corners. First, we'll need to disable the rounded corners by passing in `roundedCorner: false`.

```
map.addControl(new OpenLayers.Control.LayerSwitcher({
  div: document.getElementById('layer_switcher_control'),
```

```
  roundedCorner: false
}));
```

6. Let's create the **ex3_layerswitcher_style.css** file now. We'll specify the control's style here. As we have manually specified the `div` property when creating the control, the first thing we'll style is the div we passed in (with an ID of `layer_switcher_control`). Because we passed this in ourselves, OpenLayers does not apply any default styles to it. Let's give it a solid border and some padding. Add this to the style file:

```
#layer_switcher_control {
  border:2px solid #454545;
  padding:2px;
}
```

7. Now we need to start overriding the styles the control inherits from OpenLayers. First, we'll need to get the relevant class names. We can use Firebug to see that the `'Base Labels'` text is inside a div with a class of `baseLbl`. Since it's a heading that lists base layers below it, let's make it a bit bigger and give it a background. It also falls inside our `layer_switcher_control` div, so when we specify it in the CSS let's be as specific as we can:

```
#layer_switcher_control .baseLbl {
  background:#cdcdcd;
  font-size:1.3em;
  font-weight:bold;
}
```

8. Let's also style the label text for the actual layer names. Using Firebug, we can see that the label text is inside a `<span>` tag with a class of `labelSpan`, which is a child element of a div with the class `baseLayersDiv`. All base layers will show up in this div, while any overlay layers will show up in a div called `dataLayersDiv`. Using this information, let's apply a style to it, specifying the inheritance to access the element:

```
#layer_switcher_control .baseLayersDiv .labelSpan {
  font-style: italic;
  font-weight:bold;
}
```

9. Open up the page now and you should see the styled layer switcher div:

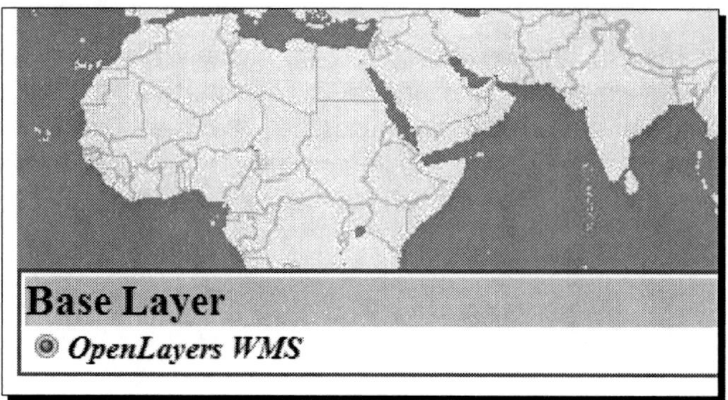

What Just Happened?

We just added a **LayerSwitcher** control outside the map and styled it. We saw how to style the div element that we created, along with styling the elements by grabbing the class names that OpenLayers generates. The LayerSwitcher control along with some others such as OverviewMap, have more elements to style than other controls. It may not be immediately obvious what elements need to be styled, but we can always use Firebug to inspect the HTML and determine the class names.

Have a Go Hero – add layers

Add more layers to the map you just created. Notice how there is now another set of elements for the overlay layers, in an element with a class that starts with '`dataLayers`'. All your overlay layers are considered to be 'data layers' and will show up here, while base layers show up in the `baseLayersDiv`. Using what you learned in the previous example, apply your own styles to the overlay layers div elements.

Other resources

A comprehensive coverage of CSS is outside the scope of this book, but hopefully this chapter has provided necessary information for styling OpenLayers elements. More extensive information on CSS can be found at the W3Schools site, located at `http://www.w3schools.com/css/default.asp`.

A developer that has proficient design skills is not a common thing—fortunately, there are resources that provide high quality, professional user interface elements. **GeoExt** is a third party library that integrates **ExtJS**, a popular JavaScript framework, with OpenLayers, and includes numerous user interface and OpenLayers map components. It does, however, require a bit of familiarity with the ExtJS library. GeoExt can be found at `http://www.geoext.org/index.html`, and the ExtJS can be found at `http://www.sencha.com/products/js/`.

Summary

In this chapter, we talked about what CSS is and what it's used for. We learned how to use CSS and HTML together, along with how to refer to elements in CSS. Then, we discussed how OpenLayers uses CSS, and how control elements get their names. Lastly, we created and applied our own custom styles to some controls.

The goal of this chapter was to provide a foundation for understanding how we style controls with CSS. If you haven't worked much with CSS before or if you're unsure how to style other types of controls then don't worry. We'll be styling controls throughout the book using the same principles we introduced in this chapter, so you'll get a lot more exposure to it.

8
Charting the Map Class

The Map class is, as you have probably figured out by now, the core piece behind your map. The map object(s) you create is the most important thing behind your map, as without a map object you can't do anything with layers or controls. In this chapter, we'll be talking about the Map class, which we've been taking for granted so far.

Understanding the Map class will enable us to do even more cool things with our applications, and provides a way for us to programmatically tell our maps what to do.

We've been using the Map class throughout the book so far without really knowing how or why. This chapter aims to not only explain how and why we've been doing things (such as using `map.zoomToMaxExtent()`), but also provide a thorough coverage of one of the core parts of OpenLayers—the **Map** class. We'll take a look at

- What the Map class is
- How the Map class relates to the other classes we've discussed
- Accessing the Map class' properties
- Using functions of the Map class
- Working with events to define and extend map behavior
- Creating a simple application that contains multiple maps

The Map class

OpenLayers' **Map** class is what drives our maps. All the things we'd like to do with our maps—moving them, zooming, adding layers—all these things are made possible by this class. We've worked extensively with it already by creating a map object, adding controls and layers to it, then telling the map to zoom to the max extent. While we've covered Layers and Controls in pretty good detail, we have yet to really discuss the functionality behind the Map class, the core component of our applications.

In OpenLayers, control and layer objects belong to a map object. Control and layer objects must be hooked up to a map if we want them to do anything. So, we need a map object to actually make a useful map—and as you might imagine, we'll see later in the chapter that it is possible to make an application that uses multiple map objects.

Creating a map object

Before we jump in, let's review the base code for instantiating a map object. We've done this many times before, but a little review won't hurt.

```
var map = new OpenLayers.Map('html_element', { options });
```

The first parameter is a string consisting of the ID of the HTML element you wish the map to be placed in (almost always a div element). The second parameter is optional, and consists of an object literal, or anonymous object, (key:value pairs) containing property and value settings.

So, there's not much new here yet. This is, essentially, all you need to set up your map object. However, as we've mentioned before, if you're using a projection other than `EPSG:4326`, such as spherical Mercator, you're going to have to set some other properties as well (such as `maxExtent` and `units`), when creating the map object.

This chapter will cover most of the properties and functions available to us through the Map class, so let's start with the properties.

Map class properties

There is a vast array of possible properties that you can pass in, and we've already seen a few of them throughout the book. There are also quite a few properties which are pretty useful which we haven't yet covered. I'll start off by introducing a few properties, and then we'll see them in action with some examples.

Throughout the explanation of properties and methods, I'll typically refer to an arbitrary map object as `map`. If your map object is called something else, then you would simply replace `map` with the name of your map object. Another quick note; while we will be talking about all these properties in the context of passing them in while creating the map object, you can call any of them at any time to get the value (e.g., calling `map.tileSize` will return the map's tile size).

> While we'll cover all the properties and functions relevant to all the examples and discussions in the book, for an always up to date and complete list you can visit the docs at `http://dev.openlayers.org/docs/files/OpenLayers/Map-js.html`.

Map properties

Let's go over the map properties that are typically passed in when creating a map object. There are other properties that we can access but shouldn't pass in at instantiation time—we'll cover those next. For now, let's focus on properties to use when instantiating map objects.

allOverlayers

`allOverlays: {Boolean} Default  is false`

The `allOverlays` property specifies whether or not the map can function without any base layers. So far, we've been using base layers in all our examples, either explicitly or implicitly (letting our layers be set as base layers automatically). By setting this property, *all* layers will act as overlay layers.

There may be times when you wish to use this—just keep in mind, when using this property, users have the ability to disable all layers and they could, in effect, see an empty map. By setting this property to `true`, third party API layers will also act as overlay layers. So, if you wish, you could use a Google maps layer as an overlay layer and make it semi transparent.

controls

`controls: {Array {OpenLayers.Control}}`

We covered controls in Chapter 6, so we don't need to go into too much depth here. We can define our map's controls when we create the map object, or we can add them via `addControl(s)` after the map object has been instantiated. After the map is instantiated, we can access its controls by calling `map.controls`. If you do not specify an array of controls for the map to use when you create it, your map will receive four default controls: **Navigation**, **PanZoom**, **ArgParser**, and **Attribution**.

displayProjection

`displayProjection: {OpenLayers.Projection}`

This is a property that is used mainly by controls which show coordinate information. By setting this property on the map object, any control that has a `displayProjection` property will be set to this value. Controls, such as the **MousePosition** control, can display coordinates in the `displayProjection`. So, your map could be in a different projection than what you wish to display the coordinates in. However, to use a `displayProjection` other than `EPSG:4326` or `EPSG:900913`, Proj4js must be included on your page.

This property comes in very handy if, for instance, your map is in a spherical Mercator projection (i.e., `EPSG:900913`), but you might wish to display coordinates in another projection, like `EPSG:4326` (to display lon/lat coordinates).

div

`div: {HTML Element or String}`

So far, we've been creating our maps like this:

```
var map = new OpenLayers.Map('map_element', {});
```

With the div property, we can instead pass in an HTML element (or the ID of the element, as above) in the options; i.e.,

```
var map = new OpenLayers.Map({'div': 'map_element'});
```

One of the advantages of doing it this way is that the `div` property is optional, so you can create a map object and choose not to place it in any div. If you do this, you can place your map in a div later by using the `render()` method.

This is actually almost the same thing OpenLayers is doing for us automatically when we pass in an HTML element during map object instantiation. When we do specify this `div` property, OpenLayers simply calls the `render()` method right then—we're just delaying this from happening and calling it manually if we choose not to specify a div. This can be useful when we only want to show the map after a user clicks on a button, for instance.

Time for Action – using the allOverlays Map property

Let's take a look at using the `allOverlays` property and not specifying a div when creating a map.

1. In your `init()` function, let's create our map object with `allOverlays` set to `true` and with some controls passed in. We will also not specify an HTML element:

   ```
   var map = new OpenLayers.Map({
   ```

```
  allOverlays: true,
  controls: [new OpenLayers.Control.Navigation(),
new OpenLayers.Control.PanZoom(),
new OpenLayers.Control.LayerSwitcher()]
});
```

2. Now, let's create a couple of layers so we can see how the `allOverlays` property works. We'll assume that you will add WMS layers to your maps for future examples.

```
        var wms_layer_all = new OpenLayers.Layer.WMS(
            'OpenLayers WMS',
            'http://vmap0.tiles.osgeo.org/wms/vmap0',
            {layers: 'basic'},
            {}
        );

        var wms_layer_labels = new OpenLayers.Layer.WMS(
            'Labels',
            'http://vmap0.tiles.osgeo.org/wms/vmap0',
            {layers: 'clabel,ctylabel,statelabel',
transparent:true},
            {}
        );
        map.addLayers([wms_layer_all, wms_layer_labels]);
```

3. Since we didn't specify a `div` when instantiating our map object, we'll have to call the `render()` function to place the map inside a div. The function takes in either an HTML element or the string of the element's ID, so let's pass in the element's ID.

```
map.render('map_element');
```

4. Finally, check to see if a center is set. If it is not, zoom to the max extent. We'll assume you do this step in future examples. You can place the call to the `render()` function after this bit if you'd like, and it will still zoom to the center or the max extent—the order in which you call `render()` and set the map's location is up to you.

```
if(!map.getCenter()){
  map.zoomToMaxExtent();
}
```

5. Take a look at the map and open the layer switcher—you should be able to turn off both layers and see an empty map now. Because we don't have a base layer and all the Overlayers are disabled by default, you'll just see a blank map until you enable a layer.

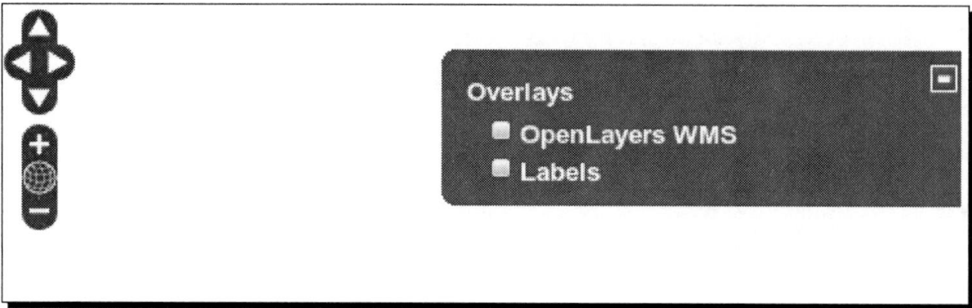

What Just Happened?

We have just looked at a few of the properties we brought up—`allOverlays`, `controls`, and (leaving out) the `div` property. We also saw how the user can potentially see no map at all by turning off all the layers.

The map will not automatically render, because we did not pass in an HTML element. Instead, we called the `render()` method and passed in an HTML element after our map object was created. There may be times when you wish to delay rendering the map, such as waiting for a user to click a button, and in those cases this is a good way to do it. We'll talk more about map methods later in this chapter, but let's get back to discussing map properties.

eventListeners

`eventListeners: {Object}`

This property accepts an anonymous object containing key:value pairs of event types (as the key) and functions to call (the values) when those events are fired. We saw this property briefly in Chapter 6, and it behaves the same way here. An example would be:

```
var map = new OpenLayers.Map('map_element', {
  eventListeners: { 'moveend': my_moveend_function }
});
```

The above code assumes that a function named `my_moveend_function` exists. We will cover this property in much more detail, along with the possible event types, later in this chapter in the section on events.

fallThrough

`fallThrough: {Boolean} Default: true`

The `fallThrough` property determines whether or not OpenLayers will allow events on the map to propagate downwards (i.e., 'fall through') to other elements on your page.

Let's go over the meaning with an example. Say your `map_element` div has an event attached to it that will show an alert when you click on it. This event is outside of OpenLayers. Now, let's assume you create a map object and attach it to that `map_element` div. If `fallThrough` is set to `true` (it is by default), you will receive the original alert by clicking on the map—the mouse click event will be allowed to 'fall through'. If it is set to `false`, you will *not* receive the alert, as OpenLayers will consume that mouse click event.

layers

`layers: {Array {OpenLayers.Layer}}`

We've encountered this property, to some degree, already. After the map is instantiated, we can access its layers by calling `map.layers`. So far, we've been creating our map object, then our layer objects, then adding the layers to the map with `addLayer()`. We can, however, use the `layers` property when instantiating our map and pass in an array of layer objects.

Passing in layers using this property when we create our map object or calling `addLayers` essentially does the same thing—use whichever method you're most comfortable with. An example would be:

```
var map = new OpenLayers.Map('map_element', {
  layers: [my_layer_1, new OpenLayers.Layer.WMS({ … })]
});
```

You can pass in layer objects that have already been created (e.g., `my_layer_1`, assuming a layer object with that name has been created), or by instantiating a layer object in the call itself (e.g., `new OpenLayers.Layer.WMS({...})`).

In the example above, the … would be replaced with the options for the WMS layer.

maxExtent

`maxExtent: {OpenLayers.Bounds} Default: bounds in decimal degrees, (-180, -90, 180, 90)`

Setting this will specify the maximum extent of your map. Tiles that fall outside of the maximum extent will not be requested, nor can users pan to a coordinate that lies outside the `maxExtent`. If you are using a different projection than the default projection, you will need to change this to reflect the world's coordinates in your desired projection.

The `maxExtent` property's data type is an **OpenLayers.Bounds** object. The **OpenLayers. Bounds** class is used to create a 'bounds' object, which contains four coordinates that make up a bounding box. The four coordinates are minimum x (left), minimum y (bottom), maximum x (right), and maximum y (top). To instantiate a bounds object, you just pass in the coordinates in the order of:

```
var bounds_object = new OpenLayers.Bounds(minx, miny, maxx, maxy);
```

minExtent

`minExtent: {OpenLayers.Bounds}`

Setting the `minExtent` will specify the minimum extent of the map. There is no default value for this property. You will usually not need to set this, unless you are specifying custom resolutions using `maxResolution`—in such case, you will usually set the values to `(-1, -1, 1, 1)`.

restrictedExtent

`restrictedExtent: {OpenLayers.Bounds}`

This property specifies the bounds the user can navigate in—meaning that the user will be able to only pan around inside the bounds specified by the `restrictedExtent` property (if it is given, and if restricting their navigation is possible).

Setting this property will still allow the user to zoom out and see parts of the map that are outside the restricted extent, but the map's center will be set to the restricted extent. If you want to limit the zoom level, you could set the `resolutions` array, `maxResolution`, or `scales` properties (covered in the following pages). This property is similar to maxExtent, however, tiles outside the `restrictedExtent` will still be requested, but the user won't necessarily be able to pan to them.

numZoomLevels

`numZoomLevels: {Integer} Default: 16`

The numZoomLevels property specifies the amount of possible zoom levels that your map will have. For many applications, giving users 16 zoom levels is not always desirable. In most cases, just specifying the numZoomLevels (along with maxExtent, if using a different projection) is all you need to do to set the number of zoom levels. We'll see, as we look at other properties, more ways to specify the number of zoom levels (some without using this property at all). However, let's look at how to use this property to set the number of zoom levels—it's pretty easy!

Time for Action – setting zoom levels and maxExtent

1. Create your map object, by specifying the numZoomLevels and adding a **PanZoomBar** control. We'll also set the numZoomLevels property to 8, meaning that only eight zoom levels will be available. Lastly, we'll set the maxExtent property to include just a subset of the world, like the following:

```
map = new OpenLayers.Map('map_element', {
  controls: [
    new OpenLayers.Control.Navigation(),
    new OpenLayers.Control.PanZoomBar(),
    new OpenLayers.Control.LayerSwitcher()
  ],
  numZoomLevels: 8,
  maxExtent: new OpenLayers.Bounds(-100, -30, 40, 30)
});
```

2. Open up the page, and you should see something like this:

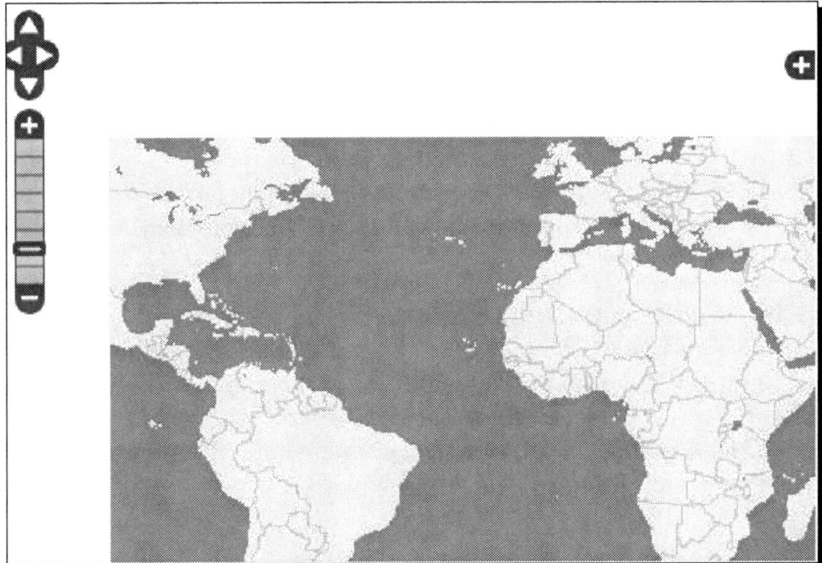

What Just Happened?

Our map has only eight zoom levels and a maximum extent of `(-100, -30, 40, 30)`. You must have noticed that the map started at a zoom level that is zoomed in a couple of times. This is mainly due to the fact that the furthest out zoom level would show more than the maximum extent of the map. Let's quickly talk about what zoom levels are.

Zoom levels accessing the `map.zoom` property (or calling `map.getZoom()`) will show your current zoom level (an `{Integer}` value). The zoom level numbers descend from 0 (the 'furthest out' zoom level—the level your map will usually start at) to the maximum zoom value minus one (since the first value starts at 0, not 1).

In our example, the highest zoom value we can have is `7`, because our `numZoomLevel` setting is 8. Since the zoom values start at 0, not 1, we have to subtract one from the maximum number of zoom levels to get the current zoom level value.

On the **PanZoomBar** control, the very bottom item on the slider represents the zoom level further out (we'll call this the minimum zoom level). The highest you can go will be referred to as the maximum zoom level. Now, if we're using a third party API layer, we can simply set `minZoomLevel` and `maxZoomLevel` on those layer properties, but to set these values for the map (and other non third party API layers), we use either **scales** or **resolutions** along with min or `maxScale`, and min or `maxResolution`.

Map properties—Continued

Let's continue our discussion on map properties.

Resolutions

`resolutions: {Array{Float}}`

This is an array of resolutions the map will use. Each value in the array is a possible zoom level. If you do not pass this in when instantiating your map (or layer), it will be automatically determined based on other properties, such as `maxExtent`. Setting this property is another way to specify the number of zoom levels on your map. The `resolutions` array descends from high values to low values.

Resolution is the width/height in map units per pixel—so, for example, 150 miles divided by 512 pixels would be a resolution of `0.29296875`. If you are using a tile cache server, you will need to specify the resolutions at which the tiles are cached (as well as set the `serverResolutions` property, which specifies the resolutions at which the tiles are cached on the server). Otherwise, you will often simply just define the `numZoomLevels` to specify how many zoom levels you want.

> Another quick note on the resolutions array is that each value in the array is half the value of the previous item. So, if the first item in your resolutions array was `0.703125`, the next value would be `0.3515625`, the next `0.17578125`, and so on.

Time for Action – using resolutions array

Setting the resolutions array is one way to specify the number of zoom levels. Let's see it in action.

1. In the map object definition specify the resolution array as the following:

```
map = new OpenLayers.Map('map_element', {
  resolutions: [ 1.40625,0.703125, 0.703125, 0.3515625,
0.17578125, 0.087890625, 0.0439453125 ]
});
```

2. Zoom around on the map. Because we've only provided five possible resolutions, you should be able to zoom in five times.

What Just Happened?

Using the `resolutions` array, we were able to specify the number of zoom levels. Unless we're using a cached tile service, this isn't necessarily the easiest way to specify the number of zoom levels. We have mentioned earlier we can also use **scales**, and we can also use `minResolution` and `maxResolution`.

Map/Layer property inheritance

Resolutions/scales/max extent etc. properties can be specified in the map object or layer objects. Preferably, they should be specified in the map, as you won't have to worry about which layers to apply the properties to. However, if you do not specify them in the map, then the settings of the base layer will be applied to the map. This isn't necessarily bad, but it can be a bit ambiguous as to what layers are controlling the resolutions, because if these properties are set in overlay layers they won't necessarily be applied.

So, to be safe, if you set those properties on the map then you don't have to worry about applying them to layers. The main exception is if you are using a third party API layer—in this case, you must set those layer properties, such as `minZoomLevel`, `maxZoomLevel`, (two third party API specific properties cannot be set on the map), and `numZoomLevels`.

If you want to set properties that mimic limiting the minimum or maximum zoom level, you can use `max/minResolution` or `max/minScale`, which we'll cover now.

Map properties discussion—Continued

Let's get back to looking at some of the remaining map properties.

maxResolution

`maxResolution: {Float or String (with value of 'auto')}. Default: 360 degrees / 256 px`

The `maxResolution` property specifies what the maximum resolution of the map can be. Or, in other words, how far 'zoomed out' the map can be. Setting this property will affect what the base zoom level is and how far you can zoom out. If you want to get the value for this property, then you can zoom to the desired zoom level and call `map.getResolution();` or access the `map.resolution;` property in Firebug to get the current zoom level's resolution.

Setting the `maxResolution` to `'auto'` is one way to make sure the map's extent 'fits' your map's div completely. Setting the property to `'auto'` can also be used with other properties to automatically generate zoom levels.

minResolution

`minResolution: {Float or String (with value of 'auto')}`

Specifying this property will limit the minimum resolution of the map—how far in the user can zoom. This property can also be set to `'auto'`, but if it is then the `minExtent` property must be set as well. If `minResolution` is not set, the number of zoom levels will be determined either by the `numZoomLevels` setting, the `resolutions` array, or the `scales` property.

Time for Action – using Min and Max resolution

Let's look at how to use the `minResolution` and `maxResolution` properties and how they affect our zoom levels.

1. Instantiate your map object, by specifying the the min/max resolution properties:

```
//Create a map with an empty array of controls
map = new OpenLayers.Map('map_element', {
    controls: [
        new OpenLayers.Control.Navigation(),
        new OpenLayers.Control.PanZoomBar(),
        new OpenLayers.Control.LayerSwitcher()
    ],
    minResolution: 0.02197265625,
    maxResolution: 0.3515625
});
```

2. You should see something like this, with limited zoom levels:

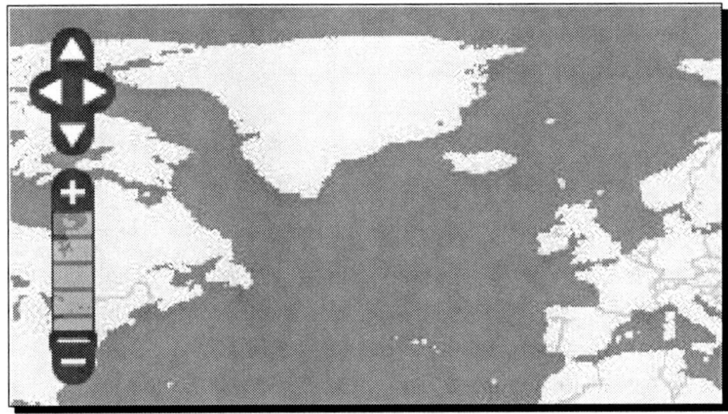

3. Now, let's recreate the map element and set the `maxResolution` and `numZoomLevels` properties:

```
map = new OpenLayers.Map('map_element', {
    controls: [
        new OpenLayers.Control.Navigation(),
        new OpenLayers.Control.PanZoomBar(),
        new OpenLayers.Control.LayerSwitcher()
    ],
    maxResolution: 0.3515625,
    numZoomLevels:8
});
```

4. The map should now show zoom levels like:

What Just Happened?

We just used the `minResolution` and `maxResolution` properties to specify the zoom levels of our map. There is another way, apart from using resolutions, to specify zoom levels and that is by using the `scales` property.

scales

`scales: {Array}`

To specify the scales, pass in an array of scale values. When using this property, do not use the `minResolution`, `maxResolution`, `minScale`, `maxScale`, `numZoomLevels`, `minExtent` or `resolutions` properties. If these properties are set, they override the `scales` property and it will not be used. You should also specify the `unit` property if your projection is using units other than `'degrees'`.

Like the `resolutions` array, scales are ordered from highest to lowest—most zoomed out to most zoomed in. You can use `map.getScale()` to get the scale of the current zoom level.

maxScale

`maxScale: {Float}`

This specifies the maximum scale of the map. This property is similar to `maxResolution`—it limits how far out the user can zoom the map. If you specify the `maxScale` property, setting the `maxResolution` or `minResolution` properties may cause errors. Use either scales or resolutions, but avoid mixing them.

minScale

`minScale: {Float}`

This property specifies the map's minimum scale. More specifically, it determines how far the user can zoom in. If you set this property, the same idea applies as with `maxScales`—do not mix scales and resolutions properties.

When setting `maxScale` and `minScale`, the `minScale` value should be *larger* than the `maxScale` value.

Time for Action – Using scales

Using scales is another way we can control the zoom levels on our map. Let's take a look.

1. Create your map object using `minScale` and `maxScale` as follows:

```
map = new OpenLayers.Map('map_element', {
    controls: [
        new OpenLayers.Control.Navigation(),
        new OpenLayers.Control.PanZoomBar(),
        new OpenLayers.Control.LayerSwitcher()
    ],
    maxScale: 27683990.15625,
    minScale: 221471921.25
});
```

2. You should see something like this:

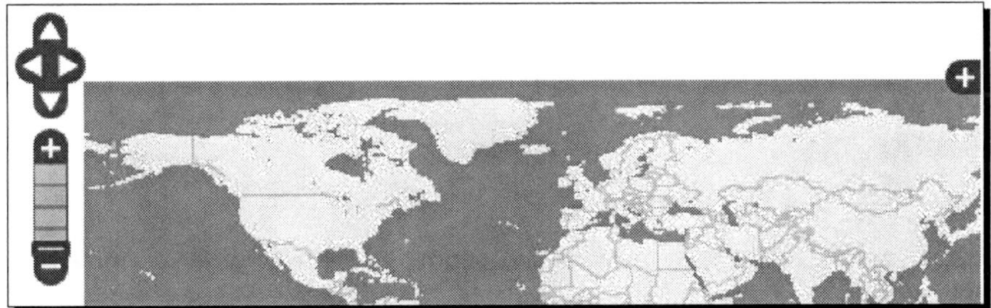

3. Now, let's go back to the code and recreate our map object. This time, we'll pass in a scales array.

```
//Create a map with an empty array of controls
map = new OpenLayers.Map('map_element', {
    controls: [
        new OpenLayers.Control.Navigation(),
        new OpenLayers.Control.PanZoomBar(),
        new OpenLayers.Control.LayerSwitcher()
    ],
    scales: [ 55367980.3125, 27683990.15625, 13841995.078125,
6920997.5390625],
});
```

4. You should see something like this:

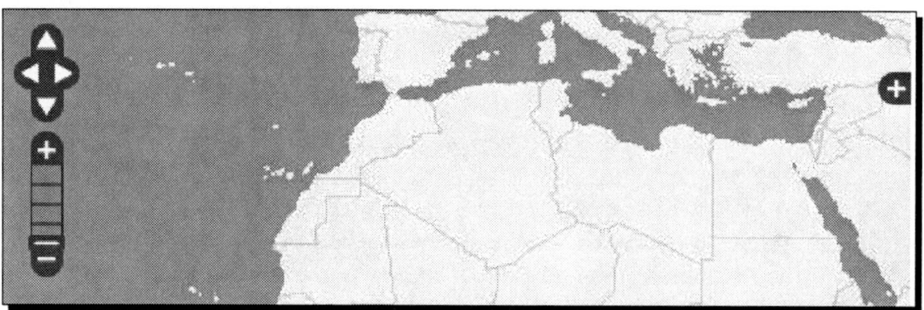

What Just Happened?

We just used scales to determine the zoom levels of our map. Using scales or resolutions comes in handy when you want to specify the maximum or minimum zoom levels, as well as if you want to specify a hard-coded array of zoom level values (and especially when you are working with a cached tile server). Let's talk about some other, non zoom level related properties now.

panMethod

`panMethod: {Function} Default: OpenLayers.Easing.Expo.easeOut`

This property specifies what type of tween animation will be used when panning the map. The default value is a function called `OpenLayers.Easing.Expo.easeOut`, which causes the animation to 'ease out' (or slow down) when the panning is finished. At the time of writing, the possible values are `OpenLayers.Easing.Expo`, `OpenLayers.Easing.Quad`, and `OpenLayers.Easing.Linear`. Each of those three base functions are divided into three further types: `easeOut` ('out' means when the animation is finished), `easeIn` (in means when the animation starts), and `easeInOut` (which means the animation will happen at both times). The docs at `http://dev.openlayers.org/docs/files/OpenLayers/Tween-js.html` will contain the most up to date possible values.

When specifying this property, use the full combination of the base class and subclass, such as `OpenLayers.Quad.easeInOut`. The animation effect will occur whenever the map is panned, such as when using the pan arrow buttons, panning the map with your keyboard, or calling `panTo()`.

panDuration

`panDuration: {Integer} Default: 50`

Specifying this will control how long panning takes to complete. Like the `panMethod` property, this property only effects the panning animation of the map.

Time for Action – working with Pan animations

OpenLayers gives us the ability to use different types of animations when the user pans the map. Using the properties we just discussed, let's learn how to customize the pan animations.

1. Create a new page from the template in Chapter 1. Define your map object like this, passing `panMethod` and `panDuration` properties:

```
map = new OpenLayers.Map('map_element', {
  panMethod: OpenLayers.Easing.Quad.easeInOut,
  panDuration: 100
});
```

2. Pan the map by clicking on one of the arrows in the control on the top left. In Firebug, call the following `panTo` function to pan the map to pass in a coordinate:

```
map.panTo(new OpenLayers.LonLat(-18,42);)
```

3. You should see an animation when panning the map.

What Just Happened?

We just used the `panMethod` and `panDuration` properties to customize our map's pan animations. Changing the `panDuration` will affect how long the animation itself lasts, and changing the `panMethod` determines which type of animation to use. By using these properties, you can mimic the way Google Maps or other third party maps function.

Have a Go Hero – use different animation types

Using what we learned from the previous section, try changing the `panMethod` property to various different possible values (such as `OpenLayers.Expo.easeInOut`) to see the different animation styles. Also, change the `panDuration` to see how much different values affect the speed of the animation.

Let's get back to some more map properties now.

projection

`projection: {String} Default: 'EPSG:4326'`

We've covered this in depth in Chapter 4, our chapter on projections, so we don't need to spend much time going over it here. Essentially, if you are using a projection other than `EPSG:4326`, then you can set the EPSG code here to specify your map's projection. All your layers should be in the same projection as your map's projection. If you do set the projection here, you will also usually have to specify related properties such as the `maxExtent`, `maxResolution`, and `units` (if the projection is not in degrees).

theme

`theme: {String or null} Default: 'theme/default/style.css'`

This property specifies the relative path (meaning, relative to the path your map page is in) to the map's theme style file—a CSS file. If you are using your own theme file, you should specify the path to the CSS file here, along with setting the `OpenLayers.ImgPath` (the path of any custom map images).

This property can also be set to `null`, in which case you can simply include CSS file link tags in your page (or put style information in `<style>` tags). See Chapter 7 for more information on using CSS to style your map.

tileSize

`tileSize: {OpenLayers.Size} Default: (256, 256)`

Specifying this will override the default tile size, which is 256 x 256 pixels. This default size (`256, 256`) is the size of tiles from third party APIs such as Google. If you are not using third party APIs, there may be a good reason to change this value. The larger the tile size, the fewer requests have to be made to the server—but the longer each tile takes to send over. Some tile cache servers may cache tiles at 512 x 512 pixels; in this case you would need to set your map size to match it. In most cases, however, you will not need to change this, but feel free to try changing the values to find a 'sweet' spot for your application. An example would be:

```
tileSize: new OpenLayers.Size(512,512);
```

unit

`unit: {String} Default: 'degrees'`

This specifies the map's units. Unless you are using a non default projection, you probably won't need to change this. Possible values are `'degrees'` or (`'dd'`), `'m'`, `'ft'`, `'km'`, `'mi'`, `'inches'`.

Map functions

We've used a few methods of the Map class already, such as `addLayers` and `zoomToMaxExtent`. In fact, we've used the more common methods at least a couple of times throughout the previous chapters. We haven't covered them in good detail yet, and there are a few functions we haven't encountered but are still quite handy, especially when developing maps with any sort of custom functionality.

This section is divided into groups of related functionality. Each group will have its own header and then lists functions alphabetically, so you can quickly find the function you're looking for.

Control related

- `addControl( control )`: Parameters—`control {OpenLayers.Control}`. This function takes in a single control object and adds it to the map.
- `addControls( controls )`: Parameters—`controls {Array {OpenLayers.Control}}`. This function takes in an array of control objects and adds them to the map.
- `getControl( match )`: Parameters—`match {String}`. Accepts one argument, the ID of a control. It will return a control object, if found, that matches the ID passed in.

  Returns: `{OpenLayers.Control}` or `null`. If no match is found, returns null.
- `getControlsBy( property, match )`: Parameters—`property {String}`, `match {String or Object}`. This is an extremely useful function that is sometimes overlooked. If you need to get control objects that match some criteria, this is the function to use. It accepts two arguments, a **property** (such as `'active'`), and a **match** (such as `true`). The **match** argument can be either a string, regular expression, or Boolean. The `property` is the string name of any property of a control—so, if you want to get all the controls that are active, you would call `map.getControlsBy('active', true);`.

  Returns: `{{Array of OpenLayers.Control objects}}` or `null`. If no match is found, returns null; otherwise, returns an array of matched control objects.
- `getControlsByClass( match )`: **Parameters**—`match {String` or `Object}`. Similar to `getControlsBy`, but instead will perform a match for class name. Calling this function and passing in a string containing the class name (or a regular expression) will return either null or an array of control objects.

  Returns: `{Array of OpenLayers.Control objects}` or `null`.

- `removeControl( control )`: **Parameters**—`control { OpenLayers.Control }`. This function takes in a single parameter, an OpenLayers Control object, and removes it from the map. Removing a control will affect the `map.controls` array, so be aware of this if you are using indexes to reference control objects in other places of your code. This is another reason why creating a variable to reference control objects is preferred, as you don't have to worry about the order of the `map.controls` array.

Time for Action – using control methods

Let's go through a quick example using some of the functions we just covered.

1. Open up an existing map (any map is fine).
2. In Firebug, input and run the following:

   ```
   var returned_controls = map.getControlsBy('active', true);
   ```

3. Now, if that array is not empty, call the following. If the array is empty, it means that there are no active controls. Try to add some controls to your map until this function returns a non empty array:

   ```
   map.removeControl(returned_controls[0])
   ```

What Just Happened?

We just got an array of controls that were active and then removed the first item in the returned array from the map. If the `returned_controls` array is empty, calling `removeControl` will not do anything (you can't remove a `null` control). Let's now look at a larger group of functions.

Extent/Coordinate/Bounds related

The following functions are all related, in some capacity, to moving or getting position information about the map.

Some of the functions will make use of the **OpenLayers.LonLat** class. This class is used to create a coordinate object, which contains a longitude and latitude value (or x and y values, depending on your projection). To instantiate a **LonLat** object, simply call the class and pass in longitude (x) and latitude (y) values (which are `{Float}` data types):

```
var my_lonlat_object = new OpenLayers.LonLat(-42.18, 42.20);
```

Methods

The methods are as follows:

- `getCenter()`: **Returns**{`OpenLayers.LonLat`}. Calling this function will return a LonLat object containing the center point of the map.
- `getExtent()`: **Returns** {`OpenLayers.Bounds`}. Returns the current extent of the map.
- `getMaxExtent()`: **Returns** {`OpenLayers.Bounds`}. Returns a Bounds object consisting of the map's max extent; essentially, it returns the value of the `map.maxExtent` property.
- `getMaxResolution()`: **Returns** {`Float`}. Returns the maximum resolution of the map.
- `getNumZoomLevels()`: **Returns** {`Integer`}. The number of zoom levels the map contains is returned.
- `getResolution()`: **Returns** {`Float`}. Returns the map's current resolution.
- `getResolutionForZoom( zoom )`: Parameters are `zoom { Integer }`. This function allows you to pass in a zoom level, `zoom` (an {`Integer`}), and receive the resolution for that zoom level. Returns: {`Float`}. Returns the resolution for a passed in zoom level.
- `getScale()`: **Returns** {`Float`}. Returns the map's current scale value.
- `getZoom()`: **Returns** {`Integer`}. Returns the current zoom level value, which is also the value of the `map.zoom` property.
- `getZoomForExtent(bounds, closest)`: **Parameters** are `bounds {OpenLayers.Bounds}`, `closest {Boolean}` (Optional). Takes in an OpenLayers.Bounds object and an optional `closest` argument (default value is `false`) and returns a level for the passed in bounds. If closest is set to `true`, a suitable zoom level is returned that may not fully contain the entire extent. Returns: {Integer}. This returns a zoom level appropriate for the passed in bounds.
- `getZoomForResolution(resolution, closest)`: **Parameters**: `bounds {OpenLayers.Bounds}`, `closest {Boolean}` (Optional). Similar to `getZoomForExtent`; takes in a resolution and optional `closest` argument and returns a zoom level. **Returns**: {`Integer`}. Returns a zoom level appropriate for the passed in resolution.
- `isValidLonLat( lonlat )`: **Parameters** are `lonlat {OpenLayers.LonLat}`. Takes in a single `lonlat` object and **returns** a Boolean specifying if the passed in coordinate is within the extent of the map. **Returns**: {`Boolean`}. Whether or not the passed in point is within the map's `maxExtent`.

- `isValidZoomLevel( zoomLevel )`: **Parameters** are `zoomLevel {Integer}`. This function accepts a single `zoomLevel` parameter and returns `true` or `false` if the passed in zoom level is within the range of map zoom levels. **Returns**: {Boolean}. Whether the passed in zoom level is within range of map zoom levels.
- `moveTo( lonlat, zoom, options )`: **Parameters** are `lonlat {OpenLayers.LonLat}`, `zoom {Integer}`, `options {Object}` (Optional). Takes in an OpenLayers.LonLat object, zoom level, and optional `options` object. This function will move the map to the specified coordinate and zoom level, but will not show any panning animations.
- `pan( dx, dy, options )`: **Parameters** are `dx {Integer}`, `dy {Integer}`, `options {Object}` (Optional). This function takes in two integer parameters and an optional `options` object. The `dx` parameter specifies the distance to pan the map in the **x** (longitude) direction and it can be either positive or negative. The `dy` parameters specifies how much to pan the map in the **y** (latitude) direction. The options object can consist of two properties: `animate` {Boolean} specifies if the panning animation will be enabled. Default value is `true`. The second property is `dragging` {Boolean}, which specifies whether or not to call `setCenter` with dragging, the default value is `false`.
- `panTo( lonlat )`: **Parameters**—`lonlat {OpenLayers.LonLat}`. Pans the map to a passed in coordinate (an `OpenLayers.LonLat` object). This will perform any associated panning animations if the passed in coordinate is within the current extent.
- `setCenter( lonlat, zoom, dragging )`: **Parameter**—`lonlat {OpenLayers.LonLat}`, `zoom {Integer}` (Optional), `dragging {Boolean}` (Optional). This function will set the map's center to the passed in coordinate and (optionally) zoom level. If `dragging` is set to `true` (it is `true` by default), `movestart` and `moveend` events will be triggered.
- `zoomIn()`: Calling `zoomIn()` will cause the map to zoom in the next zoom level, if possible.
- `zoomOut()`: Calling `zoomOut()` will cause the map to zoom out one zoom level, if possible.
- `zoomTo( zoomLevel )`: Parameters—`zoomLevel {Integer}`. Takes in a zoom level and zooms the map to the specified zoom level.
- `zoomToExtent( bounds, closest )`: **Parameters**—`bounds {OpenLayers.Bounds}`, `closest {Boolean}` (Optional). Zooms to the passed in bounds and re-centers the map. By default, `closest` is set to `false`. If it is `true`, a zoom level that most closely fits the bounds will be found, but it may not fully contain the extent.

- `zoomToMaxExtent( options )`: **Parameters**—`options {Object}` (Optional). Zooms to the map's maximum extent. An optional `options` object can be passed in that contains one property—`restricted` (`True` by default). If `restricted` is set to `true`, this function will zoom to the map's restricted extent instead.

Time for Action – using coordinate related functions

Let's put some of these functions to use!

1. Open up an existing map, any page will do.
2. In Firebug, let's call the `pan` function. We'll move -30 degrees (30 degrees left) in the x (longitude) direction, and 30 degrees up in the y (latitude) direction. In the Firebug console, input and run the following:

   ```
   map.pan(-30,30);
   ```

3. Now let's see how the `setCenter` function works.

   ```
   map.setCenter( new OpenLayers.LonLat(-42, 70), 2);
   ```

4. Zoom out now with the `zoomOut()` function:

   ```
   map.zoomOut();
   ```

5. Let's check to see if a coordinate outside the map's max extent is valid. The following should return `False`:

   ```
   map.isValidLonLat( new OpenLayers.LonLat(-190, 20) );
   ```

What Just Happened?

As you can see, it's easy to call any of those map functions we want. The prior group of functions was quite long, but it was the longest group—I promise! We'll do a quick quiz, and then take a look at some more functions.

Pop Quiz – using coordinate related functions

In most cases, it will be your map's users who will navigate the map. However, programmatically controlling map navigation is often necessary or useful. Describe two possible ways to move or set the map's center to the coordinates `(-42, 52)`.

Layer related functions

The following group of functions involves layer actions—adding layers, removing layers, etc. You've seen most of these functions already:

- `addLayer( layer )`: **Parameters**—`layer {OpenLayers.Layer}`. Takes in a layer object and adds it to the map. The layer object can be an already instantiated object, or you can instantiate a layer object on the fly in the call itself.
- `addLayers( layers )`: Parameters—`layers {Array{OpenLayers.Layer}}`. This function takes in an array of layer objects and adds them to the map. Like in the `addLayer` function, you can pass in already instantiated layers or instantiate them on the fly. It is recommended that you instantiate layer objects so you can refer to them by name, but either way is acceptable.
- `raiseLayer( layer, delta )`: **Parameters**—`layer {OpenLayers.Layer}, delta {Integer}`. This allows you to change the order layers appear on the map, allowing you to place layers above or below other layers. This function changes the order of the layer by the passed in `delta` value. If `delta` is positive, the layer is moved up in the `map.layers` array by `delta`. If it is negative, it is moved down by `delta`. We'll be using this function later in the book to move layers up and down the layer list.
- `removeLayer( layer, setNewBaseLayer )`: **Parameters**—`layer {OpenLayers.Layer}, setNewBaseLayer {Boolean}`(Optional). This function will remove a passed in layer from the map. It removes the associated HTML elements, removes the layer from the map's layer list, set's the layer's map value to `null`, and triggers a `removelayer` event. The `setNewBaseLayer` property is optional and defaults to `true`, which will attempt to set a new base layer if need be.
- `getNumLayers()`: **Returns**: `{Integer}`. Returns the number of layers on the map.

Other functions

The following functions are also very useful and will be used throughout the book, but do not necessarily fall into the above function categories:

- `destroy()`: Calling `destroy()` will do what you would imagine—it destroys the map object. After the map is destroyed, the map object is essentially made useless.
- `getLonLatFromPixel( pixel )`: **Parameters**—`pixel {OpenLayers.Pixel}`. This function returns an `{OpenLayers.LonLat}` object based on the passed in pixel—whatever coordinates are passed in that pixel is returned. An example call would be `map.getLonLatFromPixel(new OpenLayers.Pixel(250,250));`. We'll be using this function later in the book.

  Returns: `{OpenLayers.LonLat}`. Returns a LonLat object from the passed in pixel.

- `getPixelFromLonLat( lonlat )`: **Parameters**—`lonlat {OpenLayers.LonLat}`. This function will return a pixel location based on a passed in `lonlat` coordinate. The returned pixel coordinate is returned in view port coordinates (meaning, the pixel location is relative to the map div element). This function is quite useful if you want to, for instance, display another div on top of your map at a specified coordinate. We will be using this function later in the book.

  Returns: `{OpenLayers.Pixel}`. It returns an `OpenLayers.Pixel` from the passed in coordinate.

- `render( element )`: **Parameters**—`element {HTML element or String (of ID of element)}`. This function takes in a single parameter—an HTML element or the ID of an element you wish to render the map to. We saw this function in action earlier in this chapter. If you do not pass in an HTML element (or ID) to the map object when you create it, you can delay rendering and later call this render method. This function will render the map to the element that is passed in.

- `updateSize()`: This function should be called whenever the map div's size is updated. For example, if you have a resize-able div that the map is placed in, then your code should call `map.updateSize()` whenever that div is resized.

Doing stuff with events

In Chapter 6, we introduced the notion of events and how OpenLayers uses events. At the core, there are essentially two types of events used by OpenLayers: Browser events and Map events. **Browser** events are things like clicking on the map div with your mouse, while **Map** events are things such as zooming the map to some coordinate. We worked a little bit with events in Chapter 6, so let's extend that knowledge and add even more custom functionality to our map.

> We won't go over browser events much, but the ideas behind them are essentially the same as map events. A great resource to find out more about browser events can be found at `https://developer.mozilla.org/en/DOM/event`.

Map event types

There are a number of supported map event types. Let's take a look at them, and then we'll cover how to use them in your map. You can also call `map.EVENT_TYPES`, which will return an array of valid map events. Some event types will return an **event object** to the event listener. If an event object is returned, it will be specified as *Event Object* in the event type descriptions below:

- **addlayer**: This event is triggered *after* a layer is added. *Event object*: Includes a `layer` property that references the added layer.
- **changebaselayer**: Triggered after the base layer changes.
- **changelayer**: This event gets triggered after a layer's properties are changed. Specifically, it gets triggered whenever its name, order, opacity, parameters, or visibility is changed. *Event object*: Includes a `layer` property which refers to the changed layer, and a `property` property which refers to the type of property that was changed (order, opacity, etc.).
- **mousemove**: The event is triggered whenever the mouse is moved inside the map.
- **mouseout**: This event is triggered on mouseout; whenever your mouse leaves the map div.
- **mouseover**: This gets triggered whenever the map gets a mouseover event; whenever your mouse first enters the map div.
- **movestart**: Whenever the start of a drag, pan, or zoom occurs, this event is triggered. This event refers to the movement of the map itself, not just the mouse.
- **moveend**: Triggered after a drag, pan, or zoom is finished. This event refers to the movement of the map itself, not just the mouse.
- **move**: This event is triggered on any drag, pan, or zoom of the map.
- **preaddlayer**: This is triggered *before* a layer is added. *Event object*: Includes a `layer` property that references the layer to be added.
- **removelayer**: When a layer has been removed from the map, this event is triggered. *Event object*: Includes a `layer` property that references the layer that was removed.
- **zoomend**: This event is triggered after a map zoom completes.

Using map events

There are primarily two common ways to use map events. Both ways accomplish the same thing—adding listeners to the map that will do something when a specific type of event is triggered. One way is to use the `eventListeners` property when creating your map object. The other way is to use `map.events.register(type, obj, lisenter)`. We'll cover both.

Using the eventListeners property

This is a good way to add the events if you know what events you want to add to your map when you initially create the map object. To use this property, pass in an anonymous object consisting of `eventType: listenerFunction` (key: value) pairs. The `eventType` is one of the event types we described in the previous section, and the `listenerFunction` is the name of the function that will get called when that event type occurs.

Time for Action – using eventListeners

Let's demonstrate how to use event listeners. We'll start off with a simple example that will send an alert anytime the map finishes zooming.

1. The first thing we'll need to do is to create a function that will get called by the event listener when some event happens. We'll have to do this for both the `eventListeners` method and the `map.events.register` method which we'll talk about shortly. Let's create a simple function that will send an alert when the user zooms in. Place this as the first line in your `init()` function, before your OpenLayers map code:

   ```
   function alert_on_zoom(event){ alert('You finished zooming'); }
   ```

2. Next, we'll need to create our map object and pass in an `eventListeners` object. We'll want to listen for a `zoomend` event type, which is an event that happens when the map has finished zooming. So, the key inside our `eventListeners` object will be the event type, which is `'zoomend'`. The value will be the name of the function we wish to get called. Make sure that you do *not* include the parentheses, as we aren't actually calling the function—we're just setting the value to be a reference to the function, which will get called later when the event happens:

   ```
   map = new OpenLayers.Map('map_element', {
     eventListeners: {
       'zoomend': alert_on_zoom
     }
   });
   ```

3. Now, when you visit the map and zoom in, an alert box will pop up with the text **'You finished zooming'**.

What Just Happened?

We just use the `eventListeners` property of the map object to add an event listener for the `zoomend` event type. Be sure to set the value to the function's name only, do not include the parentheses, as we do not want to call the function right now. When the `zoomEnd` event occurs, it will call the `alert_on_zoom` function and pass in the event object. We'll talk about what the event object contains shortly.

Using map.events.register

Using `map.events.register` will do essentially the same thing as setting the `eventListeners` property, but we can set it after the map object has been created. The function call looks like:

```
map.events.register(type, object, listener);
```

The `type` argument refers to the `eventType`, the `object` is a reference to the map object—you will almost always simply pass in your map object—and the `listener` refers to the function that will be called when the event is triggered. The following example will do exactly the same thing as the example in the prior event listeners section. Like before, we create a function that will get called when the `zoomend` event occurs. The difference here is that we are adding the event to the map object *after* it has been created.

```
function alert_on_zoom(event){ alert('Map zoomed'); }
map.events.register('zoomend', map, alert_on_zoom);
```

Now, let's talk about the event object that is passed into the listener function.

Event object

When working with events, it's usually useful to know a bit about what occurred. The event object provides us with some information about the event. Depending on the event type, the event object will have different properties.

All event objects will have at least one property referred to as `object`, which references the map object, and an `element` property which references the HTML element the map is in. Additionally, some event types include more properties. The previous *Map event types* section includes information on the event object properties that are populated for different event types.

To access the event object properties, you just have to use `event.property`, where property is the name of the property you wish to access.

Time for Action – working with Map events

1. Before the map object is instantiated, let's create a function that will get called when the map's `zoomend` event is called. First, we'll create the function:

```
function zoomend_event(event){
  alert('Done zooming');
}
```

2. Let's add another function after that which will update the first layer's opacity to a random value when the map is finished being moved. First, create the function:

```
function update_opacity(event){
  map.layers[0].setOpacity(Math.random());
}
```

3. Now we're going to create the map object. Use the following code to instantiate the map object, passing in event listeners for `zoomend` and `moveend`:

```
map = new OpenLayers.Map('map_element', {
  eventListeners: {
    'zoomend': zoomend_event,
    'moveend': update_opacity
  }
});
```

4. Be sure to add a WMS layer to the map, along with setting the extent like we've done before. Now, open up the map and start navigating around it. When you zoom in, you should receive an alert. When you finish panning, the layer's opacity should change. Now, let's see how the events we just created can actually trigger other events. With the `moveend` event listener we have, the layer's opacity will change every time the user finishes panning. Changing the layer's opacity causes the layer's `changelayer` event to trigger. So, let's demonstrate how it works. Create a function that will send an alert containing some information about the `event` object, namely the layer's name and the property that was changed.

```
function show_layer_info(event){

  alert('Layer changed: ' + event.layer.name + ' |
Property Changed: ' + event.property);
}
```

5. Now, we'll need to register the `changelayer` event. Just like before, we'll use `map.events.register`:

```
map.events.register('changelayer', map, show_layer_info);
```

6. Open up your map now and start triggering events. You'll probably get annoyed of the alerts pretty quickly.

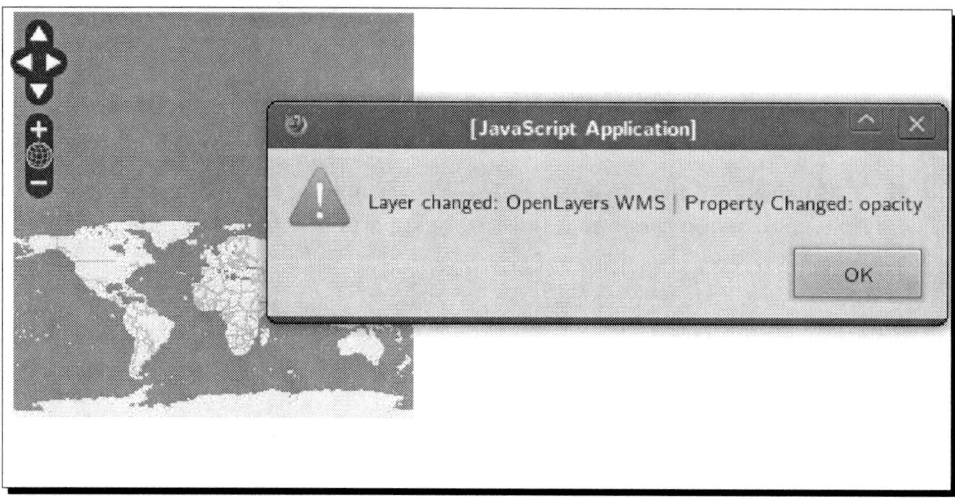

What Just Happened?

We just demonstrated how event listeners can be added to the map and trigger functions when map events happen. You probably also noticed that whenever you moved the map, the `changelayer` event got called. This is because the layer's opacity was updated, which triggers the `changelayer` event. So, one important idea to take away is that events can (and often do) call other events. We'll use events more throughout the book, so if you aren't totally comfortable with them yet—don't worry; they'll be coming up again.

Multiple maps

So far, we've only used one map in all our examples. And, for most applications, only one map is required. There are times though when having two maps is a good thing—like when you're learning about how the Map class works (although, I'm sure you can be a bit more creative).

Using multiple map objects

Making two map objects on your page isn't too hard. We just need another element to place the second map element in, along with adding controls and layers to map—things we've been doing throughout the book.

We've talked about how control and layer objects belong to a single map object. But what if you want to have multiple map objects that use the same layers? A single layer object can only belong to one map object at a time, but fortunately there is a simple way to use the 'same' layer object in multiple maps—by calling the layer's (or control's) `clone()` method.

Time for Action – using multiple map objects

We've used only one map object in all our examples up to this point. Adding multiple map objects isn't very hard though—let's figure out how it's done.

1. We're going to first have to add another HTML element for our second map, and we'll rename the first map element's ID for consistency. Edit your HTML div elements:

```
    <div id='map_1_element' style='height: 500px; float:left;
width:400px;'></div>
    <div id='map_2_element' style='height: 500px; float:left;
width:400px;'></div>
    <div style='clear:both;'></div>
```

2. Now, in your JavaScript code, let's rename the global map variable and add another one to hold our second map (right above the `init()` function):

```
var map1, map2;
```

3. Let's create our first map and its layers and controls. Nothing new here, we're mainly just renaming the map object to `map_1`, and adding a layer to it and setting the center:

```
map_1 = new OpenLayers.Map('map_1_element', {});
//Create a base layer
var wms_layer_all = new OpenLayers.Layer.WMS(
    'OpenLayers WMS',
    'http://vmap0.tiles.osgeo.org/wms/vmap0',
    {layers: 'basic'},
    {}
);
map_1.addLayer(wms_layer_all);
if(!map_1.getCenter()){
    map_1.zoomToMaxExtent();
}
```

4. Now, let's create our second map object.

```
map_2 = new OpenLayers.Map('map_2_element', {});
```

5. We haven't yet added any layers to it. In this case, we want to use the same layer that the first map has. However, since a layer object can belong only to one map at a time, we need to call the layer's `clone()` method, which will basically create a duplicate layer object.

```
var wms_layer_all_map_2 = wms_layer_all.clone();
```

6. Add the layer, then we'll zoom in with the second map and set it to a different location:

```
map_2.addLayer(wms_layer_all_map_2);
map_2.setCenter(new OpenLayers.LonLat(-42, 42), 3);
```

7. Take a look at your page. You should see something like this:

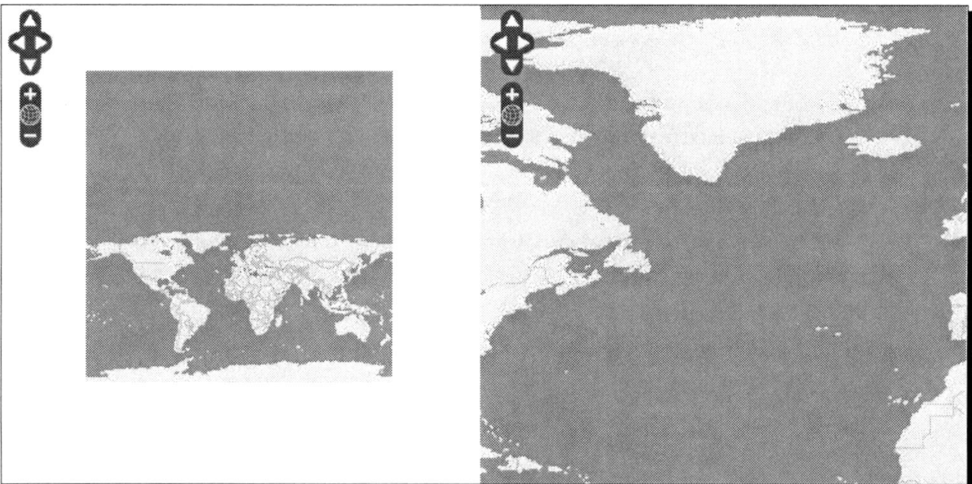

What Just Happened?

We just created two maps on the same page. We used the layer's `clone()` method to duplicate the layer object so that each map object would have the same layer, without having to manually recreate the layer object. If we were adding control objects to our maps, we would use the `clone()` method on our control objects if we wanted to duplicate them. While this is a pretty simple example, there are times when showing maps side by side would be more useful.

Multiple maps and custom events

Let's create a slightly more complicated application using multiple maps and adding event listeners. One map will show a zoomed out view of a country, and the map next to it will show a close up view. Whenever one map is moved, the other map's center point will be immediately updated. This type of mapping application can be quite useful for things such as data entry processes, where two large maps might be more usable than one large map with an overview map.

Let's put together some of the concepts we've learned in this chapter and create a similar type of application.

Time for Action – creating a multiple map and custom event application

In this example, we'll make an application that contains two maps, side by side, that update one another when moved.

1. Create a copy of the previous example. We'll be working on it as the basis for this example.

2. Let's recreate the first map objects. For this example, we'll make the first map zoomed in a bit and set a `maxResolution` so the map cannot be zoomed out more than a few times. We'll also use two control—**Navigation** and **PanZoomBar**.

```
map_1 = new OpenLayers.Map('map_1_element', {
    controls: [
        new OpenLayers.Control.Navigation(),
        new OpenLayers.Control.PanZoomBar()
    ],
    maxResolution:0.0054931640625,
    minResolution:0.00034332275390625
});
```

3. Let's also change the center point. We'll create a variable to store the starting center coordinate (which will also be used by the second map) and change the `map.zoomToMaxExtent` line. After the layer has been added to the map, use the following code:

```
var map_center = new OpenLayers.LonLat(-120, 34);
if(!map_1.getCenter()){
  map_1.setCenter(map_center);
}
```

4. Now for the second map, we'll set it at a more zoomed out level and restrict the resolutions as well. Change the second map's creation code to the following:

```
map_2 = new OpenLayers.Map('map_2_element', {
    controls: [
        new OpenLayers.Control.Navigation(),
        new OpenLayers.Control.PanZoomBar()
    ],
    maxResolution: 0.17578125,
    minResolution: 0.0439453125
});
```

5. Next, let's set the map_2 object's center point to the same center point as the first map:

```
map_2.setCenter(map_center);
```

6. Now, our two map objects are set up just the way we want them—half of our work is done. If you open the map, you should see something like this:

7. Our next goal is to add events to the map that will cause the map objects to update each other when the maps are moved. This is a little trickier than it may first sound. Let's start off by creating a function for each map that will get called when a `moveend` event is triggered.

   It is important that when calling `setCenter`, we pass in `true` as the third parameter so that the `moveend` event is not triggered. If it is triggered, we will end up with an infinite loop (not good).

```
function update_map_1(event){
  map_2.setCenter(map_1.getCenter(), null, true);
}
```

```
function update_map_2(event){
  map_1.setCenter(map_2.getCenter(), null, true);
}
```

8. Finally, let's finish up by registering the events for our two map objects.

```
map_1.events.register('moveend', map_1, update_map_1);
map_2.events.register('moveend', map_2, update_map_2);
```

9. All done! Open the page and pan around. When you finish panning around with one map, the other map will be updated.

What Just Happened?

You just created a fairly complicated mapping application with two map objects and a couple custom events. With all you've learned from this chapter and the previous ones, we can start to do some pretty interesting things. This example is just a small sample of what we can do with just a little bit of work in OpenLayers.

Summary

This brings us to the end of the core coverage of the OpenLayers library. At this point, we've covered in good detail the three 'core' classes—Layer, Control, and Map.

This chapter specifically covered the Map class, along with its properties and methods. We then went in to greater detail about map events and how to work with them. Lastly, we learned how to use multiple map objects on the same page.

Now that we've gotten the fundamentals down, we're ready to start applying those concepts and to create some really interesting mapping applications. The next chapter covers the **Vector** class, a very powerful layer class that allows us to do a lot of really neat things.

9
Using Vector Layers

At this point, we've gone over the foundation of OpenLayers. We've covered the core classes—Map, Controls, and Layers. The rest of this book will focus more on refining that core knowledge, expanding on concepts already introduced and delving a bit into more of the 'advanced' things we can do with the API.

We'll start diving into some of these advance topics starting with this chapter, covering the Vector Layer class. With it, our maps can be made even more interactive, responsive, and sleeker by showing and allowing interaction with vector data.

We'll go over how to create a vector layer, create and interact with objects in it, load data from external files (like KML), and more. Throughout this chapter, we'll go over many different types of examples and build upon them to demonstrate how the Vector Layer works.

In this chapter will cover the Vector Layer class, along with a couple of other related classes. We'll:

- Discuss what the Vector Layer class is and see how it works
- Cover properties, methods, and events of Vector Layer class
- Go over the Feature and Geometry classes
- Discuss how to create more advanced Vector layers
- Demonstrate how to use the Strategy class
- Learn about the Protocol class
- Cover the Format class

What is the Vector Layer?

OpenLayers' Vector Class is generally used to display data on top of a map and allow real time interaction with the data. What does this mean? Basically, it means we can load in data from geospatial files, such as KML or GeoJSON files, and display the contents on a map, styling the data however we see fit. For example, take a look at this map:

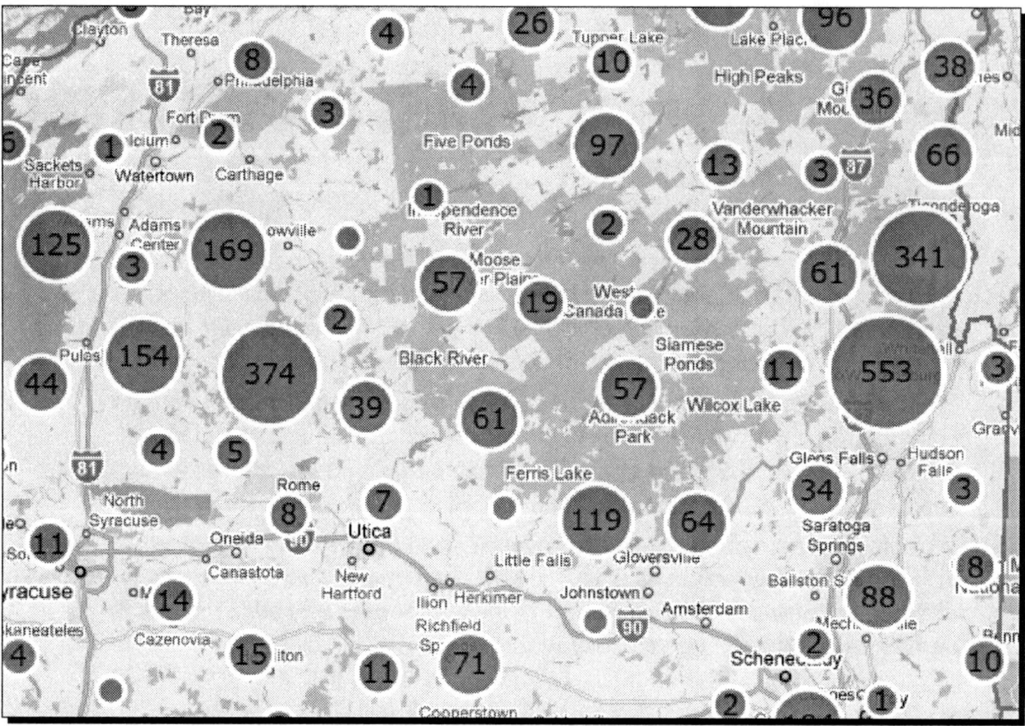

This shows a map with a Google layer as underlying base layer and a vector layer on top of it. The data (all the circles with numbers in them) are loaded in from a GeoJSON file, an open file format that many other applications support. In the vector layer, there are a bunch of data points throughout the map. Each dot on the map is an object in the vector layer, and these objects are referred to as **Features**.

In this case, each feature is actually a **cluster** of data points—the numbers in each circle represent how many points belong to that cluster. This clustering behavior is something we can use out of the box with OpenLayers via the **Strategy** class, which we'll be covering later in the chapter. Before we get to that point, let's talk about one of the main things that separate a vector layer from other layers.

What makes the Vector Layer special?

With a raster image, what you see is what you get. If you were to look at some close up satellite imagery on your map and see a bunch of buildings clustered together, you wouldn't necessarily know any additional information about those buildings. You might not even know they are buildings. Since raster layers are made up of images, it is up to the user to interpret what they see. This isn't necessarily a bad thing, but vector layers provide much more.

With a vector layer, you can show the actual geometry of the building and attach additional information to it—such as the value of it, who owns it, its square footage, etc. As we'll see later in this chapter, it's easy to put a vector layer on top of your existing raster layers and create features in a specific location. We'll also see how we can get additional information about features just by clicking or hovering our mouse over them.

The Vector Layer is client side

Another fundamental difference is that the vector layer is, generally, used as a **client side** layer. This means that, usually, interaction with the actual vector data happens only on the client side. When you navigate around the map, for instance, the vector layer does not send a request to a server to get more information about the layer. Once you get the initial data, it's in your browser and you do not have to request the same data again (in most cases, although WFS is an exception; we'll cover this later in the chapter).

Since, in most cases, the vector data is loaded on the client side, interaction with the vector layer usually happens nearly instantaneously. However, there are some limitations. The vector layer is dependent on the user's browser and computer. While most browsers other than Internet Explorer have been progressing exceptionally well and are becoming more powerful each day, limitations do exist.

Due to browser limitations, too many features in a vector layer will start to slow things down. There is no hard number on the amount of features, but generally anything over a couple hundred of features will start to slow things down on most computers. However, there are many ways around this, such as deleting features when you don't need them, and we'll talk about performance issues in more depth later.

Other uses

With the vector layer, we can display any type of geometrical object we'd like—points, lines, polygons, squares, makers...any shape you can imagine. We can use the vector layer to draw lines or polygons and then calculate the distance between them. We can draw shapes and then export the data using a variety of formats, then import that data in other programs, such as Google Earth. These are just a few basic cases though, and throughout this chapter you'll see how powerful the vector layer can be.

What is a 'Vector'?

In terms of graphics, there are essentially two types of images: **raster** and **vector**. Most images you see are **raster** images—meaning, basically, they are comprised of a grid of pixels and their quality degrades as you zoom in on them. A photograph, for example, would be a raster image. If you enlarge it, it tends to get blurry or stretched out. The majority of image files—`.jpegs`, `.png`, `.gifs`, any bitmap image—are raster images.

A **vector**, on the other hand, uses geometrical shapes based on math equations to form an image. Meaning that when you zoom in, the quality is preserved. If you were to zoom in on a vector image of a circle, the lines would always appear curved—with raster image, the lines would appear straight, as raster images are made up of a grid of colors. Vector graphics are not constrained to a grid, so they preserve shape at all scales.

Time for Action – creating a Vector Layer

Let's begin by creating a basic vector layer. In this example, after you add some points and other feature types to your vector layer, try to zoom in. You'll notice that the points you added don't lose quality as you zoom in. We'll go over how it works afterwards.

1. We'll start off by using a basic WMS layer:

```
var wms_layer = new OpenLayers.Layer.WMS(
            'OpenLayers WMS',
            'http://vmap0.tiles.osgeo.org/wms/vmap0',
            {layers: 'basic'},
            {}
        );
```

2. Now, let's create the vector layer itself. We'll use the default projection and default values for the vector layer, so to create the layer all we need to do is create it:

```
var vector_layer = new OpenLayers.Layer.Vector('Basic Vector
Layer')
```

3. Add the layers to the map now:

```
map.addLayers([wms_layer, vector_layer]);
```

4. If we looked at the map now, we would just see a simple map—our vector layer does not have any data loaded into it, nor do we have any controls to let us add vector data.

5. Let's add the **EditingToolbar** control to the map, which allows us to add points and draw polygons on a vector layer. To do so, we just need to instantiate an object from `OpenLayers.Control.EditingToolbar` and pass in a vector layer. We'll pass in the `vector_layer` object we previously created:

```
map.addControl(new OpenLayers.Control.EditingToolbar(vector_
layer));
```

6. Take a look at the map now. You should see the `EditingToolbar` control (which is basically a panel control with control buttons). Selecting different controls will allow you to place vector objects (called features) on the vector layer. Play around with the `EditingToolbar` control and place a few different points / polygons on the map:

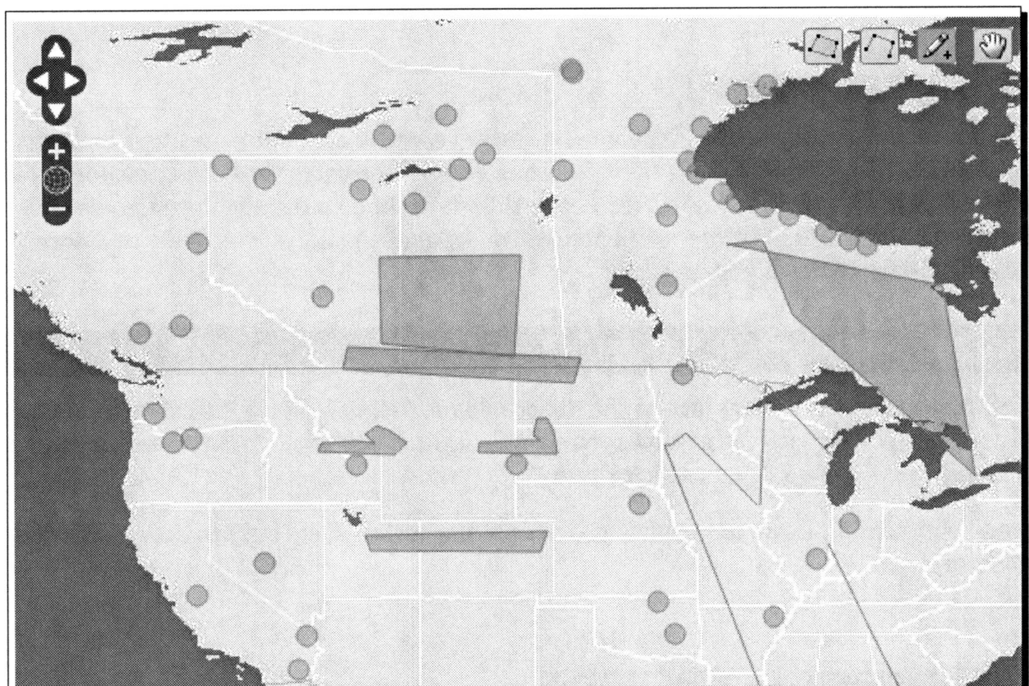

7. Now, one more step. You've placed some features (points / polygons / lines / etc.) on the map, but if you were to refresh the page they would disappear. We can, however, get the information about those features and then export it to a geospatial file. We'll work with files later, but for now let's grab the information about the features we've created. To access the information about the vector layer's features, all we need to do is access its `features` array. In Firebug, type and run the following:

```
map.layers[1].features
```

8. You should see a bunch of objects listed, each object is a feature you placed on the map:

```
[Object { layer=Object, more...}, Object { layer=Object, more...},
Object { layer=Object, more...}, ...]
```

9. Now, if you expand one of those objects, you'll get the information about a feature. The `geometry` property is an anonymous object each feature has which contains geometry information. You can also see the methods of the feature objects—try playing around with different functions. You can access the individual features by using `map.layers[1].features[x]`, where `x` is the index of the feature in the features array. For instance, to destroy the first feature which we added to the map we could use:

```
map.layers[1].features[0].destroy();
```

What Just Happened?

We just demonstrated how to create a basic vector layer and added features to it using the `EditingToolbar` control. Using the `features` array of the vector layer, we also destroyed some features. As you've just seen, it's not terribly difficult to start using the vector layer—pretty easy, in fact. The rest of this chapter will more or less build on what we just saw, so there's no need to be intimidated.

Pop Quiz – why use a Vector Layer?

Vector layers tend to be very fast, as the data can be stored entirely on the client. Interaction happens instantly, which can greatly enhance the user's experience. Come up with a couple of cases where you would use a vector layer.

Now, before we jump into more advanced uses of the vector layer, let's see how it actually works first.

How the Vector Layer works

There are primarily four things we need to cover to understand how the vector layer works.

- How the Vector Layer is rendered
- The Vector Layer class itself
- The Geometry and Feature classes
- How to use the related Strategy, Protocol, and Format classes

Let's go over rendering—fortunately, there's not much to it.

How the Vector Layer is rendered

As we discussed earlier, the vector layer doesn't use raster graphics. Other layer types use the `<img>` tag (image tag) to show images—in HTML, the image tag will only display raster images. So, we can't just use `<img>` tags like other layers. Instead, we have to use a vector image **renderer**. As we mentioned before, the vector data is not just an image, and can contain additional information such as the coordinates of the data.

The vector data must be rendered to be seen. OpenLayers supports three ways to render the vector layer: **SVG**, **Canvas**, and **VML**.

SVG

The default way to render the vector layer is to use the SVG renderer, which makes use of the `<svg>` tag. **SVG** is an acronym for **Scalable Vector Graphics**, and allows us to render vector images in the browser. All browsers (except Internet Explorer) support SVG, so by default OpenLayers uses SVG to render the vector layer.

Canvas

We can use the **Canvas** renderer, which makes use of the `<canvas>` HTML tag. Using this renderer tends to be a little slower however, as the vector is actually turned into a raster with the canvas tag—but this may be desirable in some cases.

VML

Internet Explorer does not follow web standards, and at the time of writing did not support SVG or Canvas. Fortunately, by default, OpenLayers will detect if the user's web browser does not support modern technologies and a fall back renderer called **VML** will be used (which is similar to SVG, but is Microsoft specific). SVG tends to be faster than VML, so the only case where you would want to use VML over SVG is when Internet Explorer is used.

'Renderers' array

When you create a vector layer, it looks for an array called `renderers` which contains the names of renderers, in order, to use. By default, the `renderers` array is set as:

```
["SVG", "VML", "Canvas"]
```

This means that OpenLayers will try to use SVG first, and if the browser does not support SVG it will fall back on VML—and if it does not support VML, it will try to use Canvas.

Time for Action – changing the Renderers array

Let's use the `Canvas` renderer and see what our map looks like.

1. Make a copy of the previous example. We'll just be changing one line of the code.
2. The only thing we'll need to do is set the `renderers` property when instantiating the vector layer. By default, it is set as `['SVG', 'VML', 'Canvas']`. Let's make `Canvas` the default renderer. Replace your vector layer instantiation code with:

```
var vector_layer = new OpenLayers.Layer.Vector('Basic Vector
Layer', {
    renderers: ['Canvas', 'SVG', 'VML']
});
```

3. Open up the map and draw some points. It may look similar, but you will probably notice that the lines don't look as sharp as they do when using the `SVG` renderer. If you use Firebug to inspect the map element, you'll see a `<canvas>` tag:

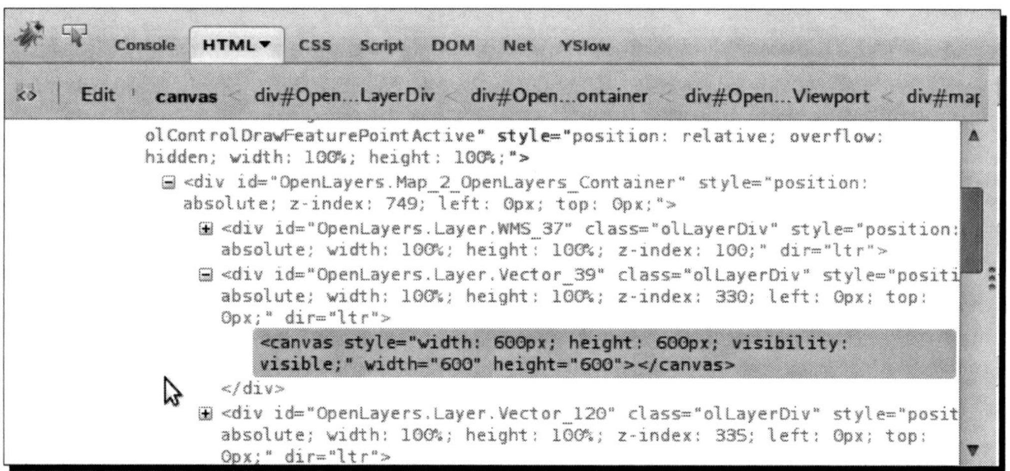

What Just Happened?

You just saw how easy it is to change the renderer used by the vector layer—although it is not usually necessary to change it.

Now that we know how the vector layer is rendered, let's talk about the class itself.

Vector Layer class

The Vector Layer, by itself, is a layer like the other layers we've discussed so far—but to really get the most out of it, we'll be working with other classes.

To even get a basic example working (like the first one in this chapter), we make use of a few other classes. Specifically, the **Vector** class makes use of the **Feature** class to show objects on the layer. But for the **Feature** class to work, it needs to use the **Geometry** class to create geometry objects. Therefore, the actual vector objects in your vector layers are Feature objects which are composed of Geometry objects—we'll cover all that soon.

Before we do that though, let's cover the Vector Layer class itself. We'll first go over the properties of the Vector class, and then the methods (in a similar manner to Chapter 3).

OpenLayers.Layer.Vector properties

Let's go over the properties that the Vector class contains. Some of them are instantiated objects from other classes, which will be covered later in this chapter.

- `drawn`: {`Boolean`}. Returns `true` or `false` depending on whether the features have been drawn or not. You do not set this property when instantiating the vector layer object.
- `features`: {`Array {OpenLayers.Feature.Vector}`}. This is an array of feature objects belonging to the vector layer. We saw this in the earlier example—by accessing this array, we can find out information about all the objects (features) which a vector layer contains. Since this is an array, you can access an individual feature by calling `vector_layer.features[X]`, where `X` is the index of the desired feature. We'll go much more in depth with how to interact with features later in the chapter.
- `filter`: {`OpenLayers.Filter`}. By assigning a filter object to a vector layer object, you can (as the name implies) filter out certain data based on the properties supplied to the filter object. This is very useful when you want to display some, but not all, features from a data source. We will go over this property thoroughly in the Filter class section in Chapter 10.
- `isBaseLayer`: {`Boolean`}. Default value is `false`. Specifies if the layer is a base layer or not. You could use a vector layer as a base layer, having an entirely vector based map instead of relying on a WMS or Google Maps Layers as a base layer.
- `isFixed`: {`Boolean`}. Default value is `false`. Determines if the vector layer will move around when the map is dragged. This can come in handy if, for instance, you want to place a marker on your map that always stayed in the center of the map (in which case you would set this property to `true`).

- `isVector`: {`Boolean`}. Returns `true` if the layer is a vector layer. You do not set this property when you instantiate the vector layer. This property is used primarily to check if an already instantiated layer is a vector layer or not. For instance, if you wanted to loop through all the layers on your map and determine if a layer was a vector layer or not, you would likely use this property.
- `protocol`: {`OpenLayers.Protocol`}. Specifies a protocol object to use for the vector layer. In the section on strategies, protocols, and formats, we talk about this in much more depth.
- `renderers`: {`Array{String}`}. Specifies an array containing strings which contain the renderers to use. Each renderer is tried, in order, and if it is not supported by the browser, the next one is tried. Earlier in the chapter we went over how to use this property.
- `rendererOptions`: {`Object`}. The renderer will use an anonymous object consisting of properties. We won't talk any more about renderers in this chapter, but the properties this object can contain are listed in the OpenLayers docs for each renderer class at `http://dev.openlayers.org/docs/files/OpenLayers/Renderer-js.html`.
- `reportError`: {`Boolean`}. Default is `true`. This property specifies whether or not to report error messages if the renderer fails to load.
- `selectedFeatures`: {`Array{OpenLayers.Feature.Vector}`}. This property contains an array of features the layer contains that are currently selected. Features can be selected by, for instance, clicking on a feature. This property is discussed more in the section on interacting with features.
- `strategies`: {`Array{OpenLayers.Strategy}`}. An array of strategy objects. Strategies tell the vector layer how to behave, such as clustering features together. In the section on strategies, protocols, and formats, we talk about this in much more depth.
- `style`: {`Object`}. Contains style information for the vector layer. Using this, we can change the color, size, etc. of features in our vector layer. We talk about this in much more detail in Chapter 10.
- `styleMap`: {`OpenLayers.StyleMap`}. A stylemap object that defines styles the vector layer will use. Chapter 10 covers the Style and StyleMap class in detail.
- `unrenderedFeatures`: {`Object`}. This contains an anonymous object of features that failed to render (if any exists). You do not set this property when instantiating the vector layer object.

OpenLayers.Layer.Vector methods

Now that we've gone over the Vector Layer class properties, let's discuss the methods we can call. We'll just cover functions specific to the Vector layer; functions that are inherited from the base `OpenLayers.Layer` parent class can be found in Chapter 3.

- `clone()`: Makes a copy of the layer and the features it contains. Returns an `{OpenLayers.Layer.Vector}` object, which is a copy of the layer.
- `getDataExtent()`: This function will return an `{OpenLayers.Bounds}` object consisting of the max extent that includes all the features of the layer.
- `refresh(obj)`: Causes the layer to request features and redraw them. If the layer is visible and in range of the map extent, the refresh event will be triggered. Takes in an optional `obj` object containing properties for event listeners.
- `assignRenderer()`: Assigns a renderer to the layer based on the layer's `renderers` property.
- `displayError()`: Shows an alert informing the user that their browser does not support the layer's renderers.

Working with features

The remaining methods that we'll discuss involve features. A feature, as we saw earlier, is an object that belongs to the vector layer. We'll cover methods first, and then walk through the related examples to show how to properly use them.

addFeatures(features, options): Calling this function will add features to the map. You must pass in at least an array of `features` objects, and you can optionally pass in an `options` object. The `features` parameter is an `{Array{OpenLayer.Feature.Vector}}`, and options is an anonymous `{Object}`.

Time for Action – adding features

Let's add some features to a map manually.

1. Make a copy of the first example—we'll just need a basic WMS base layer and a vector layer.
2. Open up the map in Firefox and enable Firebug. We'll use the JavaScript console to add features to the vector layer.

3. Let's create some features first. To do so, we'll need to make use of the `OpenLayers.Geometry` classes. Let's start off by creating a `OpenLayers.Geometry.Point` object, passing in a longitude and latitude (type and execute the following in Firebug):

```
var point = new OpenLayers.Geometry.Point(-72, 42);
```

4. Now that we have a geometry object, we can create a feature object from it. We'll use the `OpenLayers.Feature.Vector` class to create a feature object using the `point` object we just created. When instantiating, the constructor can take in three arguments—`geometry`, `attributes` (optional), and `style` (optional). We'll cover the Feature class in detail later in the chapter. Create the feature point, by passing in the `geometry` object we created above:

```
var feature_point = new OpenLayers.Feature.Vector(point);
```

5. Alright, now we're ready to add the feature to the map with `addFeatures`. Even though we are passing in a single feature, we still must pass in an array. Add it like this:

```
map.layers[1].addFeatures([feature_point]);
```

6. You should see the point added to the map:

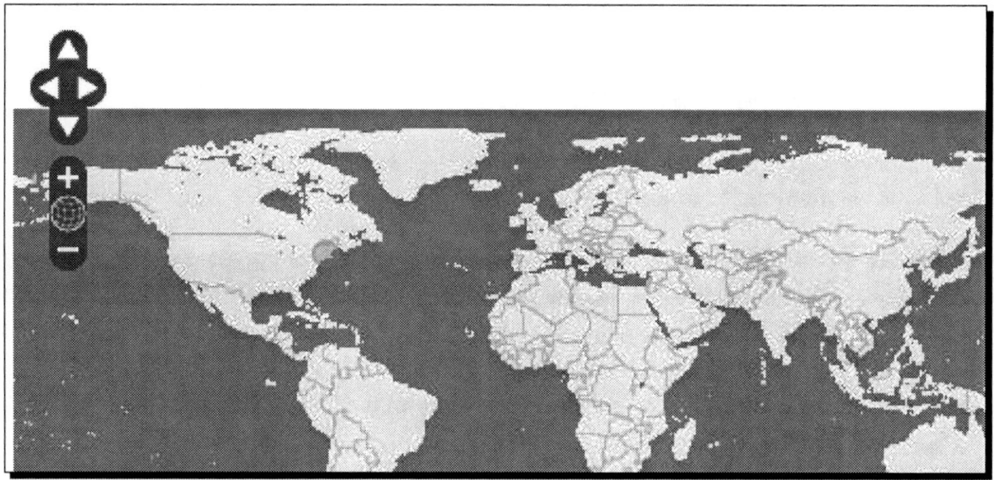

What Just Happened?

We just used the `addFeatures` method to add a feature we created from a geometry object to the map. Don't worry if the `OpenLayers.Geometry` class is new to you—we'll cover it, along with more examples of it, throughout this chapter.

Have a Go Hero – create more points

Now that you know how to add a point to the map, try to add some more points. Use the code from the previous example as a guide to add multiple Geometry Point objects to your map. Change the coordinates and see how the locations are affected. Also try to add a point outside the map's extent and see what happens.

Let's continue our discussion about the Vector Layer's methods.

Vector Layer methods (Continued)

- **removeFeatures(features, options)**: This function will remove features from the vector layer by erasing the passed in features and removing them from the layer (but the features themselves are *not* destroyed). Two events are triggered for each feature—`beforefeatureremoved` and `featureremoved`.

  This function takes in two parameters, like the `addFeatures` method. The `features` parameter is an `{Array{OpenLayer.Feature.Vector}}`, and options is an anonymous `{Object}`. The `options` parameter can accept a `silent` property which is a `{Boolean}` with a default value of `false` which determines if the events will be triggered or not.
- **removeAllFeatures(options)**: Calling this function will remove all features from the map. Like the method above, it will not destroy the features, but it will erase them from the map and remove them from the layer's feature array. It takes in one optional `options` parameter that can accept a `silent` property, if set to `true`, will suppress events from triggering.
- **destroyFeatures(features, options)**: This function will erase and destroy any features that get passed in. The difference between this function and `removeFeatures` is that `destroyFeatures` will both remove the features from the layer *and* destroy the features themselves—so you cannot add a feature back to the map that has been destroyed. It takes in two parameters—both are optional. If the `features` parameter is not passed in, *all* the features of the layer will be destroyed.

Time for Action – destroying features

Let's demonstrate the difference between `removeFeatures` and `destroyFeatures`.

1. Open up the first example from the chapter. We'll use Firebug again.

2. Before we remove features, we first need to add them to the map. We'll use the same code from the previous example. Let's create a feature object. In Firebug, type and execute:

```
var feature_point = new OpenLayers.Feature.Vector(new OpenLayers.
Geometry.Point(-72, 42));
```

3. Now, let's add it to the map:

```
map.layers[1].addFeatures([feature_point]);
```

4. We have the feature on the map now, so let's see how `removeFeatures` works. We can call this function and either pass in a feature from the `map.layers[1].features` array, or pass in a feature object we've already created. Let's use the second method:

```
map.layers[1].removeFeatures([feature_point]);
```

5. Now you should not see any features on your map. If we check the `map.layers[1].features` array, it should be empty:

```
>>>map.layers[1].features;
[]
```

6. So, as we expected, the feature we originally added to the map is no longer in the `features` array. However, the feature itself still exists. We can check this by simply typing in the feature object's name:

```
>>>feature_point

Object { data=Object, more...}
```

7. This is what the primary difference between `removeFeatures` and `destroyFeatures` is—when calling `removeFeatures`, the feature itself still exists in memory. This is not a good thing if you plan to never use the feature again. Let's see what happens when we use `destroyFeatures`. First though, we must add the feature back to the map:

```
map.layers[1].addFeatures([feature_point]);
```

8. Now we can destroy it. We'll pass in the feature by using the `map.layers[1].features` array this time when calling `destroyFeatures`:

```
map.layers[1].destroyFeatures([map.layers[1].features[0]]);
```

9. The feature should now be removed from the map. The feature object itself will be destroyed as well though. If we try to access the feature, all the attributes are null.

```
>>>feature_point.data
null
>>>feature_point.geometry
null
```

What Just Happened?

We just demonstrated the differences between `removeFeatures` and `destroyFeatures`. The former removes the features from the layer, while the latter does the same *and* destroys the feature itself so it cannot be added to the map again.

Let's continue.

Vector Layer methods (Continued)

- **drawFeature(feature, style)**: This will draw / redraw a passed in feature to the layer. You should only use this function if the feature's style has changed—it will not add a feature to the layer, and will only work after a feature has been added. The `feature` parameter is the feature you wish to draw, and the `style` parameter is an optional style `{Object}`. If no style is passed in, the layer's default style is used.
- **eraseFeatures(features)**: This function takes in an array of feature objects and erases them from the map. It does *not* remove the features from the layer object, nor does it destroy the feature object itself. Using this function, you can remove the feature from the map, but retain the feature in the layer's feature list—then you can pass the erased feature into the `drawFeature` method to reshow it.
- **getFeatureById(featureId)**: This function accepts a `{String}` consisting of a feature ID. It will return a `{OpenLayers.Feature.Vector}` object (a feature object) that corresponds to the passed in ID—if none is found, it will return `null`. The ID, if you do not set it when creating a feature object, is an automatically generated string that will be something like `OpenLayers.Feature.Vector_42`—the number is also essentially random, so you will likely only need to use this function if you set the ID of a feature when creating it. Otherwise, you may want to use the `getFeatureByFid` method.
- **getFeatureByFid(featureFid)**: This function is similar to the `getFeatureById` function, but looks for a **FID** instead of an ID. The FID is a string that normally specifies the index of the feature in the `features` array (and it may have to be set manually if not loading data from external sources). Like `getFeatureById`, it accepts a `{String}` consisting of a feature Fid. It will return a `{OpenLayers.Feature.Vector}` object (a feature object) that corresponds to the passed in FID—if none is found, it will return `null`.

- **getFeatureFromEvent(event)**: Calling this function will return either the feature passed in an `{Event}` occurred over, or return `null`. For example, if a `featureselected` event was passed in, this function would return the feature that was selected. We cover vector layer events in the next section.
- **onFeatureInsert(feature)**: This method will be called right *after* a feature is inserted into the vector layer. By default, it is an empty function. If you supply a function, it will be called after a feature is inserted. The `feature` parameter will be passed in to whatever function you create. An example call to override this function would be:

  ```
  map.layers[1].onFeatureInsert = function(feature){ alert(feature);
  };
  ```

  The above code would cause an alert to be displayed that would display the feature that was inserted into the map. The next *Time for Action* example will use this function.
- **preFeatureInsert(feature)**: This method will be called right *before* a feature is inserted into the vector layer. By default, it is an empty function. If you supply a function, it will be called after a feature is inserted. The `feature` parameter will be passed in to whatever function you create. An example call to override this function would be:

  ```
  map.layers[1].onFeatureInsert = function(feature){ alert(feature);
  };
  ```

  The above code would cause an alert to be displayed which would display the feature that was inserted into the map. The next *Time for Action* example will use this function.

Time For Action – working with feature events

Let's take a quick look at a couple of the previous Vector class methods.

1. Open up the first example from the chapter—we'll be using Firebug, and we'll just need a vector layer and EditingToolbar control. We won't be editing any code, so open up the first example and Firebug's JavaScript console.
2. We're going to add a function using `preFeatureInsert` that will display an alert containing the feature's ID. This function will be triggered before the feature is inserted into the map. Type and run the following in Firebug to create the function as follows:

   ```
   map.layers[1].preFeatureInsert = function(feature){
     alert('preFeatureInsert - ID: ' + feature.id)
   };
   ```

3. Take a look at the map now and add a point using the EditingToolbar control (or calling `map.layers[1].addFeatures()`). You should see an alert that will be triggered before the feature is added to the map that displays the ID of the soon to be added feature. Take note of the ID that the alert contains.

4. Using the ID that was in the alert, let's call the `getFeatureById` function (if you didn't get the ID, just create another feature or find the ID in the `map.layers[1].features` array). An ID that was generated for me was `OpenLayers.Feature.Vector_143`, so I'll use that—but be sure to use the one generated for you. Call the following function, substituting the ID that I used with your ID:

   ```
   map.layers[1].getFeatureById('OpenLayers.Feature.Vector_143');
   ```

   Running that should return to you the feature object.

5. Now, let's use `onFeatureInsert` to trigger a function to be called after a feature is added. Let's show an alert containing the feature's geometry information:

   ```
   map.layers[1].onFeatureInsert = function(feature){
     alert('onFeatureInsert - Geometry:' + feature.geometry)
   };
   ```

6. Now, try to add a feature. You should see two alerts—one before the point is added that displays the feature's ID, and another after the feature is added that contains geometry information.

What Just Happened?

We just used a few functions involving vector layer events. That ends our discussion on the Vector class methods section and starts our coverage of Vector Layer class events. Don't worry—it's not as long as the previous sections and you've already been exposed to the difficult event stuff in earlier chapters.

Vector Layer class events

In Chapter 8 we covered events. The same concepts we talked about there apply here, but there are a few vector layer specific event types that we'll use later in this chapter that haven't been covered yet. Let's go over the supported event types then see them in action. Because the Vector class inherits from the `OpenLayers.Layer` base class, all the event types of the Layer class can be used as well.

Vector Layer event types

All these events can be registered the same way we registered events in the previous chapter. For example:

```
vector_layer.events.register(type, obj, listener);
```

Assuming `vector_layer` is the name of your vector layer object, the previous code will register a listener for an event of a passed in type. Along with the event types of the Layer class, the Vector class supports the following event types (in alphabetical order):

- **afterfeaturemodified**: Triggered after a feature has been modified. The listener function receives a `feature` object which references the modified feature.
- **beforefeatureadded**: This event is triggered before a single feature is added to the map. The listener function will receive an object containing a feature property that references the soon to be added feature. If the listener function returns `false`, the feature will be not be added to the map.
- **beforefeaturesadded**: This event does the same thing as `beforefeatureadded`, but the listener function will accept an array of features instead of a single feature. If the listener function returns `false`, the features will not be added.
- **beforefeaturemodified**: Triggered before a feature is selected to be modified. The listener function receives a `feature` object which references the soon to be modified feature.
- **beforefeatureremoved**: Triggered before a single feature object is removed from the map, and the listener function receives a `feature` object which references the removed feature.
- **beforefeaturesremoved**: Triggered before an array of feature objects are removed from the map, and the listener function receives a `features` array which references the removed features.
- **featureadded**: Triggered right after a single feature object is added to the map, and the listener function receives a `feature` object which references the added feature.
- **featuresadded**: Like the previous type, but designed to take in an array of features. It is triggered right after an array of feature objects are added to the map. The listener function receives a `features` array which references the added features.
- **featuremodified**: Triggered when a feature has been modified. There is a slight difference between this and the `afterfeaturemodified` event. This `featuredmodified` event gets fired as soon as the feature is modified, and the `afterfeaturemodified` event gets triggered after the modification is fully complete. The listener function receives a `feature` object which references the modified feature.

- **featureremoved**: Triggered after a single feature object is removed from the map, and the listener function receives a `feature` object which references the added feature.
- **featuresremoved**: Triggered after an array of feature objects are removed from the map, and the listener function receives a `features` array which references the removed features.
- **featureselected**: Triggered after a feature is selected. The listener function receives a `feature` object which references the selected feature. Usually used when using the SelectFeature control, covered later in this chapter.
- **featureunselected**: Triggered after a feature is unselected. The listener function receives a `feature` object which references the unselected feature. Usually used when using the SelectFeature control, covered later in this chapter.
- **refresh**: This event is triggered when the vector layer makes a request for new features, or when the `refresh` method is called. Using the WFS protocol, for example, the vector layer will make additional requests for features and this event will be triggered. We go over requesting data from external sources later in this chapter.
- **sketchcomplete**: Triggered after a sketch has been completed. A sketch can be made, for example, with the `EditingToolbar` control—drawing a line or a polygon is considered a 'sketch'. When the drawing is fully complete (i.e., when you double click to finish the sketch), the `sketchcomplete` event is fired. The listener receives a `feature` object which references the sketched feature. If the listener function returns `false`, the features will not be added.
- **sketchmodified**: Triggered when a sketch is modified. If, for example, you are in the middle of drawing a polygon using the `EditingToolbar` control and move your mouse, this event is fired. The listener receives a `feature` object which references the sketched feature, and `vertex` property which references the modified point.
- **sketchstarted**: Triggered as soon as a sketch is started. If, for example, you click on the draw polygon control of the `EditingToolbar` control and place a point on the map, this event is triggered. The listener receives a `feature` object which references the sketched feature, and `vertex` property which references the starting point.
- **vertexmodified**: Whenever any vertex contained by any feature is modified this event is triggered. The listener function receives three arguments: `feature` which references the feature the vertex belongs to, `vertex` which references a point (the modified vertex), and `pixel` which contains the on screen pixel location the vertex was modified at.

Time For Action – using Vector Layer events

Now that you know the possible event types, let's play around with some.

1. Open up the first example from this chapter. We won't be editing the code, but instead we'll use Firebug again. We just need a vector layer and `EditingToolbar` control. As in the previous chapters, `map.layers[1]` is assumed to be the vector layer.

2. Open up Firebug. We'll start off by registering a `beforefeatureadded` event to the map. First, like in Chapter 8, we need to create a listener function that will get called when the event fires. We know from the previous list of event types that the listener function will receive an object containing the feature, so let's create our function with a `feature` parameter that will reference the feature. In Firebug, create a function:

```
function before_feature_added(feature){ console.log('before adding
a feature!', feature); };
```

3. All we have to do now is register the `beforefeatureadded` event on our vector layer:

```
map.layers[1].events.register('beforefeatureadded', this, before_
feature_added);
```

4. Now, look at your map and add a feature. We used `console.log` and passed in two parameters to it (a string and a feature object). Take care when using `console.log` in your applications—users without Firebug or a development console may receive errors. Since we're testing things out now though, we don't have to worry about it. Your console should log something like:

```
before adding a feature! Object { feature=Object,  more...}
```

5. The definition for this event type says we can return `false` to stop the feature from being added. To do so, we'll have to register a different event to the layer for the `beforefeatureadded` event type. Let's first *unregister* to the event, as we want to ensure that we won't run into any issues:

```
map.layers[1].events.unregister('beforefeatureadded', this,
before_feature_added);
```

6. Try to add some features to your map now. Nothing should be happening, since we unregistered the `beforefeatureadded` event. So, let's redefine the function and then register it to the layer again.

```
function before_feature_added(feature){
  console.log('feature will not be added!', feature);
```

```
    return false;
};
```

7. Now we will just register the event:

```
map.layers[1].events.register('beforefeatureadded', this, before_
feature_added);
```

8. Try to add a feature to the map. The feature should not be added, and your console should log:

```
feature will not be added! Object { feature=Object,  more...}
```

What Just Happened?

We just showed how to register and unregister an event on our vector layer that gets triggered before a feature is added to the layer. Let's take a look at one more example involving events, and then continue our discussion about how the Vector Layer class works.

Time For Actions – working with more events

In this example, we'll examine the events related to adding features to the map. We'll look at the feature added event type, which gets triggered when a feature is added to the map (either programmatically or by a user), as well as sketch events which can be triggered by the EditingToolbar control.

1. Open up the first example from this chapter. Again, we'll use Firebug.
2. This time, we'll demonstrate the `featureadded`, `sketchstarted`, and `sketchcomplete` events. Let's create three appropriate listener functions:

```
function feature_added(feature){ console.log('feature added',
feature); };
function sketch_start(feature){ console.log( 'sketch started:',
feature); };
function sketch_complete(feature){ console.log( 'sketch done:',
feature); };
```

3. Now, register the feature added event:

```
map.layers[1].events.register('featureadded', this, feature_
added);
```

4. Take a look at the map and add a feature. You should see a message after adding a point or after adding a polygon / line (sketch):

```
feature added Object { feature=Object,  more...}
```

5. Now let's register the sketch events. They will get triggered when using any of the `EditingToolbar` controls.

```
map.layers[1].events.register('sketchstarted', this, sketch_
start);
map.layers[1].events.register('sketchcomplete', this, sketch_
complete);
```

6. Now, when adding a point or creating a polygon / line, you should see a total of three messages when you finish adding the feature:

```
sketch started Object { feature=Object,  more...}
sketch done Object { feature=Object,  more...}
feature added Object { feature=Object,  more...}
```

What Just Happened?

We just demonstrated a few more event types. You can also figure out how the events propagate (which events get executed first) by viewing the console log. From the example above, we can see that the `sketchcomplete` event get executed before the `featureadded` event.

Even though we registered the `featureadded` event first, the order that we register the events in does not change the order that the events propagate in. We'll be using more of the vector layer events throughout the chapter, but it shouldn't be much more complicated than the previous two examples. So, let's get on with it!

Geometry and Feature classes

We've been using feature objects throughout the chapter so far without really talking about the **Feature** class itself. We also have hinted at the **Geometry** class, but we haven't gone into any detail so far. This section will cover both classes in a bit more detail so that you can gain a bit more confidence working with them. Don't worry—it's easy, you've already been exposed to both classes.

Before we get into the **Feature** class though, we should go over the **Geometry** class, as it's used to create the actual geometry objects that make up a feature object.

Geometry class

The **Geometry** class is, more or less, the foundation of the feature objects we've seen so far. Specifically, up to this point, we have been using the `Feature.Vector` class as the base class for our feature objects. We'll talk more about that shortly, but for now it is just important to know that the `Feature.Vector` class uses the `Geometry` class to store geometry information about a feature.

But what exactly is the **Geometry** class? In a nutshell, it stores geographic information. Remember the earlier example in this chapter where we added a feature. The code was:

```
var feature_point = new OpenLayers.Feature.Vector(
  new OpenLayers.Geometry.Point(-72, 42)
);
```

We passed in Geometry Point object (we'll get to what the subclasses are in a minute). Now, if executed and looked at it on the map, we'd see a point at the coordinate `-72, 42`. Then, if we get the feature information via something like `map.layers[1].features[0]`, we'd see information about that feature. When we look at it, we see a geometry property.

Expanding it, or using `map.layers[1].features[0].geometry`, we find out that it has a `bounds` property, along with `x`, `y`, and `ID` properties. This is how feature store geographic information in a geometry object.

Let's take a look again at the code that instantiates a geometry object: `new OpenLayers.Geometry.Point(-72, 42)`. As you might have guessed, we're using the Point subclass of the Geometry class.

Geometry subclasses—Theory

When working with the Geometry class, we actually almost always use some subclass of it. What do we mean? Think about the Layer classes we've used throughout the book—we've been using subclasses of the base Layer class the entire time (`Layer.WMS`, `Layer.Image`, etc. are all subclasses of the `OpenLayers.Layer` class).

Just like how we work with layers, we almost always work with `OpenLayers.Geometry` *subclasses* when we want a Geometry object. So far, we've only been explicitly calling the `Geometry.Point` subclass, which accepts a single X,Y coordinate and creates a geometry based on the passed in coordinate. There are many more subclasses that let us do things a bit more tricky than just working with points.

Before we cover the subclasses, let's quickly go over some of the methods available to *all* of the subclasses via the base `Geometry` class. All these methods are available to any Geometry subclass, as all the subclasses inherit from the Geometry class.

Geometry class methods

- **atPoint(lonlat, toleranceLon, toleranceLat)**: This will return a {Boolean} indicating whether the geometry object is at the passed in `lonlat`. The `lonlat` parameter is an {`OpenLayers.LonLat`} object containing a coordinate to check, and the `toleranceLon`, `toleranceLat` parameters specify a {`Float`} number which sets the threshold for the longitude and latitude, respectively. If a point lies within the threshold of the longitude and latitude, `true` will be returned—if not, `false` will be returned. The calculation which determines if the geometry is at the passed in point is an approximation based on the geometry object's bounds.
- **calculateBounds()**: Calling this function will recalculate the bounds of the geometry. It does not return anything. If you wish to see the geometry object's bounds, see `getBounds()`.
- **clearBounds()**: This function will turn the geometry object's bounds object to `null`.
- **clone()**: This function creates a copy of the geometry and returns a cloned {`OpenLayers.Geometry`} object.
- **destroy()**: Calling this function will destroy the geometry object. Note—if you call this on a geometry object that is already part of a feature object, it will not remove the geometry object from the map.
- **distanceTo(geometry, options)**: Calling this function will calculate the nearest distance between the current geometry object and a geometry object passed in. The `options` parameter can contain additional calculation options, which vary depending on the geometry subclasses. There is a `details` option which is a {`Boolean`} and can be specified for all subclasses. If `details` is set to `true` in the `options` parameter, this function will return an {`Object`} containing the distance and x0, y0, and y1,y0 values which represent the coordinates of the two geometry objects. If `details` is not set (or set to `false`), this function will by default return a {`Number`} containing the distance. Take care to mind the units that the map is in.
- **extendBounds(bounds)**: This function will extend the geometry's bounds, including the passed in `bounds` object, which must be an {`OpenLayers.Bounds`} object. If the geometry does not have a bounds set when this function is called, then it will be set.
- **getArea()**: Returns a {`Float`} containing the area the geometry object covers. This function is redefined in various subclasses, but can be called by all subclasses.
- **getBounds()**: Returns the bounds of the geometry as an {`OpenLayers.Bounds`} object. If no bounds are set, the bounds are calculated. This will return the bounds for a single geometry object—if you want to get the bounds of all the features on your layer, see the Vector class' `getDataExtent` method.

- **getCentroid()**: Returns a {OpenLayers.Geometry.Point} object containing the center point of geometry object. This function is redefined in various subclasses, but can be called by all subclasses.
- **getLength()**: Returns a {Float} containing the length the geometry object covers. This function is redefined in various subclasses, but can be called by all subclasses.
- **getVertices(nodes)**: This function returns an {Array} of all the points in the geometry object. It accepts a {Boolean} parameter which is True by default, which specifies that all vertices should be returned. If it is set to false, then if the geometry is a Line, this function will only return vertices that are not endpoints.
- **toString()**: Returns a **WKT (Well-Known Text)** {String} of the geometry object. WKT is a markup language, similar to HTML or XML, which is used to represent geometry objects. For example, when calling this function on a Geometry.Point object with a coordinate of (-72, 42) would return the WKT string "POINT(-72 42)". More information on WKT can be found at http://en.wikipedia.org/wiki/Well-known_text.

Time for Action – using Geometry class methods

Let's demonstrate some of the methods we just talked about. These methods can be applied to any geometry subclass—Point, Polygon, etc.

1. Open up the first example from this chapter. We'll use Firebug again to demonstrate the functions.

2. Before we can do anything we need some geometry objects. We won't use the Feature class here—we'll just demonstrate some geometry object methods. Because we aren't associating the Geometry objects with Feature objects this time, we won't see anything getting added to the map, as a Geometry object alone is not necessarily tied to any layer or feature. Let's create two geometry point objects with random coordinates:

```
var geom_1 = new OpenLayers.Geometry.Point(
  (Math.floor(Math.random() * 180) - 90),
  (Math.floor(Math.random() * 180) - 90)
);
var geom_2 = new OpenLayers.Geometry.Point(
  (Math.floor(Math.random() * 180) - 90),
  (Math.floor(Math.random() * 180) - 90)
);
```

3. Now we have two geometry point objects. Let's use `distanceTo` to calculate the distance between the two points. We'll calculate the distance between `geom_1` and `geom_2`. Because random numbers were used, your output for this call will likely be different:

```
geom_1.distanceTo(geom_2);
```

4. Let's use the `atPoint` method now and play around with the tolerance parameters. First, let's get the center point coordinate of the geom_1 object:

```
geom_1.getCentroid();
```

5. The returned object will have an `x` and a `y` property. Mine are `x: 27, y: 35`. Substitute your returned coordinate for the next steps. First, let's call the `atPoint` method-use the returned coordinate to make sure it works:

```
geom_1.atPoint(new OpenLayers.LonLat(27,35));
```

6. The output should be `true` if you have substituted your coordinates. Now, let's try to call it but offset our coordinate by five degrees:

```
geom_1.atPoint(new OpenLayers.LonLat(32,40));
```

7. You should have `false` returned now, since we haven't set a tolerance. Let's go ahead and do that, using `5` as a tolerance for both lon and lat:

```
geom_1.atPoint(new OpenLayers.LonLat(32,40), 5, 5);
```

8. Because our point lies within the tolerance, you should see `true` returned. If you set the tolerance as `4`, then `false` would be returned.

9. One more quick example—Let's create a line geometry object and then add it to the map. Using the `Geometry.LineString` class, we can create a single line. We just pass in an array of Point objects to create a line.

```
var line_geom  = new OpenLayers.Geometry.LineString([
  new OpenLayers.Geometry.Point(
    (Math.floor(Math.random() * 360) - 180),
    (Math.floor(Math.random() * 180) - 90)
  ),
  new OpenLayers.Geometry.Point(
    (Math.floor(Math.random() * 360) - 180),
    (Math.floor(Math.random() * 180) - 90)
  )
]);
```

10. Now let's add it to the map:

```
map.layers[1].addFeatures([new OpenLayers.Feature.Vector(line_
geom)]);
```

11. You should see a line placed randomly on the map. For example:

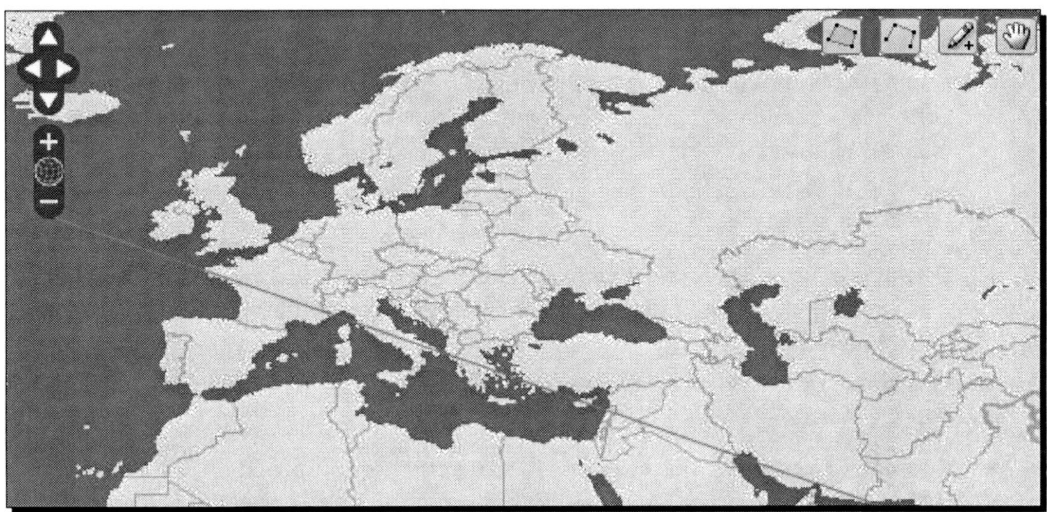

What Just Happened?

We just showed how to use a couple of Geometry class methods. Keep in mind—we only worked with the `Geometry.Point` and `Geometry.LineString` subclasses, but the methods we used (and the ones we covered) can be used for *all* Geometry subclasses.

We also saw how to create a line using the `Geometry.LineString` class. Similarly, we can create `MultiLine` strings by passing in an array of `LineStrings` to the `Geometry.MultiLineString` class. Let's take a brief look at some of the other Geometry subclasses.

Geometry subclasses

Let's take a real quick look at some of the Geometry subclasses. We won't cover their methods, but just look at how to create an object from them. All the subclasses can, again, use the methods we previously discussed—they just have slightly different implementations.

- **Geometry.Point**: Contains properties `x` and `y`. To instantiate, pass in an `x` and `y`. For example:

  ```
  var my_point = new OpenLayers.Geometry.Point(-50, 42);
  ```

- **Geometry.Collection**: This is a class that contains a collection (an {Array}) of geometry objects. Many other geometry classes, such as `LineString`, inherit from this class. To instantiate, pass in an array of geometry objects. For example, to create a geometry collection object you would pass in an array of geometry objects (assuming you have a `geom_point_object` and a `geom_line_object`):

  ```
  var geom_collection_object = new OpenLayers.Geometry.Collection([
  geom_point_object, geom_line_object ]);
  ```

- **Geometry.MultiPoint**: This is a collection ({Array}) of geometry point objects. Other classes, such as `LineString`, inherit from this class. To instantiate, pass in an array of `Point` objects:

  ```
  var geom_multipoint = new OpenLayers.Geometry.MultiPoint([ geom_
  point_1, geom_point_2 ]);
  ```

- **Geometry.Curve**: This class is similar to `MultiPoint` (it also inherits from it) but it assumes that the point objects are connected. To instantiate, pass in an array of `Point` objects:

  ```
  var geom_curve = new OpenLayers.Geometry.Curve([ geom_point_1,
  geom_point_2 ]);
  ```

- **Geometry.LineString**: This class, as we saw earlier, is composed on point objects that are connected together. It is inherited from the `Curve` class—it is basically a curve which cannot contain less than two points. To instantiate, pass in an array of `Point` objects:

  ```
  var geom_line = new OpenLayers.Geometry.LineString([ geom_point_1,
  geom_point_2 ]);
  ```

- **Geometry.MultiLineString**: MultiLineStrings contain multiple LineString objects. To instantiate, pass in an array of `LineString` objects:

  ```
  var geom_multi_line = new OpenLayers.Geometry.MultiLineString([
  geom_line_1, geom_line_2 ]);
  ```

- **Geometry.LinearRing**: This class is a version of a LineString that is closed—meaning the line 'loops back' on itself, the beginning and end points are connected. When creating the object, you can close the line yourself by making the last point equal to the first point. To instantiate, pass in an array of `LineString` objects:

  ```
  var geom_linear_ring = new OpenLayers.Geometry.LinearRing([ geom_
  point_1, geom_point_2, geom_point_3, geom_point_1 ]);
  ```

  You can also call it without passing the start point in as the end point. If you do this, it will be automatically closed for you (OpenLayers will automatically add in the start point as the end point).

- Geometry.Polygon: This class is essentially just an {Array} of LinearRing objects. For a basic polygon, you can pass in just one LinearRing object. The first LinearRing object you pass in will serve as the outer bounds of the polygon. All LinearRings objects passed in after the first will be holes within the polygon (for example, you could form a doughnut by passing in a large circle first then a smaller circle). To instantiate, pass in an array of LinearRing objects:

  ```
  var geom_polygon = new OpenLayers.Geometry.Polygon([ geom_linear_
  ring_1, geom_linear_ring_2 ]);
  ```

- Geometry.MultiPolygon: A MultiPolygon consists of multiple Polygon objects. To instantiate, pass in an array of Polygon objects:

  ```
  var geom_multi_polygon = new OpenLayers.Geometry.MultiPolygon([
  geom_polygon_1, geom_polygon_2 ]);
  ```

Geometry subclass methods

All the Geometry subclasses contain their own versions of the base Geometry class methods, along with some additional methods in some subclasses. The rest of this chapter (and book) will focus on the methods we've seen so far, so you should have all the knowledge you need to continue.

Some of the subclass methods are outside the scope of this book, but they can all be found in the official docs at `http://dev.openlayers.org/docs/files/OpenLayers/Geometry-js.html`.

Feature class

There's one more class we should cover before continuing further discussion of the Vector class. The **Feature** class is what the Vector class uses to actually show Geometry objects on the map. We've used the Feature class throughout this chapter because, well, we can't show objects on vector layers without it—so you've been exposed to a lot of the class already.

How the Feature class works

The Vector layer class has a property called `features`, which is an array of Feature objects. We've used it in this chapter so far, and we'll be using it a lot more. The feature objects are created, as you can imagine, from the **Feature** class.

The base Feature class is composed of two things—Geometry **objects** (as you've seen), and **attributes**. The attributes contain data associated with the feature.

Feature subclasses

There is only one subclass we'll be making use of—the `Feature.Vector` class. Like its parent Feature class, it is composed of a Geometry object and contains an `attributes` property. In addition, there is a `style` property which controls what the feature looks like (similar to how CSS styles HTML). We'll talk about the Style class in detail in Chapter 10.

Feature functions

There are really just a few methods we'll be using throughout the book:

- **destroy()**: Destroys the feature object.
- **clone()**: Creates a copy of the feature object and returns it, as an {`OpenLayers.Feature.Vector`} object.
- **getVisibility()**: Returns a {`Boolean`} which specifies whether the feature is displayed or not.
- **move(location)**: Moves the feature to a passed in location. The `location` can be either an {`OpenLayers.LonLat`} object, which will move the feature to a passed in map coordinate, or an {`OpenLayers.Pixel`} object which will move it to a pixel location on the screen.
- **onScreen(boundsOnly)**: Returns a {`Boolean`} indicating if the feature is within the map viewport (if it is visible on the screen). A `boundsOnly` parameter can be passed in, which is a {`Boolean`} set to `false` by default. If set to `true`, a quicker but less precise bounding box intersection method will be used.

Instantiating a feature object

To create a feature object, we just call it like:

```
var my_feature = new OpenLayers.Feature.Vector( geometry_object,
attributes, style);
```

The `geometry_object` is a geometry object (covered in the previous section). The `attributes` object is an optional object literal which will be mapped to the feature's `attributes` property, which can be used to provide additional information about the feature (such as {`'building_area': 18000, 'building_floors': 2`}). Lastly, the `style` object is an optional object specifying the feature's style (covered in more detail in Chapter 10).

Interacting with Features using Control.SelectFeature

Now that we know how to create features and put them in our vector layer, how do we interact with them? Earlier, we said that interaction with features happens nearly instantly—this is because all the vector feature data is stored in the client's browser. There is no need to request information from a server when clicking on a feature.

To make something happen when clicking on a feature, we'll need to use the **SelectFeature** control class (the `OpenLayers.Control.SelectFeature` class). This control allows us to interact with our feature objects—such as doing things whenever we mouse over or click on a feature. Let's take a look at how to use it in an example and then go over the **SelectFeature** control class itself.

Time For Action – using the SelectFeature control

Let's put together a few things we've learned so far. We'll create some points and a polygon, place it on the map, and use the SelectFeature control to allow the user to select them. We'll register the `featureselected` and `featureunselected` events so that we can fire an event when the user interacts with a feature. When those events are fired, we'll access the feature's `attributes` object and display information from it. Let's do it.

1. We'll be adding a vector layer, some features, and a SelectFeature control. The file will be referred to as `chapter9_selectFeature.html`.

2. First, let's make vector_layer a global variable like we did earlier in this chapter. Place this outside the `init` function, right after `var map;`.

```
var vector_layer;
```

3. Next, we'll add a `<div>` element that we'll output feature info to when the user clicks on a feature. Add this div after the map div:

```
<div id='map_feature_log'></div>
```

4. Now, back to the `init` function code. Add the vector layer after the WMS layer is added to the map:

```
vector_layer = new OpenLayers.Layer.Vector('Basic Vector Layer');
map.addLayer(vector_layer);
```

5. Now, let's add some features. We'll add two point features and one polygon feature. We'll pass in an attributes object (an object with key:value pairs to store data) to each feature. Let's first create the two point features:

```
  var feature_point_1 = new OpenLayers.Feature.Vector(
    new OpenLayers.Geometry.Point(6.055, 46.234),
    {
```

```
            'location': 'Cern',
            'description': "Stand back, I'm going to try science!"
        }
    );
    var feature_point_2 = new OpenLayers.Feature.Vector(
        new OpenLayers.Geometry.Point(-129, 3),
        {
            'location': 'The Sea',
            'description': 'Here be dragons'
        }
    );
```

6. Notice how we passed in two key:value pairs—`location` and `description`. These are just arbitrary keys and values—you can use whatever you like, and we'll see how to access them in a minute. First though, let's add a polygon feature. To do so, remember—we'll need to pass in an array of points into a `LinearRing` object, then pass that `LinearRing` object into the Polygon class to instantiate it. Whew. It's easier than it sounds:

```
var feature_polygon = new OpenLayers.Feature.Vector(
      //We'll make a polygon from a linear ring object, which
consists of points
    new OpenLayers.Geometry.Polygon(new OpenLayers.Geometry.
LinearRing(
    [
        new OpenLayers.Geometry.Point(-124.2, 41.9),
        new OpenLayers.Geometry.Point(-120.1, 41.9),
        new OpenLayers.Geometry.Point(-120, 39),
        new OpenLayers.Geometry.Point(-114.5, 34.9),
        new OpenLayers.Geometry.Point(-114.7, 32.7),
        new OpenLayers.Geometry.Point(-117.1, 32.5),
        new OpenLayers.Geometry.Point(-120, 34),
        new OpenLayers.Geometry.Point(-123.7, 38.4)
        //We won't pass in the first point, the polygon will close
automatically
    ]
    )),
    {
        'location': 'Fanghorn Forest',
        'description': 'Land of the Ents'
    }
  );
```

7. Now we add the features to the map:

```
vector_layer.addFeatures([feature_point_1, feature_point_2,
feature_polygon]);
```

8. Alright—nothing too new so far. Take a look at the map, and you should see the features. We can't yet interact with them though.

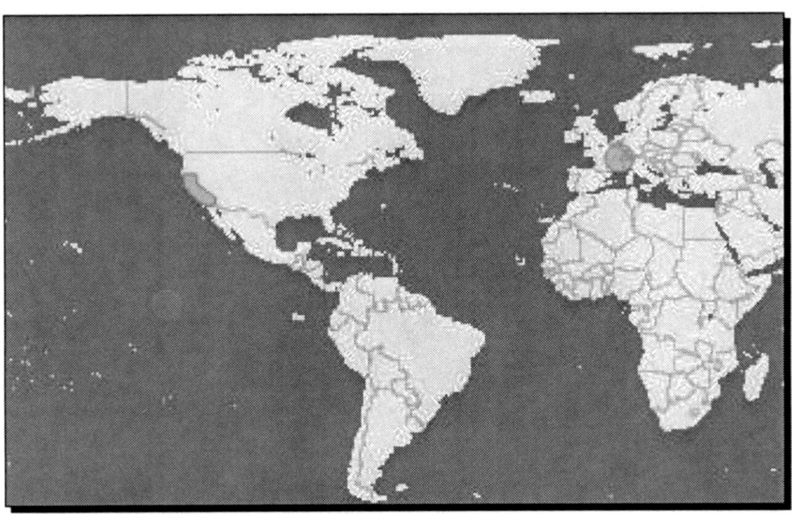

9. Now, let's make the features interactive. To do so, we'll first need a `SelectFeature` control. When we instantiate it, we pass in the vector layer that we want the control to use (alternatively, we could pass in an `{Array}` of vector layers if we wanted the control to use multiple vector layers). We'll also pass in a couple properties, which we'll cover in more detail after this example. The `multiple` property will allow multiple features to be selected at once, the `toggle` property will cause features to be unselected when selecting a different feature, and the `multipleKey` specifies which key to press to allow multiple features to be selected:

```
  var select_feature_control = new OpenLayers.Control.
SelectFeature(
    vector_layer,
    {
      multiple: false,
      toggle: true,
      multipleKey: 'shiftKey'
    }
  );
  map.addControl(select_feature_control);
```

10. At this point, the control is created and has been added to the map. However, before we can use it we must activate it by calling its `activate` method.

```
select_feature_control.activate();
```

11. Now we can select our features. Because we passed in the `multipleKey` property, we can select multiple controls by holding *Shift* and clicking on them. Holding control will toggle a feature selection. Click on a feature to see:

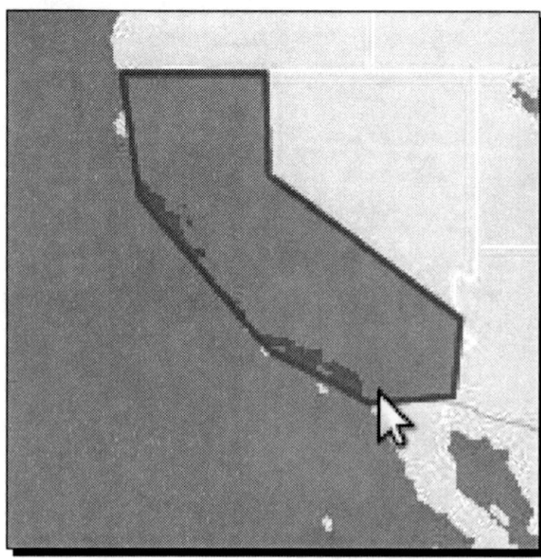

12. Now, let's do something when the user clicks on a feature. To do this, we'll create two functions that will be called when the `featureselected` and `featureunselected` events are fired (they get fired from the `SelectFeature` control). First let's create the function to call when a feature is selected. It will clear the `map_feature_log` div and then look at the `attributes` object of the passed in feature. Finally, it will loop through all selected features and display the `location` property of all selected features.

```
function selected_feature(event){
      //clear out the log's contents
      document.getElementById('map_feature_log').innerHTML = '';

      //Show the current selected feature (passed in from the
event object)
      var display_text = 'Clicked on: '
          + '<strong>' + event.feature.attributes.location + '</
strong>'
          + ': ' + event.feature.attributes.description + '<hr
/>';
    document.getElementById('map_feature_log').innerHTML =
display_text;
```

```
    //Show all the selected features
    document.getElementById('map_feature_log').innerHTML += 'All
selected features: ';

    //Now, loop through the selected feature array
    for(var i=0; i<vector_layer.selectedFeatures.length; i++){
            document.getElementById('map_feature_log').innerHTML
+=
                vector_layer.selectedFeatures[i].attributes.
location + ' | ';
        }
  }
```

13. We need a function to call when a feature is unselected now. It will do a similar thing to the previous function—display the feature the user clicked on, then show all the selected features.

```
  function unselected_feature(event){
      var display_text = event.feature.attributes.location + '
unselected!' + '<hr />';
    document.getElementById('map_feature_log').innerHTML =
display_text;

    //Show all the selected features
    document.getElementById('map_feature_log').innerHTML += 'All
selected features: ';

    //Now, loop through the selected feature array
    for(var i=0; i<vector_layer.selectedFeatures.length; i++){
            document.getElementById('map_feature_log').innerHTML
+=
                vector_layer.selectedFeatures[i].attributes.
location + ' | ';
        }
  }
```

14. Just one more thing now! We have to register the events to call those functions when a feature is selected or unselected:

```
vector_layer.events.register('featureselected', this, selected_
feature);
vector_layer.events.register('featureunselected', this,
unselected_feature);
```

15. All done! Open up your map and select some features (use *Shift* to select multiple features). You should see the log update:

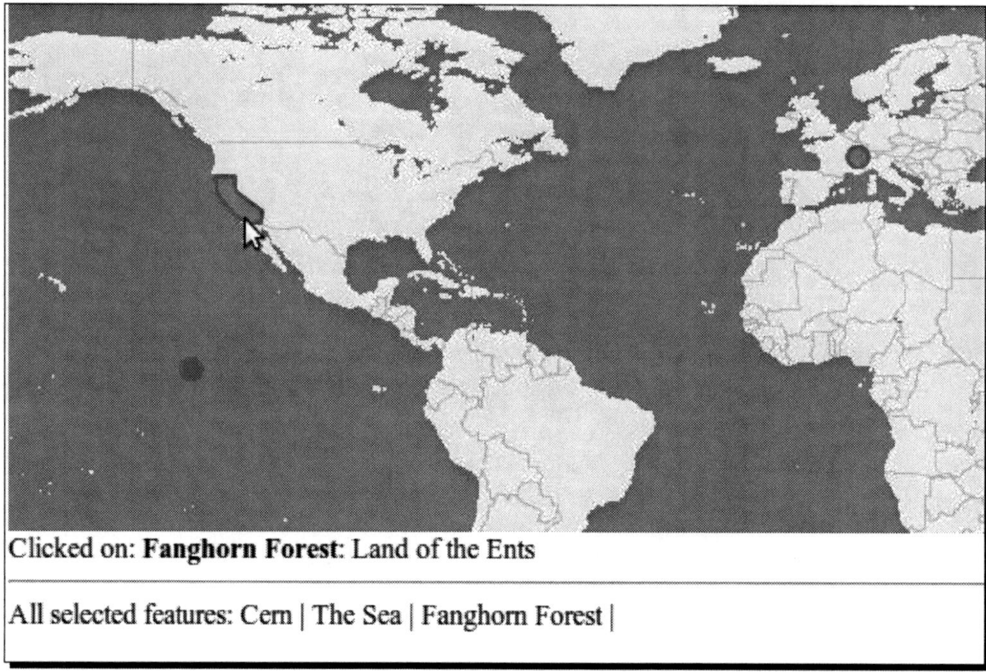

What Just Happened?

We just demonstrated how to use the `SelectFeature` control with some feature data. We'll be doing much more with the `SelectFeature` control and features throughout the remainder of the book, so if you aren't totally comfortable with it don't sweat it too much. Try to create your own functions and features. To do that, you'll need to know a little bit more about the SelectFeature class and what some of the properties of it are. Let's quickly go over them.

Control.SelectFeature class

First we'll cover the properties then look at some methods of the SelectFeature class.

SelectFeature control properties

- **box**: {`Boolean`} Specifies whether features can be selected by drawing a box. Set to `false` by default. If set to `true`, when activating the `SelectFeature` control object, you'll be able to draw a box to select features instead of clicking on features to select them.

- **clickout**: {Boolean} Determines if features will be unselected when clicking outside of any feature. Default is `false`.
- **geometryType**: {Array{String}} An array of strings which specify the only geometry types that the feature will be able to select. Each string should be the name of a Geometry class. By default, `null` is specified for this property, meaning all geometry types can be selected. For example, if you wanted the control to only allow the selection of Point objects, you would pass in this property like:

  `geometryTypes: ['OpenLayers.Geometry.Point']`
- **handlers**: {Object} This contains a reference to handler object instances.
- **highlightOnly**: {Boolean} This specifies whether features can be selected, or if features can only be highlighted. Set to `false` by default. If `hover` is set to `true`, this will do nothing.
- **hover**: {Boolean} Set to `false` by default. If this is set to `true`, features will be selected (and added to the `vector_layer.features` array) when the user mouse overs a feature—clicking on a feature will do nothing, only mousing over them will.
- **layer**: {OpenLayers.Layer.Vector} or {Array{OpenLayers.Layer.Vector}} Specifies the vector layer(s) the selectFeature control is associated with.
- **multiple**: {Boolean} Controls whether or not multiple features will be selected by clicking on them. Default is `false`. This does not mean multiple features can never be selected (you can use the `multipleKey` to select multiple features even if this is set to `false`). If set to `true`, features will not be unselected when clicking on other features.
- **multipleKey**: {String} Specifies a key to be used to allow for multiple selection of features. When holding down the key, multiple features can be selected. An example would be `multipleKey: 'shiftKey'` or `'altKey'`. Default value is `null`.
- **onBeforeSelect**: {Function} Function to be called before a feature is selected. By default, this is an empty function.
- **onSelect**: {Function} Function to be called when a feature is selected. By default, this is an empty function.
- **onUnselect**: {Function} Function to be called when a feature is unselected. By default, this is an empty function.
- **renderIntent**: {String} Used to get the style to use from the style map of the layer. Styles are covered in Chapter 10.
- **selectStyle**: {Object} Contains an object of styles. Styles are discussed later in this chapter.
- **toggle**: {Boolean} Determines whether or not to unselect a selected feature when the feature is clicked. Default value is `false`. If the `hover` property is set to `true`, this will do nothing.

- **toggleKey**: {`String`} Specifies a key that, when held down, will set the `toggle` property to `true`. When the key is released, the `toggle` property will be set back to `false`. An example would be `multipleKey: 'altKey'`. Default value is `null`.

These properties can be set when instantiating a `SelectFeature` control. To create a `SelectFeature` control object, the form for calling it is:

```
var select_feature_control = new OpenLayers.Control.SelectFeature(
  vector_layer,
  {}
);
```

The {} is the optional `options` object which can be filled with the properties we just discussed. Now, let's take a look at some of the methods of the `SelectFeature` control.

SelectFeature control methods

Let's just take a look at a few methods that we'll be using throughout the rest of the book.

- **activate()**: Activates the control, allowing us to use it.
- **deactivate()**: Deactivates the control. After calling, features cannot be selected until the control is activated again.
- **highlight(feature)**: Draws the passed in `feature` with the feature's `select` style.
- **unhighlight(feature)**: Draws the passed in `feature` with the feature's normal style.
- **select(feature)**: Selects a passed in `feature` object, adding it to the layer's `selectedFeature` array, calling the `onSelect` method, and rendering the feature as selected (applying any styles, etc.).
- **unselect(feature)**: Unselects a passed in `feature` object, removing it from the layer's `selectedFeature` array, calling the `onUnselect` method, and rendering the feature back to its normal state (applying any styles, etc.).
- **unselectAll(options)**: Calling this will unselect all features currently selected by the control. If you wish to unselect everything except a specific feature, pass it in to the `options` parameter as an `except` property.

That ends our discussion of the Feature and Geometry classes. Next, we'll be diving into the Vector class again—but this time, we'll focus on the more advanced uses.

The Vector class, part two

Now that we've gotten a bit more of an understanding as to how the vector layer works, we can start doing some more interesting things. First though, let's do a quick recap of what we've covered so far:

- The Vector class allows us to display vector objects on our map, using a variety of different renderers (SVG, Canvas, VML) to accomplish this.
- Objects, such as points and polygons, in the vector layer are `OpenLayers.Feature.Vector` class objects.
- Each `Feature` object contains a `Geometry` object which contains spatial information.
- We can use a variety of Vector, Geometry, and Feature class methods to move the feature objects on the map, add features, and get information about the feature and geometry objects on the map.

So to reiterate—so far, we've looked mainly at the Vector class itself and how to interact with features we add to it. What's left then?

Well, funny you should ask. You've probably noticed we have not spent a whole lot of time creating the actual vector layer objects. The next part of this chapter will largely focus on just that—creating vector layer objects.

Format, protocol, and strategy classes

At the beginning of the chapter, we mentioned that to really use the Vector class we actually use other classes as well. So far, we've used the `Geometry` and `Feature` class—but we've only done so *after* the vector layer was created. Let's now focus on creating more useful vector classes.

To do that, we'll need to make use of the **Format**, **Protocol**, and **Strategy** classes when we instantiate our vector layer object. Using these three classes, we can further control the Vector layer behavior.

Who invited these classes over?

So, what are these classes and why do we need them? There are a lot of good answers, and we won't be able to get to all of them in this book—but here is a short list of some of the things we can do by using these three classes:

- Load data from outside sources—KML files, GeoJSON files, WFS services, etc.
- Save the features that we create as KML or other file formats
- Group hundreds of points together using the Cluster strategy, like we saw at the beginning of the chapter
- Create even more interactive web-mapping applications

How do these three classes relate to each other, and what purpose does each one serve?

Brief overview of the three classes

These classes work together to help us define how the Vector layer behaves. We'll cover each class in more detail soon, but first let's take an overview of them.

Protocol class

The **Protocol** class controls how the Vector layer communicates with a source of data. Like the Geometry class, we actually use subclasses of the Protocol class. The two common subclasses used are `Protocol.HTTP` and `Protocol.WFS`. The HTTP protocol class allows us to communicate directly with a source that contains vector data, and the WFS protocol class lets us talk to a WFS service.

Format class

The **Format** class lets us use a type of file (such as a KML file), and turn the data in that file to actual feature objects in our map. We can also take existing feature objects and convert them to a KML, GeoJSON, etc. file format. The vision the OpenLayers developers have is to support more Formats and Protocols for the Vector class, as opposed to having specific subclasses like WFS (which is deprecated). Other layer classes, like the WMS or Google Maps layer, do not use the Format class—this is because they are raster layers, and we do not need to worry about data formats.

More technically, the **Format** class handles the serialization and de-serialization of the feature data. Serialization is a term programmers use which basically means to extract objects from your code and turn them into something like a file, or a human readable string, so those objects can be accessed outside your code. De-serialization does the opposite—it takes a file or string and turns it into an object that your code can use.

So, what does this mean in the context of OpenLayers? Using the format class, we can serialize and de-serialize feature data from a huge variety of different file formats—such as KML, GeoJSON, GeoRSS, ArcXML, etc.

Strategy class

Lastly, the **Strategy** class is used to control how requests to the server are set up and then what to do with the data returned from the server. The Strategy class is also a base class and we interact with subclasses of it. There are numerous subclasses we can use, such as `Strategy.BBOX` and `Strategy.Cluster`. Unlike the Protocol and Format classes, where we can use only one of the subclasses for each of those classes, with the Strategy class we can use multiple strategies together.

To clarify, let's look at what the `Strategy.BBOX` class does. The Strategy class is used to set up requests and determine what to do with the response. The `Strategy.BBOX` class is one subclass that handles the first part. Using a WFS server, for example, we can use the `Strategy.BBOX` class to send a request to the server that asks only for data within the viewable map extent. So, the BBOX class determines how to set up the request.

Another thing the Strategy class does is control what happens to the data returned from the server. Using a class like `Strategy.Cluster`, when the layer gets back the data it will group the returned data together in clusters. Therefore, it helps to control what happens with the results of the response to the server.

We can use the BBOX class and Cluster classes together—i.e., set up the layer to ask a WFS server for data within the map's extent, then the layer receives the data which it will turn it into clusters.

How these three classes interact

Now, you might have started to get an idea how these classes interact. The **Protocol** class determines that the data is communicated to and from the client. That data is in some format which is serialized and de-serialized by the **Format** class. Finally, the **Strategy** class tells the Vector class how to set up the request to the server and what to do with the response.

Example instantiation

Before we dive into examples or further discussion, let's take a look at how we could create a vector layer using all these three classes. The following will load in feature data from a GeoJSON file. The file must be located on the same server—if it's on a different server, or if you wish to point to an external URL, you'll need a proxy host (which we'll cover later).

```
var vector_layer = new OpenLayers.Layer.Vector('More Advanced Vector
Layer',{
    protocol: new OpenLayers.Protocol.HTTP({
       url: 'some_data.json',
       format: new OpenLayers.Format.GeoJSON({})
  }),
  strategies: [new OpenLayers.Strategy.Fixed()]
});
```

The above code would use the **HTTP** Protocol class and use the **GeoJSON** format. Notice how the format is actually part of the protocol object. The **Fixed** Strategy class is also used, which essentially just causes the vector layer to request features once and never request new features again.

That's actually pretty much all there is to it! Different formats would use a different `Format` class, and if you wanted to use other strategies you'd simply pass them into the strategies array.

That's a lot to take in. Let's go through two examples which show how to use these three classes together.

Time for Action – creating a Vector Layer

In this first example, we'll use the code similar to what we just saw above—making use of all three classes to build our vector layer, which will request data from a URL.

There are two caveats to this example. The first is that it assumes you have a file called `ex5_data.json` in the same directory as your map file. You can find it in this book's source code files at `http://vasir.net/openlayers_book/files/`.

Secondly, unless you are running this on a server, it won't work. It will need a proxy host, which we'll cover right after this example. If you do not have access to a server, you can view the example in action at the URL above.

1. Start a new map file using the base template from Chapter 1. We'll use the Protocol, Format, and Strategy classes. So first, let's create objects for each of them. Let's start with the format object, as the protocol object will use it. We'll use the GeoJSON format.

```
//Create a Format object
var vector_format = new OpenLayers.Format.GeoJSON({});
```

2. Now, let's create a protocol object using the format object just created:

```
var vector_protocol = new OpenLayers.Protocol.HTTP({
    url: 'ex5_data.json',
    format: vector_format
});
```

3. Finally, we'll create a strategy variable to use which will actually be an array of the strategy object.

```
var vector_strategies = [new OpenLayers.Strategy.Fixed()];
```

4. Now, put that together to create the vector layer and add it to the map:

```
//Create a vector layer that contains a Format, Protocol, and
Strategy class
vector_layer = new OpenLayers.Layer.Vector('More Advanced Vector
Layer',{
    protocol: vector_protocol,
    strategies: vector_strategies
});

map.addLayer(vector_layer);
```

5. If you are running this on a server, you can open up the page and you should see something like:

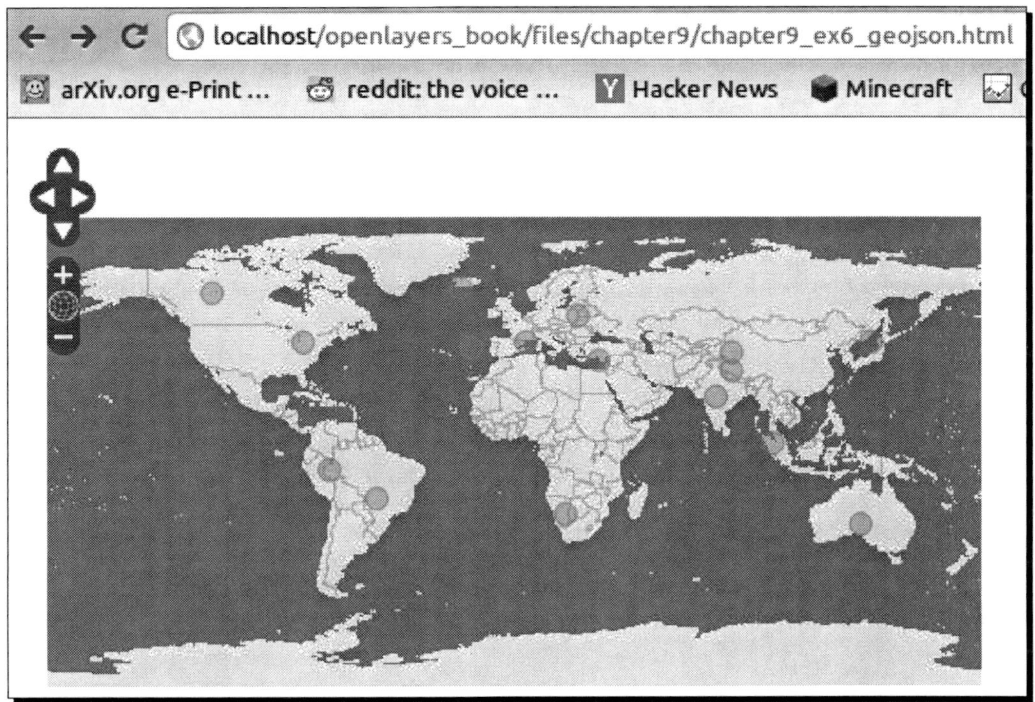

What Just Happened?

We just demonstrated how to set up a vector layer using **Format**, **Protocol**, and **Strategy** classes. If we wanted to use a, say, KML file, we would just use the `Format.KML` class and change the URL to point to a KML file.

Now, the previous example will not work if you are just running it from a folder—it needs to be on a server. Setting up a server is outside the scope of this book, but let's talk about why the previous example doesn't work if you just open it from a folder.

Cross server requests

JavaScript uses an `XMLHttpRequest` to make AJAX requests. When using the `Protocol` classes, OpenLayers makes an `XMLHttpRequest` to get the feature data from the URL. If that data file is on a different server than your map, the request will not work. JavaScript has security restrictions in place that prevent it from making these sort of cross domain requests. So, to get around this, we have to use a **proxy**. Other layer classes do not need to do this because other raster layers request images, but do not use AJAX—so the cross domain request restrictions do not apply.

Using a proxy host

A **proxy** will, essentially, make the requests to external servers instead of having JavaScript do it. We set up a proxy host with some server side script (using python, php, cgi, and so on) that will sit on our server in between our JavaScript code and external servers, so the JavaScript can (by using the proxy) talk to external servers and get around the inherent security restriction.

So, basically, JavaScript will send requests to the proxy host, and the proxy host will make external requests for JavaScript. You can write the proxy script yourself (which isn't recommended unless you really know what you're doing), or use the standard proxy host CGI file from OpenLayers. You can find it at `http://trac.osgeo.org/openlayers/browser/trunk/openlayers/examples/proxy.cgi`.

Once you have the proxy script set up on your server, you will need to tell OpenLayers to use a proxy host to make external requests. To do this, put the following in your code:

```
OpenLayers.ProxyHost = '/cgi-bin/proxy.cgi?url=';
```

You will need to replace the URL with the URL to your proxy script—this code assumes that you are using standard apache settings and are using the `proxy.cgi` file.

This step is not required for the previous example. If you have a server, running the previous example then the server does not require the use of a proxy host, as the data file is on the same server.

Using the Vector Layer without a Protocol class

If you desire to just load data from some data source, for most use cases, the standard Protocol / Format / Strategy usage we just covered will work well. However, you do not have to use those three classes together. The classes can be used somewhat independently.

For example, we could use the **Clustering** class to cluster our point data without using the Format or Protocol classes. We could use the Format class outside our vector layer to read from and output feature data in a variety of different formats.

Time for Action – using the Format and Strategy classes alone

Let's take a look at another example now. Here, we'll do something very similar to what we did in the first example—this time, however, we won't use the Protocol. Instead, we'll read in feature data as a JavaScript object and, using the GeoJSON Format class, read in the data. This way, this example *will* work without having to use a server or proxy host.

1. Create a new page using the template in Chapter 1. We'll be doing three things here—creating some feature data in GeoJSON format, creating a vector layer, and loading the GeoJSON data into it. Let's create some basic feature data. Feel free to play around with the coordinates and amount of features here:

```
var feature_data = {
            "type": "FeatureCollection",
            "features": [
                {"type":"Feature","properties":{},
"geometry":{"type":"Point", "coordinates":[-81, 42]}},
                {"type":"Feature","properties":{},
"geometry":{"type":"Point", "coordinates":[-82, 43]}},
                {"type":"Feature","properties":{},
"geometry":{"type":"Point", "coordinates":[-80, 41]}},
                {"type":"Feature","properties":{},
"geometry":{"type":"Point", "coordinates":[19, -24]}},
                {"type":"Feature","properties":{},
"geometry":{"type":"Point", "coordinates":[4, 42]}},
                {"type":"Feature","properties":{},
"geometry":{"type":"Point", "coordinates":[32, 35]}},
            ]
        }
```

2. Now, we need to create a format object to use for the `feature_object` we just created. **JSON** stands for 'JavaScript Object Notation' and **GeoJSON** is just JSON with geographic information associated with it. More information about GeoJSON can be found at `http://geojson.org/geojson-spec.html`. The data you see above is, more or less, what is in the data file from the previous example. Let's create a GeoJSON format object:

```
Create a format object var format_geojson = new OpenLayers.Format.
GeoJSON({});
```

3. Now, let's create a clustering strategy that will group points together if they fall within some distance of each other. By default, the distance is `20`—let's change it to `42`.

```
      //Create an array of strategy objects
      var vector_strategies = [new OpenLayers.Strategy.
Cluster({distance:42})];
```

4. Let's now create and add the vector layer and pass in the strategy object we just created. We don't need to pass in a protocol or format object, because our vector layer won't directly use the format object, and won't use a protocol object at all.

```
//Create a vector layer that contains a Format, Protocol, and
Strategy class
```

```
vector_layer = new OpenLayers.Layer.Vector('More Advanced Vector
Layer',{
    strategies: vector_strategies
});
```

5. Finally, we'll use the format object to read in the `feature_data` object (de-serialize it) and add the features to our vector layer.

```
//Load in the data
vector_layer.addFeatures(format_geojson.read(feature_data));
```

6. Take a look at the map. You should see three points, even though we created six. This is because the clustering strategy has grouped some of the points together.

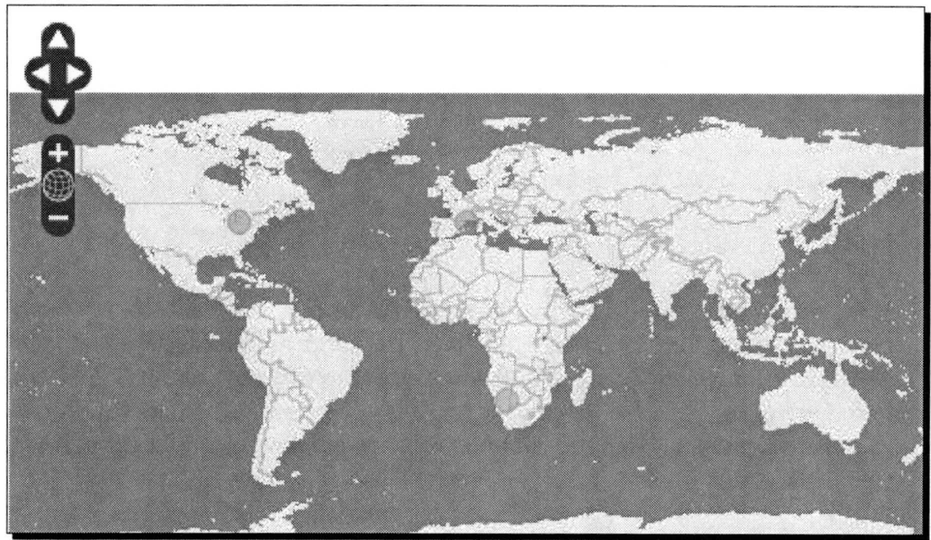

What Just Happened?

We just used the `Format.GeoJSON` class and `Strategy.Cluster` class without using the `Protocol` class. Hard coding the data, we used the `read` method of the format object to load in data and deserialize it, turning it into an array of features that we add with `addFeatures`.

If you open up Firebug and take a look at the vector layer's features (`map.layers[1].features` for example), you'll notice there are only three features listed. But we passed in six features—why is this? Since we used the `Cluster` strategy, features that are close together get clustered together and turned into a single feature. We can, however, still access the clustered features by accessing the `cluster` object of each feature (e.g., `map.layers[0].features[0].cluster`).

Now that we have a hold on how to use these classes, let's finish up by talking just a little more about the **Format** and **Strategy** classes.

Format class

The Format class is used to serialize and deserialize feature data. There are just two properties, a few methods, and a list of valid subclasses we should quickly cover.

Format class properties

You'll often run into a situation where you have a data file that is in a different projection than your map. For instance, if you are using a spherical Mercator projection for your map and the data is in EPSG:4326, you'll need to set the following two properties so that OpenLayers can transform the projection.

- `externalProjection: {OpenLayers.Projection}` This specifies the projection that the data is in.
- `internalProject: {OpenLayers.Projection}` This specifies the projection that the map (or the geometries that will be returned) is in.

By default, you can only use the spherical Mercator and EPSG:4326 projections. If you wish to use a different projection, you will need to include the Proj4js library, which was covered in more detail in Chapter 4.

Format class methods

There are two primary methods that all subclasses share.

- `read(data)`: Deserializes passed in data. There are other parameters that differ between subclasses. The return type also differs, but is often an array of feature objects.
- `write(features)`: Serializes passed in features and returns a string. The returned string will be in whatever format the format object is in—i.e., if you are using a KML format object, the returned string will be in a valid KML format.

Most subclasses extend the above methods, allowing more parameters to be passed in. Full coverage is outside the scope of this book, but can be found in the docs at `http://dev.openlayers.org/docs/files/OpenLayers/Format-js.html`.

Format subclasses

There are a myriad of subclasses available to us. Because new formats are often added, check the docs for a complete up to date list. At the time of writing, valid subclasses were:

ArcXML, Atom, GeoJSON, GeoRSS, GPX, JSON, KML, OSM, OWSContext, SOSCapabilities, Text, WFS, WKT, WMSGetFeatureInfo, WMTSCapabilities, XML

Strategy class

The strategy class is used to determine how the vector layer will request data and what it does with the feature data. Strategies can be used together—for example, the `BBOX` and `Cluster` strategies can be both used at the same time. Each subclass is quite different from each other, so let's take a look at each of the subclasses.

Strategy.BBOX

This class is used to display data that is within the map's extent. When used with the WFS protocol, it will set up the request to grab only the data that falls within the map's extent. If you are working with a lot of feature data, using the BBOX strategy will be quite helpful, as you'll only get back the data that is within the visible extent. This is possible only with some sort of feature server though—a static file won't know what to do with the requests passed in map extent, and will always return back every feature which the static file contains.

Strategy.Cluster

This will cluster features together based on a `distance` and optional `threshold` parameter. Features in the vector layer's feature list will be replaced with cluster features, and each cluster contains all of its features' information in a `cluster` object property.

The `distance` property specifies an {`Integer`} pixel distance between clusters. If a point falls within the distance, it is added to the cluster. Default value is `20`.

The `threshold` property is an optional property which determines whether or not features will be clustered depending on how many features are found. By this, if the `threshold` is set at `4`, it means that at least four features must be found to create a cluster. If there are three features that fall within the `distance`, then they will not be clustered as they don't meet the `threshold` value.

Strategy.Filter

The **Strategy.Filter** class is used to limit features that get added to the vector layer. It uses the **OpenLayers.Filter** class to do comparisons on feature data. To use this strategy, you must create a **OpenLayers.Filter** object, which is covered in detail in the next chapter.

Strategy.Fixed

This strategy is used to request features once and never request them again. There is a `preload` property that will load data before the layer is visible, which is `false` by default. If set to `true`, data will be loaded before features are drawn, but can slow down your map.

Strategy.Paging

Using this strategy, features can be grouped into 'pages,' which means you'll receive groups of your data. If you have tons of data, this is a very useful strategy. There is a `length` property which takes in an `{Integer}` which specifies the number of features per page. The default value is `10`.

Another property, `num`, contains an `{Integer}` of the current page number. To use this strategy, you will need to call the `pageNext()` and `pagePrevious()` methods to advance through the pages.

Strategy.Refresh

This strategy will refresh the vector layer, causing features to be re-requested and redrawn. It can be called manually, or an interval can be set and it will refresh at the passed in interval.

The `interval` property is a `{Float}` in milliseconds which, if set to a number greater than 0, specifies how often to automatically refresh the vector layer. By default, it is set to `0`, and will not automatically refresh.

There is a `force` property as well, which will force the layer to be refreshed. It is set to `false` by default.

There are a few relevant methods to use:

- **refresh()**: Causes the layer to be refreshed
- **reset()**: Resets the timing interval (if set)
- **start()**: Begins the auto-refresh behavior based on the `interval` property
- **stop()**: Ends the auto-refresh

Strategy.Save

Using this strategy, features can be saved to a server. The server must allow saving, such as a WFS server using transactions. When the `save()` method is called, changes will be attempted to be saved to the server.

There is also an `auto` property which can be set to a {`Boolean`} or {`Float`} (in seconds). If set to `true`, which will save immediately after the features are modified (or deleted). If set to a number, the features will be saved at the passed in interval.

Summary

This ends the chapter on the Vector Layer class. We talked about what the Vector Layer class is and how it works. We also went over the properties, methods, and events of Vector Layer class and demonstrated them with examples. The Feature and Geometry classes were also covered, along with their properties and methods. Lastly, we learned about the Strategy, Protocol, and Format classes and how to create a vector layer with them.

In the next chapter, we'll work more with the Vector Layer. We'll learn how to style our Vector layers, along with learning how to use the Rule and Filter classes to give us complete control over how our vector layer looks.

10
Vector Layer Style Guide

At this point, you're hopefully getting pretty comfortable with OpenLayers. We've talked about how to customize the appearance of Controls (UI elements), but we haven't talked much about how to customize the appearance of the map itself.

In this chapter, we'll make things look pretty (more or less). We'll:

- Learn how to style Vector layers in OpenLayers
- Discuss the Style class and demonstrate how to use it
- Go over the StyleMap class
- Work with the Rules class
- Learn about the Filter class

Let's get to it!

Styling the Vector Layer

In the last chapter, you saw how powerful the vector layer can be. In this chapter, we'll go a bit deeper and talk about how to customize the appearance of the features within your vector layer. The way vector layer styling works is similar to how we customized the appearance of our control objects, but instead of using CSS, we use **Style** and **StyleMap** objects with the vector layer. We can style the vector layer this way because the vector layer does not use raster images—it uses SVG (or Canvas or VML) elements that can be styled, similar to how HTML elements can be styled with CSS.

Changing the feature styles, such as changing the color of our features from the default orange to blue, is quite easy. But changing colors of a vector layer's features is perhaps just one of the most basic things we can do. By using the **Rule** and **Filter** classes, we can specify *how* (and what) features should be styled. For example, we could color points differently depending on their geographic location or depending on the values of properties contained in their `attributes`.

We can do much more than just modify colors. We can change the sizes, opacities, line styles, and a variety of other properties. Style properties can be set arbitrarily, or be based on properties of individual feature objects themselves.

Applying styles

We can do a lot, but how? There are three different ways to apply styles to a vector layer.

- Use the StyleMap and Style objects.
- Apply a symbolizer (an anonymous object with style properties) directly to the layer.
- Apply a symbolizer directly on a feature. This primarily only occurs when reading in data from a source like a KML file.

The first way is what we'll be using throughout this chapter. A **StyleMap** is, essentially, a mapping of **Style** objects to various 'states', or **intents**, of feature objects. For example, the `default` intent is what a feature object is normally set as. When you select it, it then receives the `select` intent, and any styles mapped to that intent.

The **Style** object contains a style symbolizer, or numerous style properties and values. We use symbolizers to define style, and we can use symbolizers on Style objects, directly on layer objects, or directly on an individual feature.

What are symbolizers?

A **symbolizer** is just an an anonymous object consisting of `key:value` pairs that contains style properties, similar to CSS. For example, { `fillColor: '#336699', strokeWidth: 4` } is a symbolizer which tells the feature to have a fill color of `#336699` (light blue), and a stroke width of `4` pixels. We'll cover a full list of valid properties later in this chapter.

We use symbolizers when we create **Style** objects to specify the style properties to apply to our features. We can apply a symbolizer directly to the vector layer object, or read in style information from a source file (such as a KML file).

Before we dive into the **StyleMap** and **Style** classes, let's first take a look at an example so we can better wrap our heads around what we intend to do in this chapter.

Time For Action – applying some basic Styling

Applying styles is pretty easy, as you'll see:

1. We'll be doing a few things in this example. First, we'll create a vector layer. Then, we'll add some features to it. Nothing new so far. Then, we'll style the layer by creating a StyleMap and Style object and applying them to the vector layer.

2. Add a WMS layer to the map (like in previous chapters) then create and add a vector layer to the map:

```
vector_layer = new OpenLayers.Layer.Vector('Basic Vector Layer');
map.addLayer(vector_layer);
```

3. Let's add some feature points. We'll create a loop which will create ten randomly placed feature objects and add them to the vector layer. These coordinates will be different each time you refresh the page, as they are being randomly generated:

```
for(var i=0; i<10; i++){
    vector_layer.addFeatures([new OpenLayers.Feature.Vector(
        new OpenLayers.Geometry.Point(
            (Math.floor(Math.random() * 360) - 180),
            (Math.floor(Math.random() * 180) - 90)
        )
    )]);
}
```

4. Now, let's add some style to our vector layer. We'll be using a **StyleMap** object and apply a style to the 'default' intent (the 'normal state' of the features) so all features will receive the style. First, we'll need to create a **Style** object which will be used by the **StyleMap** object that gets applied to the layer. The Style object consists of a **symbolizer**, as we previously mentioned, that contains `key:value` pairs of styles to apply to the features (similar to CSS):

```
var vector_style = new OpenLayers.Style({
    'fillColor': '#669933',
    'fillOpacity': .8,
    'strokeColor': '#aaee77',
    'strokeWidth': 3,
    'pointRadius': 8
});
```

5. Next, we create a StyleMap object and use the Style object we just created to define the layer's 'default' intent style.

```
var vector_style_map = new OpenLayers.StyleMap({
    'default': vector_style
});
```

6. Finally, we set the StyleMap object to the vector layer.

```
vector_layer.styleMap = vector_style_map;
```

7. You should see a bunch of green dots similar to the following. The actual point locations will be different for you, as the points are randomly generated:

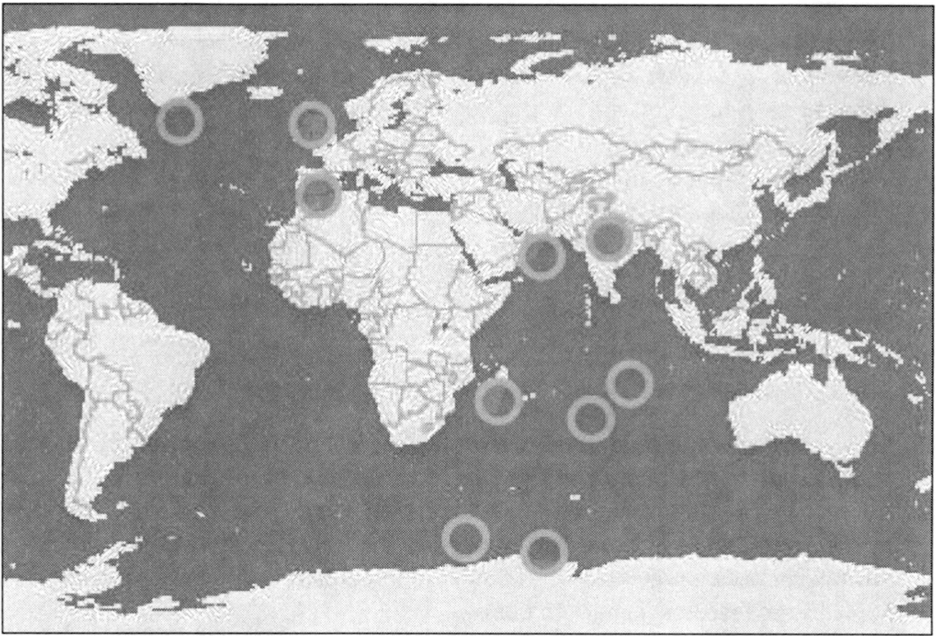

What Just Happened?

We just used the StyleMap and Style classes to apply a custom style to our vector layer. The Style object we created (the `vector_style` object) contains properties which determine what the features will look like. If you were to create an empty style object (with no `key:value` pairs, just an empty set of brackets `{}`), no styles would be applied to the layer—you would be overwriting the default style with a blank, empty style.

We only used a few symbolizer properties, such as `strokeColor`, but we'll go over a full list of valid symbolizer properties later in this chapter. For now, let's first talk more about how the StyleMap and Style classes work.

The StyleMap class

The **StyleMap** class tells the vector layer what **Style** objects to use when the features are in a certain 'state', or what OpenLayers refers to as **intent**. As the previous example showed, there's really not much in using this class. To create a **StyleMap** object you pass in an **intent** as the key (as a `{String}`), and a **Style** object is used as the value. For example, as in the previous example, `'default'` is the desired intent and the `vector_style` object is the desired style object to use for that intent. This causes the `vector_style` to be applied to the `'default'` intent:

```
var vector_style_map = new OpenLayers.StyleMap( {'default': vector_
style} );
```

What is an 'intent'?

The 'intent', short for **render intent**, is a way to specify how features should be drawn, or what features should look like when in different 'states'. There are only three default intents we can use:

- `'default'`: This is the intent used most of the time. If a feature is not in the two next intents, it is in this 'default' intent.
- `'select'`: Features are in this intent only when they are selected. When unselected, they return to the 'default' intent.
- `'temporary'`: This intent is used when features are being drawn or 'sketched'; e.g., via the EditingToolbar control. When the feature is finished being sketched, it is returned to the 'default' intent.

When creating a StyleMap object, if you specify a style object for only one intent, then all intents will receive that style object.

For instance, in the previous example, we applied a style object only to the default intent—because we applied it to only one intent, all other intents receive that style. If we were to select one of the features, we would see no changes in the feature's style because we did not specify a separate `'select'` intent style object.

The Style class

The **Style** class is used to specify the styles a vector layer should use. As mentioned a couple of times before, it's quite similar in principle to how we use CSS to style our controls. The difference is that with the vector layer we are directly embedding the style in the JavaScript code itself, using an anonymous object which is referred to as a **symbolizer**.

When we talk about symbolizers, we're just referring to an anonymous object that defines styles (or, by some stretch, their 'symbol'). The term 'symbolizer' is maybe not the best term that could have been used, but it's part of the OpenLayers vocabulary so we need to learn it.

To create a Style object, we just pass in a symbolizer (an anonymous object) that defines the layer's style. As in the previous example:

```
var vector_style = new OpenLayers.Style({
    'fillColor': '#669933',
    'fillOpacity': .8,
    'strokeColor': '#aaee77',
    'strokeWidth': 3,
    'pointRadius': 8
});
```

That's essentially all there is to it for creating a style object! A `context` property can also be specified, which can be used to provide additional variables to be used for the style class with **attribute replacement**—we'll talk about that soon.

After creating our style object, we can then use it with a StyleMap object. We could also apply the symbolizer (but not the `vector_style` object itself) to the layer's `style` property and 'skip' the StyleMap object step—although, it is recommend that you do it this way, as it's a bit limiting and it's not as 'clean' or modular as using a StyleMap object.

Rules and **filters** can also be applied to our style objects to get even more fine grain control over feature styles, as we'll see soon. First, let's go over the valid symbolizer properties.

Symbolizer properties

The following properties can be used when creating a style symbolizer. Some properties will only affect certain types of geometries (e.g., the `font` type properties apply only to `text` features). We'll go over some of the more common symbolizer properties first, and then cover the remaining properties.

List of common symbolizer properties

- **cursor**: The cursor style to use when the mouse is over a feature. Can be any valid CSS cursor style, such as `help`, `move`, `cursor`, `crosshair`, `text`, `wait`, `pointer`, or `progress`.
- **fillColor**: Color of the fill area, a six digit RGB value. Example: `#000000` would be black (`00` red, `00` green, and `00` blue.) `#ffffff` would be white.

- **fillOpacity**: Specifies the opacity of the filled area, ranging from `0` to `1` (`1` being fully opaque, `0` being fully transparent).
- **fontColor**: The font color, a six digit RGB value. Example: `#000000` would be black (`00` red, `00` green, and `00` blue.) `#ffffff` would be white.
- **fontFamily**: Specifies the font family to use for labels. Similar to the CSS `font-family` property. An example value would be `Arial` or `sans-serif`.
- **fontOpacity**: Opacity of font, ranging from `0` to `1` (`1` being fully opaque, `0` being fully transparent).
- **fontSize**: Specifies the size of the font. Can be any valid font-size CSS value, such as in pixels (e.g., `'18px'`) or em units (e.g., `'1.2em'`).
- **fontWeight**: The font weight to be applied. Can be a valid CSS font-weight property, such as `normal` or `bold`.
- **graphicName**: Specifies the type of the graphic to use when rendering points. The default value is `'circle'`, and will cause points to be rendered as circles. Other possible values include `'square'`, `'star'`, `'x'`, `'cross'`, and `'triangle'`. Other styles, such as fill and stroke properties, will still be applied to the type of shape drawn. For example, `'graphicName': 'square'` will produce a square for points instead of a circle.
- **label**: Text to apply to a feature. The value of this property is a `{String}` type, for example, `label: 'My Label'`.
- **labelAlign**: Determines where to align the label (if one is provided). Unlike the `align` property in CSS, the `labelAlign` property takes in one or two characters, one for horizontal alignment and one for vertical alignment. The possible horizontal values are 'l' (left), 'c' (center), and 'r' (right). Possible vertical values are are 't' (top), 'm' (middle), and 'b' (bottom). The alignment refers to a point relative to where the text would be, which means a 't' (top) alignment would actually put the label at the bottom, since the insertion point is to the top of the text (a little confusing, but it might help to think of the alignment as 'opposite' of where you want the labels to be). A valid value is any single or two letter combinations of the horizontal and vertical values—such as 'r' (right) or 'lb' (left bottom).
- **labelSelect**: If set to `true`, labels can also be selected with the `selectFeature` control. Default value is `false`.
- **labelXOffset**: How far, in the X direction, to offset the label (in pixels).
- **labelYOffset**: How far, in the Y direction, to offset the label (in pixels).
- **pointRadius**: Specifies how large, in pixels, the radius of point features will be. Default value is `6`.
- **stroke**: Specifies whether to show a stroke. Set to `false` if you wish to have no stroke shown.

- **strokeColor**: Color of the stroke, a six digit RGB value. Example: `#000000` would be black (`00` red, `00` green, and `00` blue.) `#ffffff` would be white.
- **strokeDashstyle**: Type of style applied to the strokes. Can be either `'dot'`, `'dash'`, `'dashdot'`, `'longdash'`, `'longdashdot'`, or `'solid'`.
- **strokeLinecap**: The type style to be applied to the line caps. Can be either `'but'`, `'round'`, `'square'`.
- **strokeOpacity**: Opacity of strokes, ranging from `0` to `1` (`1` being fully opaque, `0` being fully transparent).
- **strokeWidth**: Stroke width, in pixels.

Time for Action – common style examples

Let's take a look at what some of these common properties do through an example. We'll also demonstrate how to use two different intents—the `default` intent and the `selected` intent.

1. Make a copy of the previous example's file. We'll be using the same code, but modifying the feature styles a bit. We'll also use the `select` intent, so we'll need two style objects. Let's first recreate the default style object:

```
var vector_style = new OpenLayers.Style({
    'cursor': 'pointer',
    'fillColor': '#787878',
    'fillOpacity': .8,
    'fontColor': '#343434',
    'pointRadius': 14,
    'strokeColor': '#232323',
    'strokeDashstyle': 'dot',
    'strokeWidth': 3
});
```

2. Now, let's create a style object to use when the feature is selected. We'll change the border to solid, change the fill color, increase the point's radius a little bit, change the `graphicName` to `'square'`, and add a label that will display 'X'.

```
var vector_style_select = new OpenLayers.Style({
    'fillColor': '#ffffff',
    'fillOpacity': .9,
    'graphicName': 'square',
    'label': 'X',
    'pointRadius': 16,
    'strokeColor': '#343434',
    'strokeDashstyle': 'solid',
```

```
    'strokeWidth': 4
});
```

3. Update the StyleMap object now to include the newly added `vector_style_select` style object:

```
var vector_style_map = new OpenLayers.StyleMap({
    'default': vector_style,
    'select': vector_style_select
});
```

4. Finally, we'll just add a `selectFeature` control that will allow us to select a feature.

```
//Add a select feature control
var select_feature_control = new OpenLayers.Control.SelectFeature(
    vector_layer
);
map.addControl(select_feature_control);
//Activate the control
select_feature_control.activate();
```

5. Now, take a look at the map and select a feature. You should see the style change:

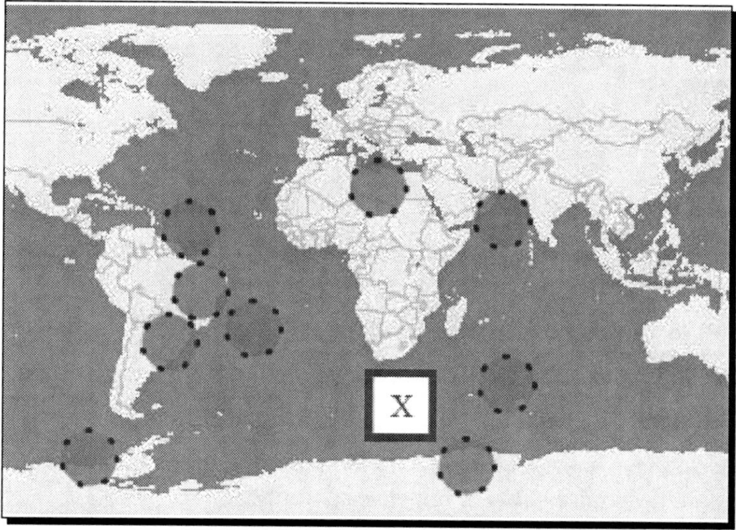

What Just Happened?

We practiced using common symbolizer properties and demonstrated how to add multiple Style objects to a StyleMap object with two intents. So far, you might not be too impressed. We've styled some features, and while there's a ton of customization we can do, we haven't done anything too fancy yet.

Have a Go Hero – style layers

Now that you're a little more familiar with how to use symbolizers, open up the previous example and change some of the symbolizers. Test different property and value combinations—different colors, opacities, background colors, etc. See if you can come up with something that looks a little better than grey and black circles.

Before we go into attribute replacement, our next topic, let's look at the remaining symbolizer properties we haven't covered yet.

Remaining symbolizer properties

- **backgroundGraphic**: Specifies the URL of an image to use. This will be placed under the `externalGraphic` (if one is set).
- **backgroundGraphicZIndex**: Specifies the z-index (order of what gets placed on each other) of the `backgroundGraphic`.
- **backgroundHeight**: Determines the height of the background image. If none is specified, `graphicHeight` is used.
- **backgroundWidth**: Height of the background image, if one exists. If this property is not set and an image is provided, the `graphicHeight` property will be tried to use.
- **backgroundXOffset**: Specifies how far, in the X direction, to offset the image (in pixels).
- **backgroundYOffset**: Specifies how far, in the Y direction, to offset the image (in pixels).
- **display**: If set to `none`, the symbolizer styles will not be applied.
- **externalGraphic**: Specifies the URL of an image to use (instead of the stroke and fill properties) when feature points are shown.
- **fill**: If set to `false`, no fill will be shown.
- **graphic**: Setting to `false` will disable any graphics from being shown.
- **graphicHeight**: The height, in pixels, of an external graphic (if it exists).
- **graphicOpacity**: Specifies the opacity of associated graphic, ranging from `0` to `1` (`1` being fully opaque, `0` being fully transparent).
- **graphicTitle**: This specifies tooltip text that will appear when mousing over an external graphic (if one is provided).
- **graphicWidth**: The width, in pixels, of an external graphic (if it exists).
- **graphicXOffset**: How far, in the X direction, to offset the external graphic (in pixels).
- **graphicYOffset**: How far, in the Y direction, to offset the external graphic (in pixels).

- **graphicZIndex**: Specifies the z-index of the external graphic. A higher z-index means it will appear over elements with lower z-indexes.
- **rotation**: Specifies how much to rotate a feature in a clockwise direction around its center. Values range from `0` to `360`, default is `0`. A value of `180` would be upside down.

Pop Quiz – determining which attributes to use

There are two ways we can specify an image: using the `background` or using the `externalGraphic` properties. When using them together, it is important to keep in mind how each of them work. If we want to show an image of a marker, and a separate image of the marker's shadow, how would we do it?

Attribute replacement

One easy, but powerful, thing we can do with feature styles is called **attribute replacement**. It's a way to use a feature's attributes in the layer's style definition, like a variable. When creating the symbolizer, you can set the value of any property in a format of:

```
${variable_name}
```

Where `variable_name` is the name of a property contained in a feature's `attributes` property. For example, let's say all our features have an attribute property called `'size'` with random integer values. If we wanted to assign the `pointRadius` to each feature's `size` property, we would use:

```
{ 'pointRadius': ${size} }
```

What happens then is that when each feature is styled, the `${size}` is replaced by the feature's `attribute.size` property (if one exists). The best way to further explain this is through an example. Let's take a look, then go even further in depth.

Time For Action – working with attribute replacement

Let's demonstrate how to use attribute replacement to change the style of features based on their attribute.

1. Make a copy of the previous example. We'll be changing it slightly to demonstrate attribute replacement. To do so, we'll first need to give our features some attributes that we can access. Modify the `addFeature` code in the `for` loop to add attributes as follows:

```
for(var i=0; i<10; i++){
    vector_layer.addFeatures([new OpenLayers.Feature.Vector(
```

```
            new OpenLayers.Geometry.Point(
                (Math.floor(Math.random() * 360) - 180),
                (Math.floor(Math.random() * 180) - 90)
            ),
            {
                //Attributes go here
                size: 5 + (Math.floor(Math.random() * 20)),
                label: 'F' + i,
                strokeWidth: (Math.floor(Math.random() * 10))
            }
        )]);
    }
```

2. Now, we just need to modify the `vector_style` style object to include attribute replacements so we can use the `size`, `label`, and `strokeWidth` properties of the features we just created. The syntax to do so is `'${variable_name}'`, where `variable_name` is the name of the feature property we want to use. Modify the `vector_style` object as follows, changing the `label`, `pointRadius`, `strokeDashStyle`, and `strokeWidth`:

```
var vector_style = new OpenLayers.Style({
    'cursor': 'pointer',
    'fillColor': '#787878',
    'fillOpacity': .8,
    'fontColor': '#343434',
    'label': '${label}',
    'pointRadius': '${size}',
    'strokeColor': '#232323',
    'strokeDashstyle': 'solid',
    'strokeWidth': '${strokeWidth}'
});
```

3. Open the map. We used randomized values, so when you refresh your map you should see something different each time. You should see something similar to this, but with different point locations and sizes:

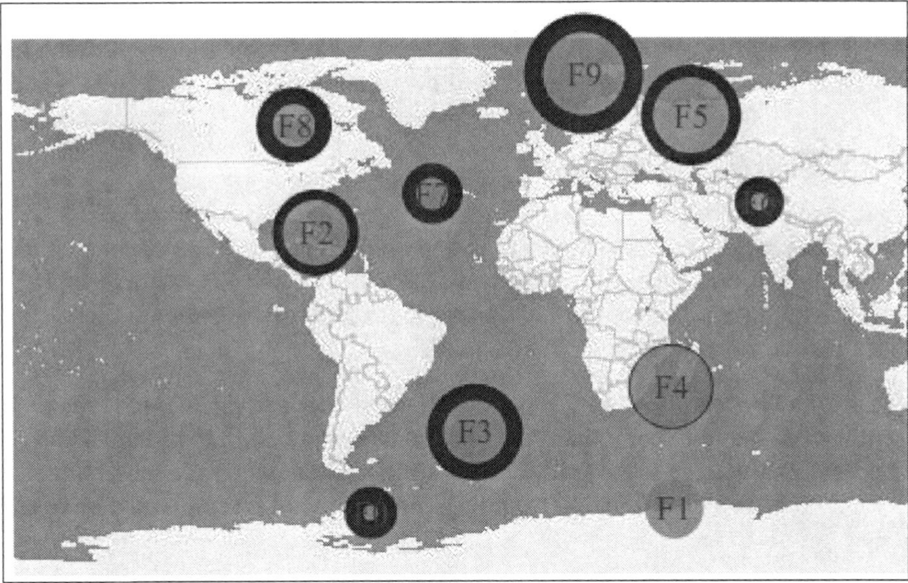

What Just Happened?

We just demonstrated how to use attribute replacement when creating our styles. Changing the point radius for features based on attributes is a fairly common practice, but as you've seen we're not just limited to a few properties—we can change any of the properties using attribute replacement. This can be quite powerful, and we'll be using it throughout the rest of this book. However, attribute replacement is just the tip of the iceberg.

Rules and filters

For even more fine grained control, we can style objects by using the **Rule** and **Filter** classes. These two classes allow us to apply different styles to different features based on some arbitrary 'rules' we choose. We can use the feature's `attributes` property to apply certain styles if one (or more) of the properties match some value we choose.

How do we follow rules?

Rules allow us to apply symbolizers when certain conditions occur. Those conditions are handled via the **Filter** class. We can have multiple rules and filters, and even use logical operators (such as OR and AND) with them. Before we talk about that though, there are two ways we can use rules.

The first is by using the `addUniqueValueRules` method of the StyleMap class. This allows simple property matching and is fairly straightforward to use. We'll go over this method first.

The second way, using custom rule and filter objects, is a bit complicated, but allows us snowflake level control over what styles get applied. We'll cover this, along with the Rule and Filter classes themselves, after we discuss how to use `addUniqueValueRules`.

Using addUniqueValueRules

The easiest way to use rules is to use the `addUniqueValueRules` method of the StyleMap class. It allows us to do a sort of value look-up and apply different styles depending on a property's value. More concretely, let's say we had a bunch of point features which represented settlements. Each feature has an attribute property called `settlement_type`, with values such as 'village', 'city', or 'metropolis'.

Now, let's also say we want to style our points differently depending on what type of settlement it is. We want to color them differently, make the point radius larger, and change the stroke size. We could, in theory, just use attribute replacement and embed these values with each feature, but a more elegant and easy to maintain way would be to use `addUniqueValueRules`.

With this method, we could create three different symbolizers and have the proper styles applied to different settlement types. If the `settlement_type` property's value matches `'village'`, for instance, it would get a certain style, and if it matched `'city'` it would receive a different style, etc. If this explanation was confusing, don't worry, we'll go over it in an example briefly.

Calling the addUniqueValueRules function

First, let's look at the general syntax for calling the `addUniqueValueRules` function:

```
style_map_object.addUniqueValueRules(intent, property, symbolizer_
lookup, context);
```

The intent parameter

The `intent` parameter specifies the desired intent—usually `'default'`.

The property parameter

The second parameter, `property`, is the property of the feature you want to check—e.g., `'settlement_type'` as in our previous explanation.

The symbolizer_lookup parameter

The `symbolizer_lookup` parameter is an anonymous object containing `key:value` pairs to use if the rule matches. The key specifies a value of the passed in `property`, and the value specifies the symbolizer to apply if the property matches that value. It might make a bit more sense to take a look at how it would appear in the code, for example:

```
var symbolizer_lookup = {
  'village': {pointRadius:5, strokeWidth:2},
  'city': {pointRadius:10, strokeWidth:4}
}
```

This applies the `'village'` symbolizer if the feature's `settlement_type` property is `'village'`, and applies the `'city'` style symbolizer if the property is `'city'`. The symbolizers will extend whatever default symbolizers are already associated with the StyleMap object. Lastly, and importantly, if the property you search for contains a value that does not exist in the `symbolizer_object`, the feature will not receive a style. So, it is best to use this function when you know what to expect from the property values—if you don't, you can create custom rules, which we'll cover next.

The context parameter

The last argument, `context`, is an optional (usually not included) object which specifies an anonymous object to check the `property` against. If no `context` is passed in, `features.attributes` are used by default (normally, this is what you want to happen).

Time For Action – using addUniqueValueRules

Now that we know about `addUniqueValueRules`, let's see it in action.

1. We're going to use a basic vector layer with some randomly generated features and `settlement_type` properties. Add a WMS layer. Then, we need a vector layer:

   ```
   vector_layer = new OpenLayers.Layer.Vector('Settlement Vector
   Layer');
   map.addLayer(vector_layer);
   ```

2. Now, let's create an anonymous object consisting of integer values as the keys and our desired `settlement_type` values as the values. We do this because we'll need a way to randomly pick what type of settlement a feature should be.

   ```
   var  settlement_values = {
        0: 'hut',
        1: 'village',
        2: 'city',
        3: 'metropolis',
   ```

```
        4: 'facebook'
    }
```

3. Ok, let's now create 20 random points. Using code similar to the previous example, we'll create twenty random points and assign a random settlement type to each feature using the `settlement_values` object we just created.

```
for(var i=0; i<20; i++){
    vector_layer.addFeatures([new OpenLayers.Feature.Vector(
        new OpenLayers.Geometry.Point(
            (Math.floor(Math.random() * 360) - 180),
            (Math.floor(Math.random() * 180) - 90)
        ),
        {
            'settlement_type': settlement_values[(Math.floor(Math.
random() * 5))]
        }
    )]);
}
```

4. Next, we'll need to create a `StyleMap` object. We won't apply any style objects to any intents this time, we'll just leave it empty. Keep in mind—if you just added an empty `StyleMap` object to your vector layer, you would still see the default layer styles as we haven't overwritten the symbolizers that the intents use.

```
var vector_style_map = new OpenLayers.StyleMap({});
```

5. We're almost ready to call the `addUniqueValueRules` method. Before we do that though, we'll need to create an object that contains symbolizers to use for each value we find. So, we need to create an object that contains a symbolizer for each of the values in `settlement_type`. This object will be the `symbolizer_lookup` object that we previously discussed. Let's go ahead and set up symbolizers for all the values of the `settlement_values` we previously created (feel free to define your own styles here if you'd like):

```
var symbolizers_lookup = {
  'hut': {
    'fillColor': '#ababab', 'fillOpacity':.8, 'pointRadius':4,
'strokeColor': '#454545', 'strokeWidth':2
  },
```

```
  'village': {
    'fillColor': '#FFFA93', 'fillOpacity':.8, 'pointRadius':8,
'strokeColor': '#AFAB57', 'strokeWidth':4
  },
  'city': {
    'fillColor': '#aaee77', 'fillOpacity':.8, 'pointRadius':12,
'strokeColor': '#669933', 'strokeWidth':5
  },
  'metropolis': {
    'fillColor': '#BD1922','fillOpacity':.8,  'pointRadius':16,
'strokeColor': '#812B30', 'strokeWidth':6
  },
  'facebook': {
    'fillColor': '#336699','fillOpacity':.8,  'pointRadius':26,
'strokeColor': '#003366', 'strokeWidth':2
  }
}
```

6. Whew—now we can call the `addUniqueValueRules` function. We'll use the `'default'` intent, as we want to see these styles applied by default. The property we want to use is the `'settlement_type'` property. Finally, we'll pass in the `symbolizer_lookup` object we created above.

   The symbolizers we use in the `symbolizer_lookup` object will also extend whatever style is already applied to the StyleMap—however; in this case, we haven't defined any style objects to use so the symbolizers will just extend the default style. Let's call the function as follows:

   ```
   vector_style_map.addUniqueValueRules('default', 'settlement_type',
   feature_symbolizers_lookup);
   ```

7. Finally, we need to hookup the StyleMap object to our vector layer. We just set the vector layer to use the `vector_style_map` object:

   ```
   vector_layer.styleMap = vector_style_map;
   ```

8. You should now see something like the following on your map. If some point types are missing, don't worry! Since the points are randomly generated, you will sometimes not see certain settlement types—refreshing your map will generate new points:

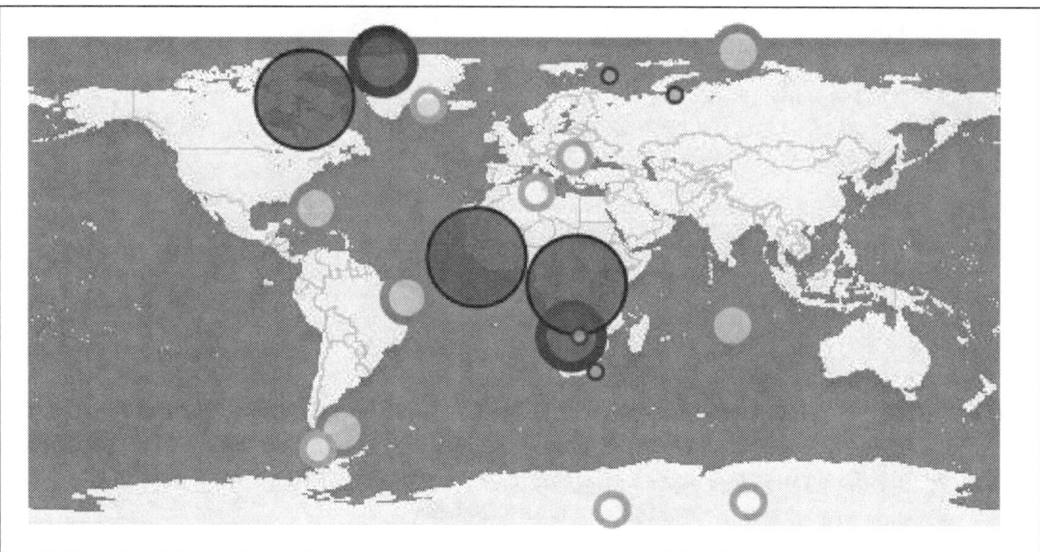

What Just Happened?

We just used a 'shortcut' for creating rules. This doesn't mean that this is something you should avoid doing though. The method is pretty fast, does its job well, and is easy to read and understand. Just keep in mind that if you don't define a symbolizer for a value that gets found, the feature containing that value may not have a style. If you're in the situation where you need to do this sort of property value checking on known values, `addUniqueValueRules` is a good way to solve the problem.

However, there is an even more powerful way to customize styles—by using custom Rules and Filters.

Rules and filters

So far, we've pretty much just been doing a one to one match on properties to specify style. With attribute replacement, we directly replace a value. With `addUniqueValueRules`, we see if a property is equal to something. So far, we haven't had much flexibility.

By using Rules and Filters, we can be as flexible as we want. We can do comparisons on properties, such as styling a feature a certain way if, for instance, it has a property less than or greater than some value. We can create filters to check for a multitude of different types of comparisons (greater than, less than, equal to, etc.), and have filters interact with each other.

How do they work?

A filters object belongs to a rule object. A rule object belongs to a style object. Each style object can have multiple rules, and rules can interact with each other depending on how their filters are defined.

How do we use them?

To use custom rules and filters, we just need to associate them with a style object. The general syntax to define a rule and add it to a style object is:

```
var my_rule = new OpenLayers.Rule({
  filter: new OpenLayers.Filter({}),
  symbolizer: { key:values }
});
style_object.addRules([my_rule]);
```

The filter object determines how the rule will be applied (such as checking to see if a property is greater than some value). We'll cover the Filter class in more detail after an example, as we can do lots of complex things with filters. This may all sound a bit abstract, so let's jump into an example to see how it works, then cover both classes in detail.

Time for Action – using rules and filters

Let's use rules and filters to assign different styles to feature objects based on their attributes.

1. Let's jump in to using rules and filters. Add a WMS layer to the map. We'll also need a vector layer, so add in a vector layer:

```
        vector_layer = new OpenLayers.Layer.Vector('Basic Vector
Layer');
        map.addLayer(vector_layer);
```

2. Next, we'll need some features. We'll generate some random feature points again, and we'll create a property for each object called `population` which contains a random number between 0 and 2000:

```
for(var i=0; i<20; i++){
  vector_layer.addFeatures([new OpenLayers.Feature.Vector(
```

```
    new OpenLayers.Geometry.Point(
      (Math.floor(Math.random() * 360) - 180),
       (Math.floor(Math.random() * 180) - 90)
    ),
    {
      'population': Math.floor(Math.random() * 2000)
    }
  )]);
}
```

3. Now we need to create a style object—rules are applied directly to style objects, and filters are applied directly to rules. So, let's create the objects in order, starting with the style object:

```
var vector_style = new OpenLayers.Style();
```

4. Let's now create three rules. For each rule, we'll pass in an object with two keys: `filter` (which will be a Filter class object) and `symbolizer` (which is a familiar symbolizer object). The filter object will need a filter `type`, which we'll cover after this example, and a `property` which the rule will match on (in this case, `population`). We'll also need to specify the value (or range of values) we want to match for each rule. The value parameter depends on the filter type, and we'll be using either `value` or `lowerBound` and `upperBound`. Let's create the first rule which will handle `population` values less than 500:

```
var rule_pop_low = new OpenLayers.Rule({
  filter: new OpenLayers.Filter.Comparison({
    type: OpenLayers.Filter.Comparison.LESS_THAN,
    property: 'population',
    value: 500
  }),
  symbolizer: {
    fillColor: '#ababab', fillOpacity:.8,
    pointRadius:8, strokeColor: '#454545',
    strokeWidth:2
  }
});
```

5. Now we'll take care of the second rule, which handles `population` values between a `lowerBoundary` of `500` and an `upperBoundary` of `1500`. The boundaries are inclusive; meaning values of `500` and `1500` will be matched. Notice how we don't have a `value` property like in the previous rule—the values here are determined by the two boundary properties:

```
var rule_pop_mid = new OpenLayers.Rule({
  filter: new OpenLayers.Filter.Comparison({
    type: OpenLayers.Filter.Comparison.BETWEEN,
    property: 'population',
    lowerBoundary:500,
    upperBoundary:1500
  }),
  symbolizer: {
    fillColor: '#aaee77', fillOpacity:.8,
    pointRadius:14, strokeColor: '#669933',
    strokeWidth:5
  }
});
```

6. Our last rule will match `population` values above `1500`:

```
var rule_pop_high = new OpenLayers.Rule({
  filter: new OpenLayers.Filter.Comparison({
   type: OpenLayers.Filter.Comparison.GREATER_THAN,
    property: 'population',
    value: 1500
  }),
  symbolizer: {
    fillColor: '#BD1922', fillOpacity:.8,
    pointRadius:20, strokeColor: '#812B30',
    strokeWidth:5
  }
});
```

7. Almost done—now we need to add those three rules to the style object. We pass in an array of the rule objects to the `addRules` method:

```
vector_style.addRules([rule_pop_low, rule_pop_mid, rule_pop_
high]);
```

8. Now create a `styleMap` object and apply the style object to it and set the vector layer to use it:

```
var vector_style_map = new OpenLayers.StyleMap({
    'default': vector_style
});
vector_layer.styleMap = vector_style_map;
```

9. Take a look at the map now. You should see something like this, but with different point locations and colors, as the values were randomized:

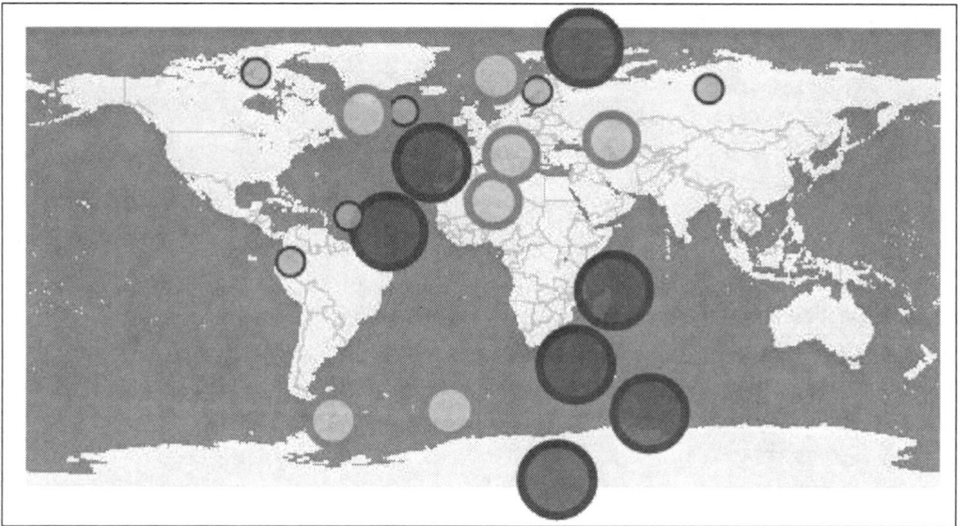

What Just Happened?

We just showed how rules and filters are used. We used three rule objects, each with a different filter object. The `type` property of the filter objects determine the type of comparison that will be applied. So, in the previous example, if a feature had a property of `'population'` with a value less than `500`, the `rule_pop_low` rule would be applied to it. Now that we have a basic understanding of how it's used, let's look more closely at the two classes.

OpenLayers.Rule class

When you want to be very specific about the types of styles that get applied to feature objects, the best way to do it is by using the **Rule** class. When you create a rule object, you specify a **Filter** object, a `symbolizer` to apply to the feature if the rule matches, and an optional `name` property which specifies an arbitrary name for the rule.

Rule objects are applied to style objects, and you can have virtually as many rules on a style object as you want. The syntax for creating a rule object, as mentioned previously, is:

```
var my_rule = new OpenLayers.Rule({
  filter: new OpenLayers.Filter({}),
  symbolizer: { key:values }
});
style_object.addRules([my_rule]);
```

As we saw in the previous example, it's not too hard to create and apply multiple rules to a style object. We only used a single filter for each rule object in the previous example, but OpenLayers makes it easy to specify multiple filters to give you even more control over your feature styles.

Rules are used in accordance with filters—it's the filters that do the work in determining if the rule will be applied to a feature. So, let's take a look at the Filter class, and how we can use it to customize our feature styles even more.

OpenLayers.Filter class

The **Filter** class controls the logic of match feature property attributes to see if a rule should be applied or not. We can use a single filter, like in the previous example, or we can combine filters together (e.g., if `property1` is greater than 500 and another `property2` is less than 200, then apply the style).

Filters can also be spatial—we can check to see if features intersect geometry objects, are within some distance of a point, and more. To do all these things, we use subclasses of the base Filter class, similar to how we use subclasses of the Layer class and other classes.

Filter Subclasses

There are four subclasses we'll cover here—**Comparison**, **FeatureId**, **Logical**, and **Spatial**.

Filter.Comparison

The **Comparison** class is the filter class we've been using so far. Like the name implies, this class will compare properties based on the specified parameters of the filter object. The type of comparison applied is specified by the `type` property. We also have to specify a value to check for—most filters use the `value` property (but some use different properties, such as `lowerBoundary` and `upperBoundary`). Finally, we must also specify a `property` to check for in the feature.

For instance, let's take a look at the filter object used in the `rule_pop_low` rule from the previous example:

```
var rule_pop_mid = new OpenLayers.Rule({
  filter: new OpenLayers.Filter.Comparison({
  type: OpenLayers.Filter.Comparison.GREATER_THAN,
  property: 'population',
  value: 1500
}),
```

Here, we ask OpenLayers to do a `GREATER_THAN` comparison type, which looks at the `population` property of the features and matches it if the value of `population` is greater than (but not including) `1500`.

Filter.Comparison Value property

All **Filter.Comparison** objects must have some accompanying value property. Almost all filter comparison types, like the `GREATER_THAN` type we just demonstrated, simply use the `value` property. Others, like the `Comparison` type, use the `lowerBoundary` and `upperBoundary` properties. Without specifying the value a filter should look for, the filter won't work (it wouldn't know what to compare).

Let's take a look at the different **Filter.Comparison** types available.

Filter Comparison types

Unless otherwise specified, each comparison `type` will have a corresponding `value` property. The `value` property is an `{Integer}` type, unless otherwise specified.

Filter Type: BETWEEN

`BETWEEN`: Checks to see if a property is between two values. This does not use the `value` property—instead, you specify `lowerBound` and `upperBound` values to check between. The values are inclusive—so if the `lowerBound` is `500` and the `upperBound` is `1500`, it will match values in between and including `500` to `1500`. Example constructor call:

```
var my_filter = new OpenLayers.Filter.Comparison({
  type: OpenLayers.Filter.Comparison.BETWEEN,
  property: 'population',
  lowerBoundary:500,
  upperBoundary:1500
});
```

Filter Type: EQUAL_TO

`EQUAL_TO`: Checks if a property is equal to a specified `value`. Example constructor call:

```
var my_filter = new OpenLayers.Filter.Comparison({
  type: OpenLayers.Filter.Comparison.EQUAL_TO,
  property: 'population',
  value: 1337
});
```

Filter Type: GREATER_THAN

`GREATER_THAN`: Checks if a property is greater than, but not including, a specified `value`. The following example constructor call would match anything greater than (but not including) `1000`—so the smallest value it would match would be `1001`:

```
var my_filter = new OpenLayers.Filter.Comparison({
  type: OpenLayers.Filter.Comparison.GREATER_THAN,
  property: 'population',
  value: 1000
});
```

Filter Type: GREATER_THAN_OR_EQUAL_TO

`GREATER_THAN_OR_EQUAL_TO`: Checks if a property is greater than or equal to a specified `value`. The following example constructor call would match the value `1000` and anything greater:

```
var my_filter = new OpenLayers.Filter.Comparison({
  type: OpenLayers.Filter.Comparison.GREATER_THAN_OR_EQUAL_TO,
  property: 'population',
  value: 1000
});
```

Filter Type: LESS_THAN

`LESS_THAN`: Checks if a property is less than, but not including, a specified `value`. Example constructor call—this would match anything below `1000`, but would not match the value `1000`:

```
var my_filter = new OpenLayers.Filter.Comparison({
  type: OpenLayers.Filter.Comparison.LESS_THAN,
  property: 'population',
  value: 1000
});
```

Filter Type: LESS_THAN_OR_EQUAL_TO

LESS_THAN_OR_EQUAL_TO: Checks if a property is less than, or including, a specified value. Example constructor call—this would match anything below 1000, and would also match 1000:

```
var my_filter = new OpenLayers.Filter.Comparison({
  type: OpenLayers.Filter.Comparison.LESS_THAN_OR_EQUAL_TO,
  property: 'population',
  value: 1000
});
```

Filter Type: LIKE

LIKE: Checks if a property contains a value, which in this case is a {String}. For example, if the property's value was 'village' and the value you specify to check for is 'village', then it would match. The value you specify is also a regular expression—which means you can pass in various special characters to match on. For example, * will match zero or more instances of any character. If you just want to see if a certain string is contained within the property, you can simply set the value to that string without worrying about what regular expressions are. Example constructor call:

```
var my_filter = new OpenLayers.Filter.Comparison({
    type: OpenLayers.Filter.Comparison.LIKE,
    property: 'settlement_type',
    value: 'village'
})
```

More information on regular expressions can be found at http://en.wikipedia.org/wiki/Regular_expression.

Filter Type: NOT_EQUAL_TO

NOT_EQUAL_TO: Checks to see if a property is *not* equal to some value passed in, which is an {Integer} type. An example constructor call would be the following, which would match everything that did not have a population property equal to the value 1000.

```
var my_filter = new OpenLayers.Filter.Comparison({
  type: OpenLayers.Filter.Comparison.NOT_EQUAL_TO,
  property: 'population',
  value: 1000
});
```

Filter.FeatureId

This will filter features based on Feature IDs. This is useful particularly when working with WFS services or SLDs. With WFS, FeatureID is a way to reference a unique feature. WFS servers return data about features, each one containing a FeatureID which uniquely identifies it. SLDs can also identify features by a unique FeatureID. This can be useful if you know the IDs of specific features you want styled. When using the FeatureID filter, it expects an array of **fids** during instantiation:

```
var my_filter = new OpenLayers.Filter.FeatureId({
  fids: ['fid1', 'fid2']
});
```

Feature.Logical

We've already practiced applying filters to rules, but what about applying a filter object to another filter object? Why would we want to do this? Well, it allows us to use logical operators with filters. Meaning, we can create really complex filters quite easily.

There are three types of logical operators that we can use:

- **OpenLayers.Filter.Logical.AND**: Checks if multiple filters match
- **OpenLayers.Filter.Logical.OR**: Checks if at least one of the multiple filters match
- **OpenLayers.Filter.Logical.NOT**: If the filter does *not* match

We can combine these filters together to create very specific rules, giving us very fine grain control over what features should get styled. To create a logical filter, you simply specify the `type` (which is one of the three logical operators above) and an array of `filters` which contains other filter objects.

For example,

```
var my_logical_filter = new OpenLayers.Filter.Logical({
  type: OpenLayers.Filter.Logical.AND,
  filters: [
    new OpenLayers.Filter.Comparison({
      type: OpenLayers.Filter.Comparison.LESS_THAN,
      property: 'population',
      value: 1000
    }),
    new OpenLayers.Filter.Comparison({
      type: OpenLayers.Filter.Comparison.LIKE,
      property: 'settlement_type',
      value: 'village'
    })
  ]
});
```

The above filter uses the AND logical operator and two comparison filters. The result is that this logical filter will match only features that match both the comparison filters (`population` less than `1000` and `settlement_type` contains `'village'`).

Let's go over this with an example.

Time For Action – figuring out logical filters

In this example, we'll use a few logical filters and some random points with random `population` and `settlement_type` values.

1. Add in a WMS and vector layer.

```
        vector_layer = new OpenLayers.Layer.Vector('Basic Vector
Layer');
        map.addLayer(vector_layer);
```

2. Now, we'll need to create an anonymous object containing some settlement value that we'll pick from at random:

```
var settlement_values = {
    0: 'village',
    1: 'city',
}
```

3. Let's create some feature. We'll create twenty features, using some random `population` and `settle_type` values in each feature's `attribute` property:

```
for(var i=0; i<20; i++){
    vector_layer.addFeatures([new OpenLayers.Feature.Vector(
        new OpenLayers.Geometry.Point(
            (Math.floor(Math.random() * 360) - 180),
            (Math.floor(Math.random() * 180) - 90)
        ),
        {
             'population': Math.floor(Math.random() * 2000),
      'settlement_type': settlement_values[(Math.floor(Math.
random() * 2))]
        }
    )]);
}
```

4. Like before, we'll now need a style object to apply filters to:

```
var vector_style = new OpenLayers.Style();
```

5. Now comes the 'hard' part. We'll create a logical filter that checks two comparison filters. It will see if the `population` is lower than `1000` and the `settlement_type` is `'village'`. This is all that's to it:

```
var filter_village_low_pop = new OpenLayers.Filter.Logical({
  type: OpenLayers.Filter.Logical.AND,
  filters: [
    new OpenLayers.Filter.Comparison({
      type: OpenLayers.Filter.Comparison.LESS_THAN,
      property: 'population',
      value: 1000
    }),
     new OpenLayers.Filter.Comparison({
      type: OpenLayers.Filter.Comparison.LIKE,
      property: 'settlement_type',
      value: 'village'
    })
  ]
});
```

6. Next, we'll create another logical filter. This one will check to see if the `population` is between 100 and 1500 *and* check to see if the `settlement_type` is `'village'`.

```
var filter_village_high_pop = new OpenLayers.Filter.Logical({
  type: OpenLayers.Filter.Logical.AND,
  filters: [
    new OpenLayers.Filter.Comparison({
      type: OpenLayers.Filter.Comparison.BETWEEN,
      property: 'population',
      lowerBoundary: 1000,
      upperBoundary: 1500
    }),
     new OpenLayers.Filter.Comparison({
      type: OpenLayers.Filter.Comparison.LIKE,
      property: 'settlement_type',
      value: 'village'
    })
  ]
});
```

7. Now we'll create one more filter. This one will use the **OR** logical operator to see if the `population` is above `1500` or if the `settlement_type` is `'city'`. So, even if `settlement_type` is `'city'` and the population is say, `500`, it will get matched because at least one of the filters matches:

```
var filter_city = new OpenLayers.Filter.Logical({
    type: OpenLayers.Filter.Logical.OR,
    filters: [
        new OpenLayers.Filter.Comparison({
            type: OpenLayers.Filter.Comparison.GREATER_THAN,
            property: 'population',
            value: 1500
        }),
    new OpenLayers.Filter.Comparison({
            type: OpenLayers.Filter.Comparison.LIKE,
            property: 'settlement_type',
            value: 'city'
        })
    ]
});
```

8. Ok—now we'll just create some rules and apply the filters to them. Each rule will be applied to one of the filters we just created.

```
var rule_village_low_pop = new OpenLayers.Rule({
    filter: filter_village_low_pop,
    symbolizer: {
        fillColor: '#ababab', fillOpacity:.8,
        pointRadius:8, strokeColor: '#454545',
        strokeWidth:2
    }
});
var rule_village_high_pop = new OpenLayers.Rule({
    filter: filter_village_high_pop,
    symbolizer: {
    fillColor: '#FFFA93', fillOpacity:.8,
    pointRadius:8, strokeColor: '#AFAB57',
    strokeWidth:4,
    }
});
var rule_city = new OpenLayers.Rule({
    filter: filter_city,
    symbolizer: {
    fillColor: '#BD1922', fillOpacity:.8,
```

```
        pointRadius:16, strokeColor: '#812B30',
        strokeWidth:6,
        fontSize:'.8em', fontColor: '#efefef',
        label: '${population}'
        }
});
```

9. Last thing—we need to add the rules to the `vector_style` object, create a `style_map` object and apply the style object to the `'default'` intent, and finally set the vector layer's StyleMap to the style map object.

```
vector_style.addRules([rule_village_low_pop, rule_village_high_
pop, rule_city]);

var vector_style_map = new OpenLayers.StyleMap({
    'default': vector_style
});

vector_layer.styleMap = vector_style_map;
```

10. You should see something like the following, with different distributions of points and colors since the values were randomized:

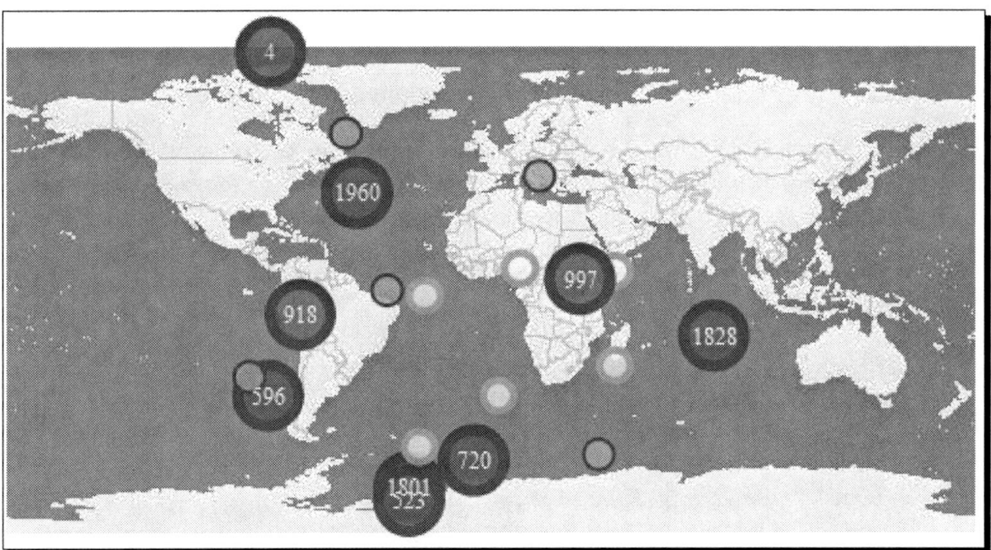

What Just Happened?

We just demonstrated how to use logical filters in our map. We can mix and match the different logical operators to create even more complex filters, allowing us to style features exactly how we want to. There's one more feature class to cover—**Feature.Spatial**.

Feature.Spatial

The **Feature.Spatial** class allows us to filter features based on their geographic information. This class is used when *creating* a vector layer. It differs from the previous logical filter, as we don't typically add this to a rule after a vector layer has been created—it's used to specify the features returned from a source like a WFS server. If you are creating a vector layer which uses the WFS protocol, this is a very useful filter.

When creating a spatial filter, a `type` and `value` must be specified. The value will be either a `{OpenLayers.Bounds}` or `{OpenLayers.Geometry}` object, depending on the `type`. Some types also allow for additional `distance` and `distanceUnits` parameters. Let's take a look at some of the types:

- **OpenLayers.Filter.Spatial.BBOX**: Specifies features to match that fall inside a bounding box, set by an `{OpenLayers.Bounds}` object in the `value` property
- **OpenLayers.Filter.Spatial.CONTAINS**: Used to check if an `{OpenLayers.Geometry}` object specified by the `value` property contains a feature
- **OpenLayers.Filter.Spatial.DWITHIN**: Specifies if a feature is within some distance specified by the `distance` property
- **OpenLayers.Filter.Spatial.INTERSECTS**: Used to check if a feature intersects an `{OpenLayers.Geometry}` object specified in the `value` property
- **OpenLayers.Filter.Spatial.WITHIN**: Used to check if a feature is completely within an `{OpenLayers.Geometry}` object specified in the `value` property

So, to use this filter, you'll usually use it when instantiating your vector layer. We won't do an in depth example, as it follows the general format of our previous examples. However, an example instantiation call using the Spatial filter would look like this:

```
var my_vector_layer = new OpenLayers.Layer.Vector(
  'My WFS Layer',
  {
    protocol: new OpenLayers.Protocol.WFS({
      url: wfs_server
    }),
    filter: new OpenLayers.Fitler.Spatial({
      type: OpenLayers.Filter.Spatial.BBOX,
      value: new OpenLayers.Bounds(-180,-90,0,0),
      projection: new OpenLayers.Projection('EPSG:4326')
    })
});
```

Summary

We've reached the end of our discussion about the core components of OpenLayers. This was the last chapter that deals specifically with defining parts of the OpenLayers API. In this chapter, we discussed styling vector layers in OpenLayers. We covered the Style and StyleMap classes, and went over how to work with the Rules and Filter classes.

The next chapter will be similar to the latter part of this chapter. Instead of going over more of the OpenLayers library (you know enough now to be dangerous), we'll go over the process of creating a web application using OpenLayers. We'll put together the things we've learned throughout this book to demonstrate how everything 'fits together', and what a typical development process looks like.

11
Making Web Map Apps

By now, we've covered all the parts of OpenLayers that are essential for making our own web map application. So far, we've been focusing on how to use the various different parts of OpenLayers. In this chapter we'll put together those pieces that we've learned and demonstrate how to create an actual web map application with OpenLayers.

While we won't be introducing many new things in this chapter, we will be putting them together in ways we haven't before. Throughout this chapter, we'll:

- Cover common development strategies
- Learn how to interact with third party data
- Build a web-mapping application from scratch using Flickr
- Deploy our applications and discuss what deployment means
- Discover how to build the OpenLayers library file

Development strategies

In this chapter, we'll be developing a web map application that loads in data from a third party source (Flickr). The examples have been structured with **iterative development** in mind. What this means is that you start small and make many changes, gradually building up your web map from nothing into something useful.

Iterative development is an important, popular, and effective way to develop applications. The core idea is that you create something simple, get it working, and then improve it. You can figure out more quickly what does and doesn't work by improving on and learning from previous iterations.

Another strategy we'll make use of is **modular programming**. What this means, essentially, is that we try to keep things as discrete (or modular) as possible. By doing so, once we know a component works, we don't have to worry about it later.

Creating a web map application using Flickr

Because OpenLayers is so flexible, it's easy to make third party software and data work with our maps. Sharing geospatial data is becoming more popular, with services such as Flickr and Twitter freely offering geospatially embedded data. Being able to visualize data often helps us to understand it. Using OpenLayers, we can place geospatial data (say, twitter posts or Flickr images) on a map and get a clearer picture about the data.

Note on APIs

Many popular sites provide an **API (Application Programmer Interface)** which allows programmers to interact with their data. For instance, both Flickr and Twitter provide APIs that enables developers to view recent updates (photo uploads and tweets). These APIs (but not all APIs) let us get geospatial data that we can use with OpenLayers. Flickr provides some very easy to use methods to retrieve data with associated geographic information, so we'll focus this chapter on building a web-mapping application around Flickr.

Accessing the Flickr public data feeds

While Flickr provides a very robust developer API, we'll only interface with Flickr via URL calls which provide access to feeds. Feeds provide information about data, and we can get different kinds of feeds (e.g., a specific user's feed or the feed for all users combined). It's really quite easy to do so; we just make a call to a URL and specify certain parameters. The base URL we'll call is `http://api.flickr.com/services/feeds/geo/?format=kml`.

The `format` parameter can be a number of values—JSON, RSS, SQL, etc. We'll be using KML and JSON in this chapter. When calling this URL, a file in the format you ask for will be returned which contains information about the latest photos uploaded that have geographic information associated with them (that's what the `geo` in the URL is for).

Flickr's API documentation can be found at `http://www.flickr.com/services/api/`. More information about the Flickr feeds can be found at `http://www.flickr.com/services/feeds/`.

Specifying data

We can refine what data is returned by adding additional parameters to the URL. You can specify a user's ID via the **ID** key, a group via the **g** key, and tags via the **tags** key. You can also specify other things, such as a certain coordinate and radius—for now, we'll just be focusing on the **tags** key.

How we'll do it

Let's create a web map application that will pull in data from Flickr and display it on a map. This will allow us to see, geographically, where photos were submitted from. We could, for example, search for 'bird photos' and get an idea where some particular bird species might be common (or at least, commonly photographed and uploaded to Flickr). We'll break down the development of this application into a few different examples, so let's get started.

Time For Action – getting Flickr data

The first step in our application will require us to get data from Flickr. We'll request some data and then save it to the server.

1. The first step is to figure out what sort of data we want to get. We'll use the URL we mentioned before, but we'll also specify a tag. Let's use 'bird' as a tag. Open up this URL in your web browser, and you should be able to download it as a KML file `http://api.flickr.com/services/feeds/geo/?format=kml&tags=bird`.
2. Save the file as `flickr_data.kml` and place it in your map directory.
3. Open up the file and take a look at it. We won't be editing it, but just take a look to see how the data is structured. Notice that there are `style` tags—if we want, we can directly apply the styles from the file to our map (as we'll see soon).

What Just Happened?

We just downloaded the latest images in KML format that contained a tag called 'bird.' When you call the URL and pass in some tag, Flickr will return back to you the latest images uploaded that have some geographic information associated with them.

Have a Go Hero – accessing the Flickr API

Make a request to the URL from the previous example. Try changing the `tags` parameter and notice how the returned file is different. Based on the parameters in the URL, Flickr will return different data.

Why did we do this?

You may be wondering why we downloaded the KML file. If you remember from Chapter 9, we could just create a vector layer and point to the Flickr URL instead of a local file. However, if we download the KML file we then have direct control over it; we can modify it. When we're in the 'development mode', we want to keep things as easy to debug and fix as possible.

Reducing possible errors

Once we get the code working to load the KML file we downloaded (in the next example), we don't need to worry about it anymore. When we develop our application and find bugs or errors with it, we don't have to spend much time tracking them down. We get the static file working, and we move on to the next task. We don't have to worry about the Flickr API going down, our requests not completing, or other things—we can focus on other parts. Once we get more parts of our application working, then we'll switch to using the dynamic URL. For now, let's use the static file.

> Because we'll be loading in a file, you must run this code on a server. You can run it on localhost—if you don't have a server, you can download Apache for windows at `http://www.apachefriends.org/en/xampp.html`.
>
> The reason it needs to run on a server is because the KML file is loaded via an AJAX call, and the files must reside on the same domain as the originating request. See Chapter 9 for more details on loading files.

Time for Action – adding data to your map

Time to get back to coding. Now that we have the data from Flickr from the previous example, let's add it to our map. We'll create a Google Maps base layer and then a vector layer filled with the Flickr data on top of it.

1. First, we need to make sure the `flickr_data.kml` file is in the same directory that we'll be creating our map in. Save the file in your server's document root folder, which may be something like (with Xampp on windows) `c:/xampp/htdocs` or on OSX (with Xammp, `http://www.apachefriends.org/en/xampp-macosx.html`) in `/Applications/XAMPP`, or on Linux: `/var/www/`. We'll refer to it as `example_1.html`.

2. Now let's create the map. We won't be using a WMS layer this time—instead, we'll just be using a Google base map and place our vector layer on top of it. Make sure to first add the reference to the Google Maps API in the `<head>` section:

```
<script src="http://maps.google.com/maps/api/js?sensor=false"></
script>
```

3. Now, create and add a Google Maps layer.

```
var google_map = new OpenLayers.Layer.Google(
            'Google Layer',
            {}
     );
 map.addLayer(google_map);
```

4. We'll now need a vector layer. We'll have to define it's projection as `EPSG:4326` because that's the projection the coordinates in the KML file are in. If they were in a different projection, we would define it as whatever projection they were in (although, we would need Proj4js to do projection transformations).

We'll use the `HTTP` protocol because we'll be accessing the KML file from our local server. This is why we can't simply open up the page in a folder—when we do so, the protocol is `file:///`, so we must open it from our local web server (provided you have one installed, see the previous note).

Inside the protocol, we'll set up a `format` object from the `KML` class and set `extractAttribtues` to `true` so we can access the attributes associated with each image. Finally, we'll use a `Fixed` strategy.

```
var vector_layer = new OpenLayers.Layer.Vector('Flickr Data',
        {
            projection: new OpenLayers.Projection('EPSG:4326'),
            protocol: new OpenLayers.Protocol.HTTP({
                url: 'flickr_data.kml',
```

```
                    format: new OpenLayers.Format.KML({
                        extractAttributes: true
                    })
                }),
                strategies: [new OpenLayers.Strategy.Fixed()]
        }
    );
```

5. And add it to the map:

```
map.addLayer(vector_layer);
```

6. We should see some points now that show the location of the images that were uploaded. Open up the page via localhost, for example: `http://localhost/openlayers_book/chapter_11/code/example_1.html`.

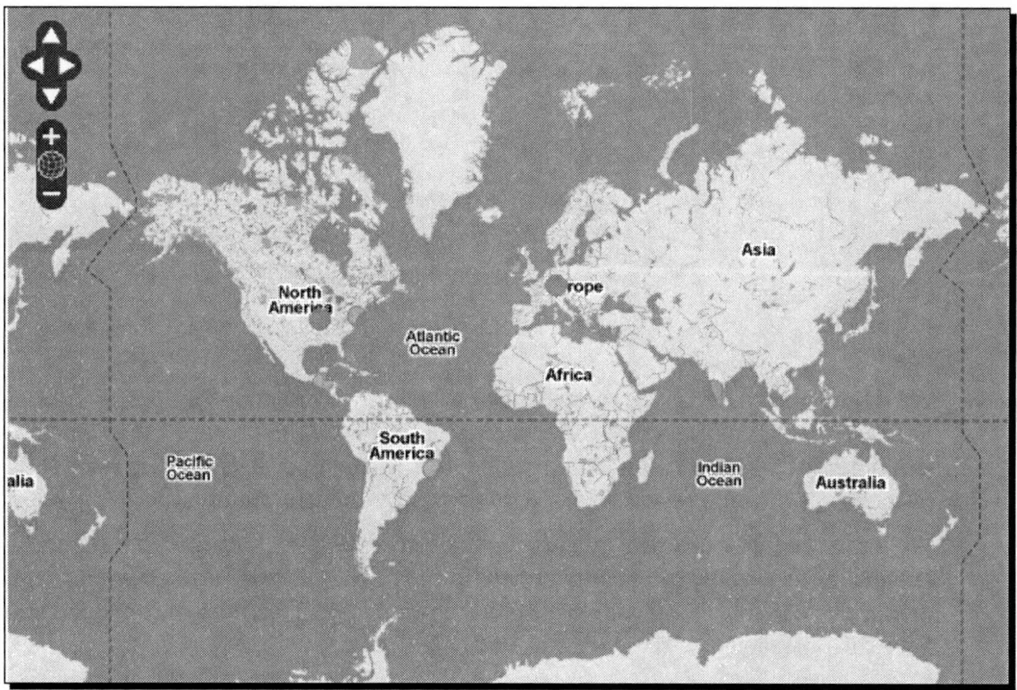

7. Now, let's take a look at what `extractAttributes` is used for. When we set it to `true`, attributes from each feature in the KML file is applied to the `attributes` property of each feature object. More bluntly—it takes attributes from the file and applies them to your points. Bring up Firebug and, in the console, access one of the feature objects:

```
map.layers[1].features[0].attributes
```

8. You should see an object that contains three properties: `Snippet`, `name`, and `styleUrl`. These are somewhat arbitrary properties, specified in the KML file for each photo, and with `extractAttributes: true` we can access them. The `styleUrl` is a reference to a style tag inside the KML file—we'll talk about it in the next example.

What Just Happened?

We just loaded in the KML file and used `extractAttributes` to look at the properties that each photo contains. Flickr is providing these attributes—the attributes in the KML file gets applied to our feature objects. Another property we can use is `extractStyles` to apply the styles from the KML file to our features.

Time for Action – extract style

The `extractStyles` can be used to style the vector layer based on the styles specified in the KML file. Because the Flickr KML file provides style information, we can use this property—let's see how.

1. If the KML file you are working with contains style information, we can directly access and use it. In this case, Flickr is providing us with a KML file embedded with style tags, so let's use it.

2. We'll specify `extractStyles: true` inside our vector layer creation call. In the format value setting, add it in, and be sure to include the comma:

```
...
format: new OpenLayers.Format.KML({
                    extractAttributes: true,
                    extractStyles: true
                })
...
```

3. Now open the page and you should see thumbnails of the images:

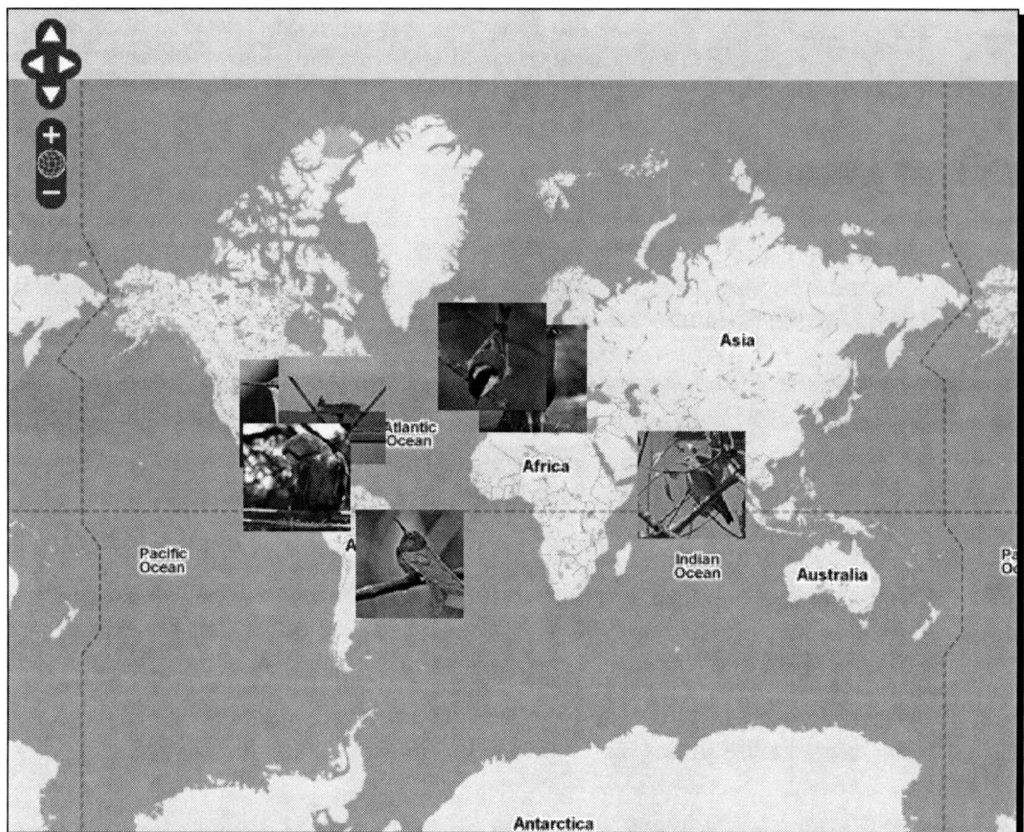

What Just Happened?

Using `extractStyles`, our features went from the default orange dots to thumbnails of the actual uploaded photos. When this property is used, style definitions in the KML file are applied to the `style` property of each feature. KML files can include style information—that is why we can use the `extractStyles` property with the KML format. OpenLayers will parse the style information from the KML file and generate the necessary style definitions.

Turning our example into an application

So far, we've accessed data from Flickr, saved it to a file, and added it to our map. This is pretty cool, but we really haven't done much else than just load in the data, from an OpenLayers point of view. It's useful, but we really haven't created a full featured 'web application' just yet. So, let's focus on how to build a more useful web-mapping application.

To do this, we'll basically need to do two general things:

1. Add some interactivity to our map.
2. Use 'live' data. We shouldn't have to manually download a KML file every time we want new data—our web application should do it automatically.

Let's focus on the first part, and then change the data source after we develop some interactivity.

Adding interactivity

In the previous example, each feature received an `externalGraphic` property because we used `extractStyles` (causing thumbnails to be displayed for each feature)—but it's hard to see where they are on the map, especially when zoomed out. We'll need to address that. We want to show the photos, but we also want to show where they are.

To accomplish this, we could revert back to using point features and making use of the `selectFeature` control. But what if too many features are too close to each, making it harder to select them? That's what the **cluster** strategy is for, so we'll use it as well.

Selecting features

What should happen when we select a feature? We'll need to show information about the feature we clicked on, and that information is the Flickr photo itself and any associated attributes. So, let's keep things a little simple for now and show the photo(s) information below the map when a feature is selected.

Time for Action – adding some interactivity

In this example, we'll be using the **cluster** strategy, **selectFeature** control, and showing photo information on selection. As we go along, feel free to tweak the examples yourself, change the functionality, or anything else—that's the best way to learn!

1. Make a copy (or direct edit) of the code from the previous example. We'll be improving it.
2. We'll keep `extractAttributes` and `extractStyles`. Even though we specify `extractStyles`, we're going to be using a custom `styleMap` object. We're doing this so that we can still access the thumbnail image location (which is set as `externalGraphic` in the feature's `style` object when using `extractStyles`). Make sure the `format` object looks like the following:

```
...
format: new OpenLayers.Format.KML({
  extractAttributes: true, extractStyles: true
```

```
})
...
```

3. Let's add a `cluster` strategy to the vector layer now so our points cluster. Our `strategies` array should now look like the following:

```
strategies: [new OpenLayers.Strategy.Fixed(),
             new OpenLayers.Strategy.Cluster()]
```

4. Let's take a quick look at the map to make sure it works. Since we have used the cluster strategy, we won't see the thumbnails that we would have (like in the previous example). Remember to access it from `http://localhost/...`:

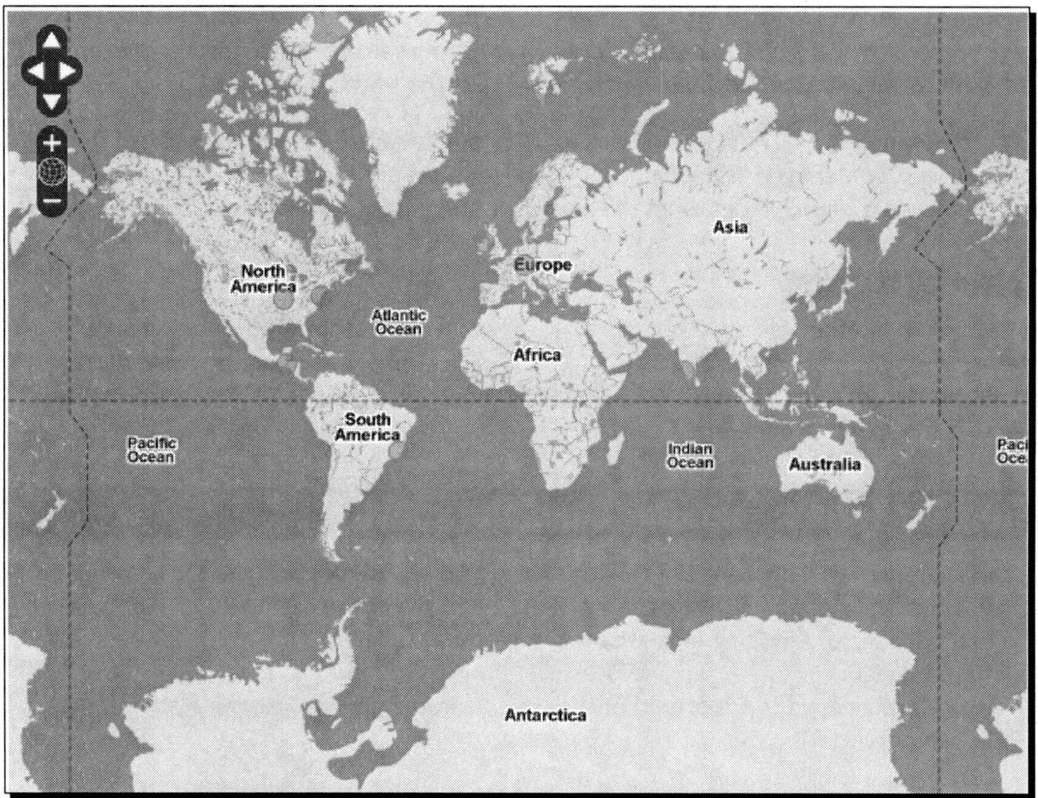

5. So far, so good. Our points look kind of small though, and we can't visually distinguish how many points are in a cluster. Let's change that. We'll make the clusters larger depending on how many points the cluster contains. When using clustering, each feature belongs to a cluster, and we can access the number of features in a cluster through `feature.attributes.count`. Let's also add a label to each feature showing the number of points it contains. We'll also pass in a second `context` object when instantiating the style object, which allows us to define the values of variables to use with attribute replacement. The `context` object will contain a function that returns some value which will be used with the attribute replacement.

```
//Create a style object to be used by a StyleMap object
var vector_style = new OpenLayers.Style({
    'fillColor': '#669933',
    'fillOpacity': .8,
    'fontColor': '#f0f0f0',
    'fontFamily': 'arial, sans-serif',
    'fontSize': '.9em',
    'fontWeight': 'bold',
    'label': '${num_points}',
    'pointRadius': '${point_radius}',
    'strokeColor': '#aaee77',
    'strokeWidth': 3
    },
    //Second parameter contains a context parameter
    {
        context: {
            num_points: function(feature){ return feature.
attributes.count; },
            point_radius: function(feature){
                return 9 + (feature.attributes.count)
            }
        }
});

//Create a style map object and set the 'default' intent to the
var vector_style_map = new OpenLayers.StyleMap({
    'default': vector_style
});

//Add the style map to the vector layer
vector_layer.styleMap = vector_style_map;
```

6. Let's take a look. The size and labels should change for each cluster:

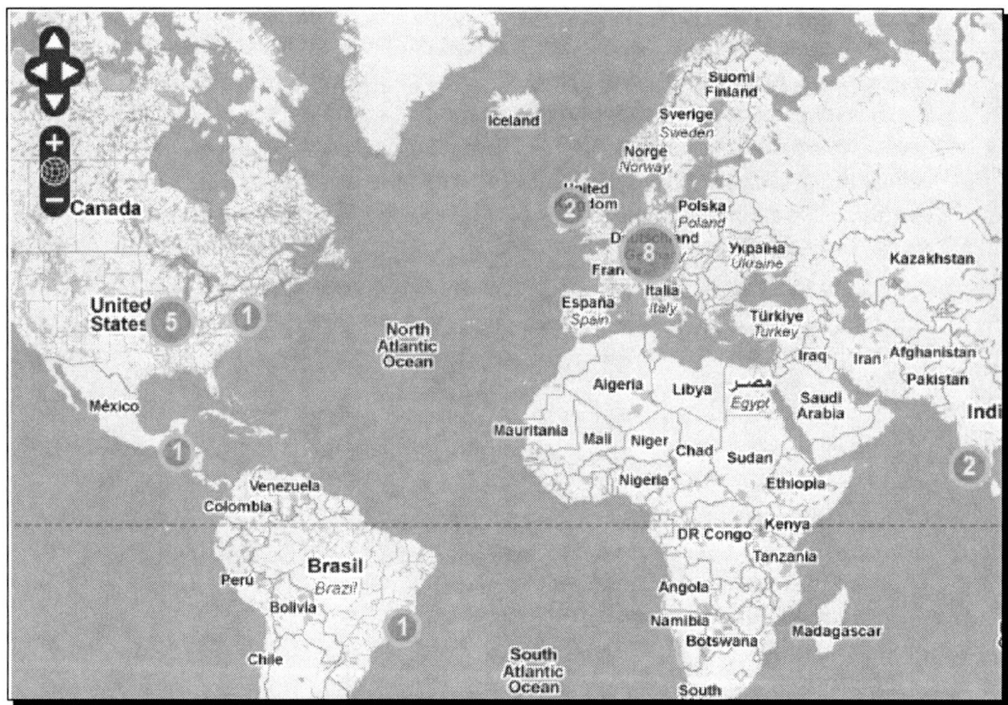

7. The first part of our plan is done—we've successfully added clusters. Now, we need to add feature selection ability. Let's create a `selectFeature` control. We'll add events soon, but for now let's just create the control and add it to the map and then activate it.

```
//Add a select feature control
var select_feature_control = new OpenLayers.Control.SelectFeature(
    vector_layer,
    {}
)
map.addControl(select_feature_control);
select_feature_control.activate();
```

8. Now, if we select a feature it won't look quite right. This is because we haven't defined a style for the `select` intent. Let's go back and define a style object and add it to our `vector_style_map` object:

```
var vector_style_select = new OpenLayers.Style({
    'fillColor': '#cdcdcd',
    'fillOpacity': .9,
    'fontColor': '#232323',
```

```
    'strokeColor': '#ffffff'
})
//Create a style map object and set the 'default' intent to the
var vector_style_map = new OpenLayers.StyleMap({
    'default': vector_style,
    'select': vector_style_select
});
```

9. On to the last part—creating the events. Our plan is to have some photo information display when we select features. Let's go ahead and get the framework for that set up first by simply creating a div that will appear below the map. In your HTML code, add the following:

```
<div id='photo_info_wrapper'></div>
```

Let's now create a function that will be called when we select a feature. It will need to update the `photo_info_wrapper` div with information about the photo(s) contained in the selected cluster. We'll need to create a loop that will look at each feature in the selected cluster, pull out its attributes, and update the HTML of the div. This will all happen in a function that gets called when a feature is selected, and we also need to create a function that will clear the div when a feature is unselected. We'll need to grab properties from the feature's `attributes` property, which are filled by the earlier `extractAttributes` parameter when creating the vector layer. We'll also access the `style` property of the features (which is populated by the `extractStyles` parameter we used earlier) to get the `externalGraphic` location. Let's create the functions:

```
function on_select_feature(event){
    //Store a reference to the element
    var info_div = document.getElementById('photo_info_wrapper');
    info_div.innerHTML = '';

    //Store the clusters
    var cluster = event.feature.cluster;

    //Loop through the cluster features
    for(var i=0; i<cluster.length; i++){
        //Update the div with the info of the photos
        info_div.innerHTML += "<strong>"
            + cluster[i].attributes.name
            + "</strong><br />"
            + "<img src='" + cluster[i].style.externalGraphic + "'
/>"
            + cluster[i].attributes.Snippet
            + "<br /><hr />";
```

```
        }
    }
    function on_unselect_feature(event){
        //Store a reference to the element
        var info_div = document.getElementById('photo_info_wrapper');

        //Clear out the div
        info_div.innerHTML = '';
    }
```

10. Now, we just need to register the events.

```
vector_layer.events.register('featureselected', this, on_select_
feature);
vector_layer.events.register('featureunselected', this, on_
unselect_feature);
```

11. Now, when we click on a cluster we should see information about the points as follows:

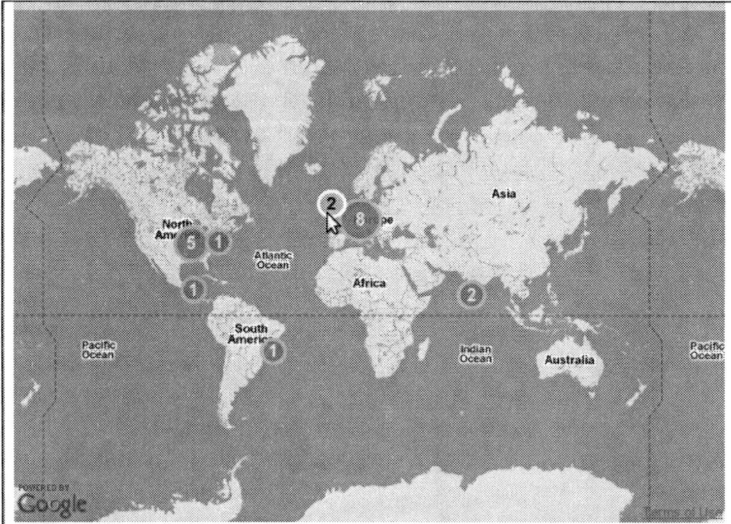

What Just Happened?

We just added some interactivity to our map. It's nothing too complex, although at first glance the code may seem daunting. We didn't really do anything 'new' though. We registered a couple of vector layer events that get fired when selecting a feature and then show information about the features selected. From here, you could change the application a bit with ease—such as changing how and what is shown. This example is to be used more or less as a guide to help you create your own applications. Let's take this example further; but first, we'll need to use realtime data.

Using real time data with a ProxyHost

The data we've loaded (`flickr_data.kml`) is from a third party source, but it's only fresh up to the point that we download it. Let's address the second point we came across previously:

Use 'live' data, and not download a KML file ourselves when we want new data

What we need to do is access the data in real time. To do this, we'll need to use a **ProxyHost**. This term is discussed in more detail in Chapter 9, but it's essentially a way to circumvent the cross domain request restraints of AJAX by calling on some server side script to make requests for us (acting as a proxy).

Time for Action – getting dynamic data

Let's specify a ProxyHost and get data from Flickr in real time.

1. We can use the example we just created, as we'll only be adding two things to it.

2. First, we'll need to define the URL of our proxyhost. It can be a CGI script, python script, etc. A CGI script is provided by OpenLayers at `http://trac.osgeo.org/openlayers/wiki/FrequentlyAskedQuestions#ProxyHost`.

   If you use that file, be sure to have Python installed. By default, the file would go in `c:/xampp/cgi-bin` using Xampp on Windows or on Linux: `/usr/lib/cgi-bin` or `/var/www/cgi` (the location may vary between distributions). In your code, specify the ProxyHost, changing the URL to point to your ProxyHost:

   ```
   OpenLayers.ProxyHost = '/cgi-bin/proxy.cgi?url=';
   ```

3. Next, we'll need to add the Flickr domain to the allowed host variable in the proxy file. Edit the proxy file and add the Flickr URL to the list of `allowedHosts` (near the top of the file provided by OpenLayers). At the time of writing, the last item in the list is `'vmap0.tiles.osgeo.org'`. Add a comma after the last item and then add `'api.flickr.com'` to the list:

```
allowedHosts = [ …, 'vmap0.tiles.osgeo.org', 'api.flickr.com']
```

4. Lastly, we'll just change the URL that the vector layer points to. In the `protocol` object in the vector layer, we'll need to change the `url` value and add a `params` object which specifies additional GET variables that will be appended to the URL call. In this case, we'll want to specify the `format` and `tags` params:

```
...
protocol: new OpenLayers.Protocol.HTTP({
                url: 'http://api.flickr.com/services/feeds/geo/',
      params: {'format':'kml', 'tags':'bird'},
…
```

5. That's it! Now, assuming you've set up the ProxyHost properly, you should see nearly the same thing as before. The only difference is the data is likely to be different, as you're now tapping into the stream in real time.

What Just Happened?

We just used a **ProxyHost** and pointed our vector layer to the actual Flickr API URL. Why didn't we do this at first? Again, to cut down on the things we need to worry about when developing the application. Now that we've got a little bit of interactivity and a live URL, let's take it a step further.

Wrapping up the application

Showing bird pictures from around the world is nice—but what about giving users the ability to show a photo with *any* tag they want? That's what we'll do next.

Recap

So far, we've created a map that lets users interact with Flickr data. As far as we're concerned, we're more or less done with the interaction part. Now we'll focus on changing the 'data source' part. Currently, we're only asking for photos with the tag `bird`, but we want to allow that to be any tag.

An important concept in application development is to keep things **modular**. This basically means that we try to write out applications in such a way that we can take out and put in different parts without drastically changing the rest of our code. In this case, we're going to leave the interaction part of our code alone (what we've done so far at least) and focus mainly on the code that retrieves data.

The plan

What needs to happen? Well, let's think through this. We want the user to be able to specify any tag they want. We want to allow multiple tags. This means we'll need to change the URL that the vector layer is pointing to, but only after they specify the tags. We'll be able to do this by changing the `params` property of the vector layer's `protocol` object. Right now, the `tags` is hard-coded as `'bird'`, but this will be a variable based on user input.

Changing the URL

So, we know we need to allow a variable which specifies the `tags` parameter in the URL to be based on user input. We'll need to create an input box that will allow the user to specify tags. We'll also have a submit button that will, when clicked, call a function that updates the vector layer's URL with the specified parameters.

Time For Action – adding dynamic tags to your map

Let's add some more interaction to our map now. We'll add an input box that will change the requested Flickr data based on the user's input.

1. Open up the previous example, we'll be adding to it. First, we'll need to add an input box and button to the HTML page. We'll create a div that holds them and place it right next to the map. Right after the map div, add the following:

```
    <div id='input_wrapper' style='position:absolute; left:610px;
top:0;'>
        <input type='text' id='input_tags' value='bird' />
        <input type='button' id='input_submit' value='Show Data'
/>
    </div>
```

2. Next, we'll need to create a function that will get called when the `input_submit` button is clicked. This function does three things. First, it will set the `tags` parameter of the vector layer to be equal to whatever value is in the `input_tags` input box. Secondly, it will call the vector layer's `refresh()` method which updates the vector layer and makes a new request for data based on the new parameters. Lastly, it will clear out the `photo_info_wrapper` div's HTML. You can add this at the bottom of the `init()` function.

```
function update_vector_layer(){
            //Change URL based on input tags
            vector_layer.protocol.options.params['tags'] =
document.getElementById('input_tags').value

            //Refresh the layer with the new params
            vector_layer.refresh();

            //Lastly, clear out the div that shows photo info
            document.getElementById('photo_info_wrapper').
innerHTML = '';
        }
```

3. Lastly, we'll need to make the `input_submit` button call the function when it is clicked. Now, we're going to be using JavaScript's built in event handling— but it's quite similar to what we do in OpenLayers. We just call the `addEventListener` method of an element. To get that element, we'll use `document.getElementById` like we've been doing throughout the book. When calling it, we pass in the event type (`'click'` in this case), the name of a function to call, and a Boolean that specifies how the event propagates (if you're not sure about this, just leave it as `false`).

```
document.getElementById('input_submit').addEventListener(
   'click',
            update_vector_layer,
   false);
```

4. Open up the page and you should see an input box next to the map. When you change the value and hit the button next to it, the `update_vector_layer` function will get called and refresh the vector layer. Try typing in various tags (or multiple tags separated by a comma) and hitting the button:

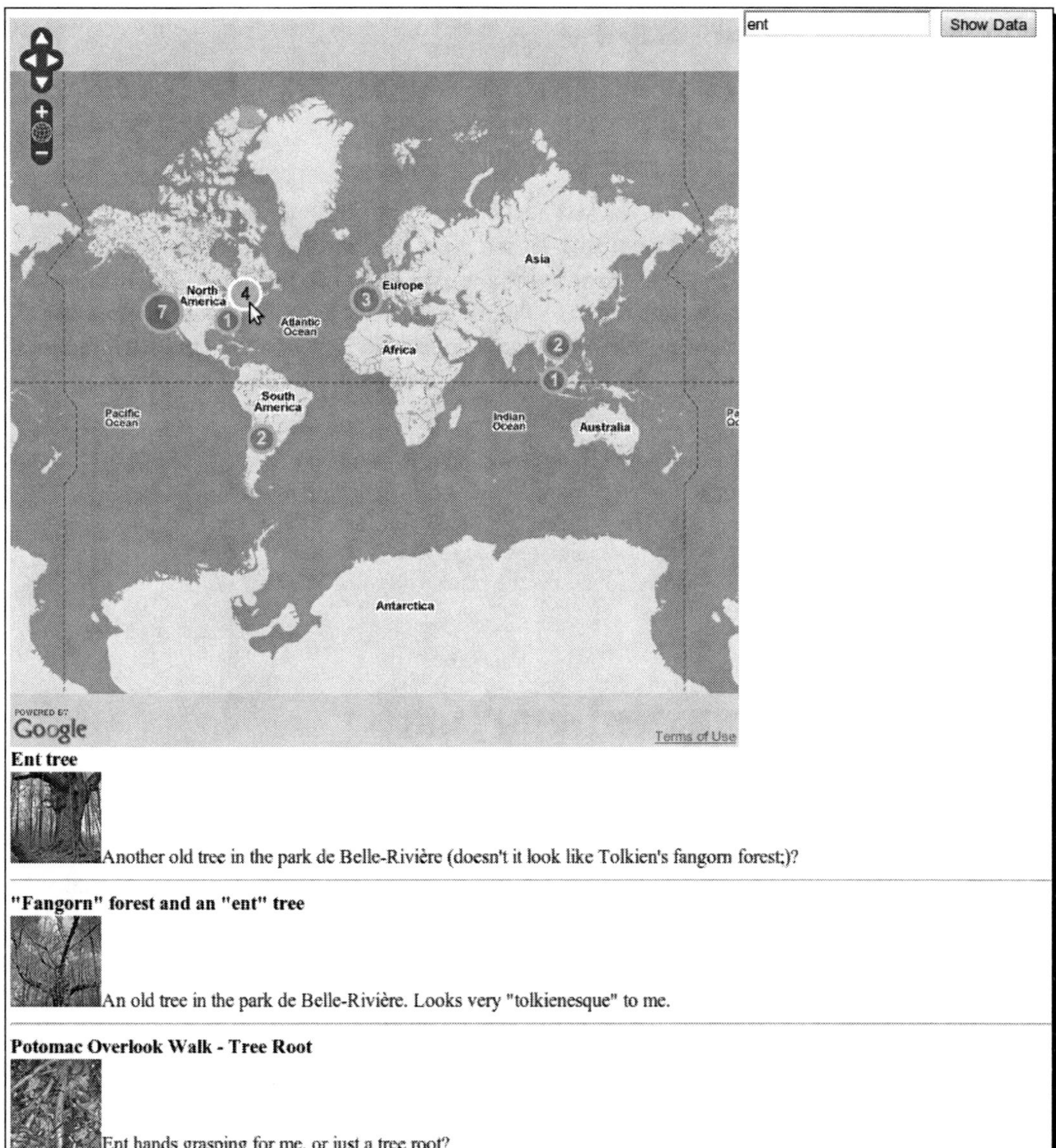
ent
Show Data
North America
Atlantic Ocean
Europe
Asia
Africa
South America
Pacific Ocean
Indian Ocean
Australia
Antarctica
POWERED BY
Google
Terms of Use
Ent tree
Another old tree in the park de Belle-Rivière (doesn't it look like Tolkien's fangorn forest;)?
"Fangorn" forest and an "ent" tree
An old tree in the park de Belle-Rivière. Looks very "tolkienesque" to me.
Potomac Overlook Walk - Tree Root
Ent hands grasping for me, or just a tree root?

What Just Happened?

We just updated our Flickr application to allow user input that affects what data is shown. We did this in a sort of modular way—we didn't have to change any of the previous code we wrote. Instead, we just updated the data source and added additional functionality. Now that we've written an application, let's talk a little bit about how to deploy it.

Deploying an application

What does it mean to **deploy** an OpenLayers (or any other) application? Basically, deploying something means that we're switching from a development mode to a production mode; we're releasing something for the rest of the world to see.

The production application should be as fast and bug free as possible. Because we want the production version to be accessed as quickly as possible, this will often include removing things we used in the development environment and tweaking the production environment to better handle a lot of users. It also means using files that are as small in size as possible. One of the first things we should do to deploy our application is to use the OpenLayers build script to create a library file which is much smaller in file size.

> There are many other things we can do to better prepare our production environment, such as using caching as well as combining and minimizing our JavaScript files. These, and other practices, are outside the scope of this book, but further information can be found on the book's website at `http://vasir.net/`.

Building the OpenLayers Library file

OpenLayers provides an easy way to configure the library file that gets included in your page. Throughout the book, we've been including a file called `OpenLayers.js`, which is a file that contains *all* the functionality (classes, functions, and so on) that OpenLayers provides. So far, this has been great—we've been developing up to this point, so we want to be sure that we have access to all the classes that we may use. What's my point here?

Always try to serve small files

Well, the `OpenLayers.js` file we've been using is around 920 KB! That's almost a megabyte—quite a large file to load, especially since it contains only JavaScript code. Even though large file sizes aren't as much of an issue as they were years ago, when everyone was on slower connections, a one megabyte JavaScript file in a production environment is something we want to avoid if at all possible.

We want all our files in a production environment to be as small as they can absolutely be. This will allow users to download the files faster (since there is less to download) which decreases the page's loading time (saves on bandwidth expenses). Faster page loads (even if the speed is only perceived) will greatly enhance the user's experience. Fortunately, we can greatly reduce the size of the OpenLayers library file with a build tool provided by OpenLayers.

Using the OpenLayers build file

When you download the OpenLayers archive file, there is a folder inside it called as `build`. Inside that, there is a file called `build.py`, which is a python script that creates an `OpenLayers.js` file based on a separate build configuration file. Building the library this way is called a **single file build**, as all the JavaScript code behind OpenLayers is contained in a single file.

So, what we can do is tell the build script to create an `OpenLayers.js` file that includes *only* the classes our application needs. This means that we can't access other classes, but in a production environment we won't need to, as the code won't be changing—that's what development is for. The benefit to doing this is because if the file has less code in it, the file size will be smaller.

Configuring the build script

When the build script runs, it looks for a configuration file to determine which classes to include and exclude when creating the `OpenLayers.js` file. There are two configuration files OpenLayers ships with by default:

- **full.cfg**: Causes the build script to include everything
- **lite.cfg**: Includes just a minimal amount of classes to create a WMS or tiled layer, and does not include controls

You can create your own files by copying one of these files and specifying the files you want to include. When creating your own build configuration file, you must include at least the section labeled `[first]` from the `full.cfg` or `lite.cfg` files.

The `[include]` section specifies what files should be added to the `OpenLayers.js` output file. If left blank, *all* files will be included. Otherwise, only files specified in this section get included. To find out what files should be included here, look at your code and whenever you see a reference to the class (e.g., when calling `new OpenLayers.Classname`), it means you'll need to include that class here.

The build script will automatically look for class dependencies, so you do not need to specify a parent class. For example, if you wish to include an individual control class, you can specify that class name and the build script will automatically include the base `Control.js` file.

The `[exclude]` section will be read in if the `[include]` section is left blank. These are classes that will *not* be included in the final build file. However, if you specify classes in the `[include]` section, this section will be ignored and only the classes in the `[include]` section will get included.

Time for Action – building a Config file

Let's take a look at how to write a build config file.

1. Copy the `lite.cfg` file found in the build directory and name the copied version `example_1.cfg` (or whatever you'd like, but that's what we'll refer to it as).
2. Let's manually specify some files. We'll add in a couple controls. Add in the following and then save the file. The full file should look like this:

```
# Config File
[first]
OpenLayers/SingleFile.js
OpenLayers.js
OpenLayers/BaseTypes.js
OpenLayers/BaseTypes/Class.js
OpenLayers/Util.js
[last]
[include]
OpenLayers/Map.js
OpenLayers/Layer/WMS.js
OpenLayers/Control/LayerSwitcher.js
OpenLayers/Control/Navigation.js
OpenLayers/Control/Scale.js
[exclude]
```

What Just Happened?

We just created a configuration file for our build named `example_1.cfg`. We'll be using this file to build the `OpenLayers.js` file. Notice that we did not have to include the base `Control.js` class—the build script will automatically look for and include the dependencies.

Pop Quiz – using the Build script

Now that you know how to use the build script, can you come up with some reasons why you think using it would be a good idea? What are some of the benefits of using it? What would be a downside of using it?

Running the build script

To build the `OpenLayers.js` file, we must run the `build.py` script. This will require Python installed on your computer, which can be downloaded for free at `http://www.python.org/`—download either the 2.6 or 2.7 version.

When the script is run, it will look for a configuration file and build a combined `OpenLayers.js` file depending on the configuration file. It will automatically include the class dependencies. Lastly, it will also **minify** (remove whitespace and unnecessary characters) the combined JavaScript code and create an `OpenLayers.js` file in the build directory. From there, you can copy the file and use it in your production code.

To run the script, on Linux you can simply `cd` into the directory and run:

```
./build.py config_file.cfg
```

Where `config_file.cfg` is optional. If not included, the `full.cfg` file will be used.

On Windows, you can use the command prompt to `cd` into the directory and run the build file the same way. You can also hit Start then select Run and copy the location of the `build.py` file from the Windows Explorer's address bar and paste it, along with the name of the config file. For example,

```
c:\users\your_name\Download\OpenLayers\build\build.py config_file.cfg
```

Time for Action – running the Build script

Let's take a look at how to run the script now.

1. Execute the build script with the config file we created in the previous example. Depending on your operating system (refer to the commands we just talked about):

   ```
   ./build.py example_1.cfg
   ```

2. You should see the output after running the command which informs you what the script is doing. In this case, it merged a total of 34 files and the final file size was just over 160 KB. That's a *huge* decrease from the original 920 KB!

What Just Happened?

We just run the build script and an `OpenLayers.js` file was produced. Depending on your own application, you would create a build script and specify the classes your code uses. Then, you would run the build script with that configuration file and copy the outputted `OpenLayers.js` file over to your production code base.

Doing it this way, you cut down the time users have to wait to load your page, as the file size will be smaller and take less time to download.

Summary

You've reached the end of the book! In this chapter we built a simple web map application that grabs Flickr data based on user input. We covered some development concepts throughout the chapter, such as attempting to keep our code modular. We learned how to interact with other third party APIs, and built an application from the ground up. Lastly, we talked about deployment and learned how to use the OpenLayers build script. Now that you've finished reading this book (I hope you've enjoyed it), you should be able to go out and make your own impressive web maps!

All code samples throughout this book, along with more deployment and JavaScript optimization techniques and more can be found at this book's website, `http://vasir.net/openlayers_book/`.

Pop Quiz Answers

Chapter 2: Squashing Bugs With Firebug

Answer: 2

Chapter 3: The 'Layers' in OpenLayers

Answer: 4. There will be an error because the variable b cannot be accessed outside the test function.

Chapter 4: Wrapping Our Heads Around Projections

Answer: There are a variety of reasons why other projections would be useful. Other projections preserve different attributes, and you would likely want to use a different projection if your map was aimed at showing close up areas. The EPSG:4326 projection would not be well suited for showing locations near the poles.

Chapter 6: Taking Control of Controls

Answer: 3—TYPE TOOL

Chapter 7: Styling Controls

Answer: There are numberless ways to access the element, here are just a few possible ways:

- #inner_most
- #outter_div .paragraph_style #middle_div #inner_most
- div p div span
- #outter_div p #middle_div #inner_most
- div #inner_most

Chapter 8: Charting the Map Class

Answer: A couple of possible ways would be to use `map.setCenter(new OpenLayers.LonLat(-42,52));`, `map.panTo(new OpenLayers.LonLat(-42,52));`, or create a bounds object containing the coordinate and call, for example: `map.zoomToExtent(new OpenLayers.Bounds(-43, 51, -41, 53));`.

Chapter 9: Using Vector Layers

Answer: There is really no 'right' answer. Any application that involves clients interacting with data would be a great use case for the vector layer. For example, a real estate site that mapped houses and displayed information about them would be a great use for the vector layer.

Chapter 10: Vector Layer Style Guide

Answer: We would set the background property to contain the drop shadow image, and the `externalGraphic` property to contain the image of the marker. We could also adjust the image offsets to give it a more realistic effect if necessary.

Chapter 11: Making Web Map Apps

Answer: Any number of reasons would be good, particularly reasons involving reduced file size. The smaller the file size, the faster the users can download the file. This also saves on bandwidth costs. The only real downside is that once the file is created by the build script, it will be harder for humans to read.

Index

D

E

F

G

H

M

N

R

S

T

U

V

W

X

Y

Z

Thank you for buying

OpenLayers 2.10 Beginner's Guide

About Packt Publishing

Packt, pronounced 'packed', published its first book "*Mastering phpMyAdmin for Effective MySQL Management*" in April 2004 and subsequently continued to specialize in publishing highly focused books on specific technologies and solutions.

Our books and publications share the experiences of your fellow IT professionals in adapting and customizing today's systems, applications, and frameworks. Our solution based books give you the knowledge and power to customize the software and technologies you're using to get the job done. Packt books are more specific and less general than the IT books you have seen in the past. Our unique business model allows us to bring you more focused information, giving you more of what you need to know, and less of what you don't.

Packt is a modern, yet unique publishing company, which focuses on producing quality, cutting-edge books for communities of developers, administrators, and newbies alike. For more information, please visit our website: `www.packtpub.com`.

About Packt Open Source

In 2010, Packt launched two new brands, Packt Open Source and Packt Enterprise, in order to continue its focus on specialization. This book is part of the Packt Open Source brand, home to books published on software built around Open Source licences, and offering information to anybody from advanced developers to budding web designers. The Open Source brand also runs Packt's Open Source Royalty Scheme, by which Packt gives a royalty to each Open Source project about whose software a book is sold.

Writing for Packt

We welcome all inquiries from people who are interested in authoring. Book proposals should be sent to author@packtpub.com. If your book idea is still at an early stage and you would like to discuss it first before writing a formal book proposal, contact us; one of our commissioning editors will get in touch with you.

We're not just looking for published authors; if you have strong technical skills but no writing experience, our experienced editors can help you develop a writing career, or simply get some additional reward for your expertise.

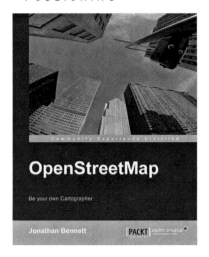

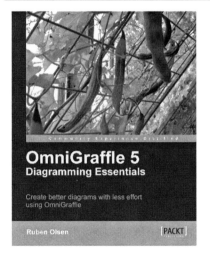

CPSIA information can be obtained at www.ICGtesting.com
Printed in the USA
BVOW082128260212

283844BV00003B/80/P